Upris

The Who

Bakers' Book

Uprisings
The Whole Grain Bakers' Book

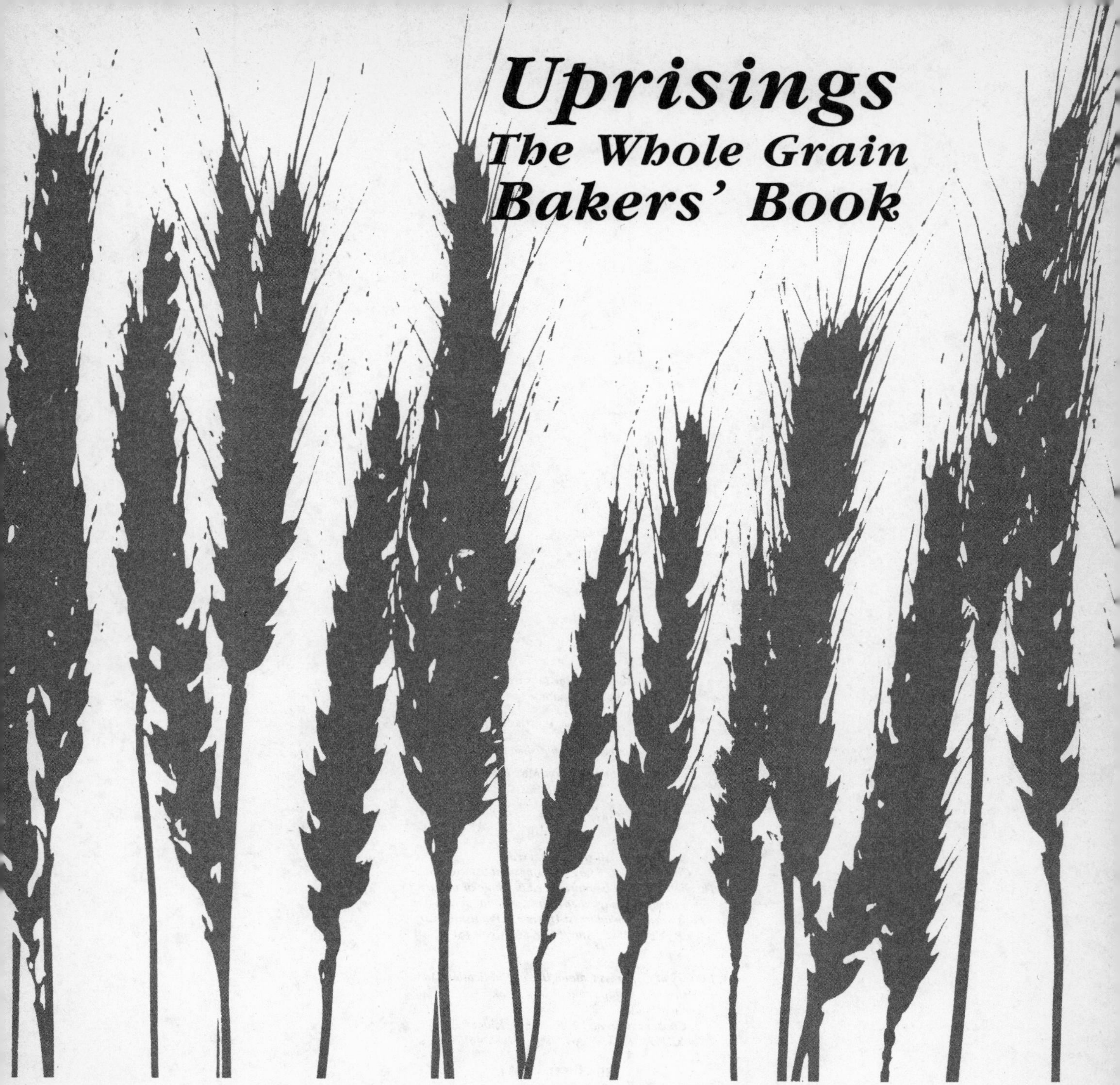

Edited by Michael Arthur, Kathy Gaskin, Lew Kidder and Jean Marvel

1983

BANTAM BOOKS
TORONTO • NEW YORK • LONDON • SYDNEY • AUCKLAND

UPRISINGS: THE WHOLE GRAIN BAKERS' BOOK
A Bantam Book/published by arrangement with the author

PRINTING HISTORY

First edition published 1983

Bantam edition/May 1986

Cover art by Bascove.

Library of Congress Cataloging-in-Publication Data
Uprising: the whole grain bakers' book.
Includes index.
1. Cookery (Cereals) 2. Baking. I. Kidder, Lew.
TX808.U67 1986 641.6'31 85-48109

ISBN 0-553-34260-6

Published simultaneously in the United States and Canada

PRINTED IN THE UNITED STATES OF AMERICA

SEM 0 9 8 7 6 5 4 3 2 1

Foreword

Welcome to *Uprisings*, the whole grain bakers' book. *Uprisings* has been collectively compiled by experienced bakers from many small independent bakeries. It draws its inspiration from a number of uprisings—of grain, of bread, and of people. The most basic of these is the grain growing from the earth, nourished by the rain and sun. Wheat, rye, corn, barley, buckwheat, millet, rice—these are the fundamental ingredients of whole grain baked goods. Bakers, with a little help from yeast and other leaveners, create another uprising, as dough rises to produce fresh-baked loaves, filling our senses. The third uprising is the cooperative ethic of the bakeries we work in. There are no bosses, no employees. Instead we all do the work together, sharing the responsibilities and the rewards. Our businesses put priority on serving the needs of the community, not on making profits for a select few.

We think it's a great loss that so many of us are unfamiliar with these uprisings. Few people enjoy the delights of eating fresh whole grain bread, let alone those of making it themselves. It's also a loss that so few people have the satisfaction of helping to run their own workplaces, doing interesting work that meets real needs. Cooperative whole grain bakeries are part of a rising tide of people taking more responsibility for what goes on in our lives. We want more and more of us to regain power over our food, our work, our health and well-being—in short, our personal, social, and economic existence. To achieve this, we heartily encourage these and other kinds of uprisings in all areas of our lives.

Cooperative Whole Grain Educational Association

The CWGEA was organized in the United States in 1978 to bring our far-flung members closer together. Incorporated in 1983 as a non-profit corporation exclusively for educational and charitable purposes, its Articles of Incorporation are these:

1. To provide education for members, including regular newsletters and conferences.
2. To foster good health by supporting nutritional awareness through education, including conducting nutritional education in public schools and other institutions.
3. To support international harmony among our members through education and meetings.
4. To insure that no part of the net earnings of the Corporation shall inure to the benefit of any member or individual.
5. To insure that this association is open to all people regardless of race, color, creed, sex, age, or national origin.

The CWGEA has begun building networks to make information, resources, and raw materials available to cooperatively run whole grain bakeries across North America. Regional coordinators have been set up, and a newsletter is published. Every summer, a conference is organized by members, with workshops, guest instructors, recipe exchanges, and extensive informal discussions. Members travel great distances for the week-long gathering in a park location, to share, to enjoy, and to be recharged with collective energy.

The CWGEA (originally entitled the Whole Grain Collective Bakers International) has had an international perspective from the start, with contacts in Canada, South America, and Europe. We feel it's especially important to share across national boundaries, increasing our knowledge of techniques and of grains other than wheat, and bringing to all people the consciousness of whole foods, self-reliance, and working cooperatively. Our food system now functions globally, and hence it is important that an awareness of its nature and of the alternatives to it be spread across the world.

CWGEA, P.O. Box 2755, Ann Arbor, MI 48106

How Uprisings Was Put Together

Uprisings originated as an idea at the 1980 CWGEA Conference. A collectively compiled book for the home baker was envisaged, featuring recipes created in more than thirty cooperative whole grain bakeries across North America. *Uprisings* would highlight the ease of baking at home, and the importance of whole foods and cooperative work.

The project was directed by a small coordinating collective based at Wildflour Community Bakery Cooperative in Ann Arbor, Michigan. Over a period of two and a half years, many volunteers have been recruited to the project, contributing their skills at all stages of the book's development. Much of the work involved test-baking the hundreds of recipes selected and sent in by the workers at collective bakeries around the country. In Ann Arbor, each recipe was reduced to home baking size, baked by a volunteer and tasted by a group. The recipe was evaluated, retested and rewritten if necessary, and finally accepted or rejected for publication. Recipes have been selected for a variety of reasons; many for sheer lusciousness, some for their simplicity or innovativeness, others for special dietary characteristics.

In harmony with the collective energy of the project, each bakery's section has been separately hand-written and illustrated by volunteers. Most of these people are part of the Ann Arbor community, but some are based as far away as Arizona, New York, and Florida. The text was written by the coordinating team, with contributions from other bakers.

Like any collective process, the creation of *Uprisings* had many problems, but also its own unique rewards. None of us would have done it any other way. It would be impossible to list everyone who contributed. The satisfaction for all of us is that, working together, we each played a part in the making of *Uprisings*. And to everyone using this book, we hope that the love that went into it brings you joy, and inspires you to create uprisings of your own!

Contents

Introduction — What's in Uprisings 1
Whole Grains — It's Living 2
Cooperation — It's Working 9
Bread and Nutrition 11
Foods for Whole Grain Baking 16
Grains 16
Liquids 21
Leaveners 22
Sweeteners 23
Salt 25
Fats and Oils 26
Dairy Products 27
Eggs 27
Other Ingredients 27
How to Bake 31
Useful Tools 31
Yeasted Breads 32
Sourdough Breads 37
Unyeasted Breads 38
Essene Bread 38
Quick Breads and Muffins 40
Cakes and Brownies 40
Pies 41
Cookies 41
Substituting Ingredients 42
Problems and Solutions 44
Equivalents of Weights and Measures 46
The Bakeries 47
Bakery Locations 48
Alvarado Street Bakery *50*
Peasant Bread 51
Carrot Celery Bread 52
Potato Dill Bread 53
Arcata Co-op Bakery *54*
Nine-Grain Bread 55
Wheat Sprouts Bread 56
Sweet Oat Bread 57
Sesame Soya Bread 58
Carrot Cake or Muffins 59
Applesauce Cake or Muffins 60
Pumpkin Cupcakes and/or Cake 61
Carob Coconut Brownies 62
Pumpkin Cookies 63
Sunny Date Chews 64
Muesli 65
The Bakery Cafe *66*
Tahini Coffee Cake 67
Pudin de Pan 68
Sesame Halvah, Carob-Coated 69
Blue Heron Bakery *70*
Potato Buttermilk Bread 71
Hearty Whole Grain Black Bread 72
Cheesecake 73
Cinnamon Rolls 74
Carob Chip Bars 76
Coconut Dream Bars 76
Walnut-Raisin/Date-Cashew Ultimate Oatmeal Cookies 77
Blue Mango Restaurant *78*
Fruit Bars 79
Banana Creme Cake 80
Dharma Crumbs Bakery *81*
Herb Bread 82
Raisin Date Bars 84
Carob Tofu Bars 85
Raisin Sunnies 86
Carob Chip Chews 87
Good Bread Bakery *88*
Grandpa's Farm Bread 89
Hearth Rye Bread 90
Rice Bread 92
Honey Bear Bakery *93*
Pita or Pocket Bread 94
Bagels—Sesame Garlic or Plain 95
Roll-ups 96
Ginger Bears 98
Sesame Dream Bars 99
Peanut Granola Chews 100
Little Bread Company *101*
Sesame Chews 103
Carob Chews 104
Maple Granola 105
Peanut Cashew Crunch Granola 106
Aunt Louise's Coco-Date Granola 106
Holy Granola 106
Manna Bread Bakery *107*
Rice Bread 108
Sourdough Bread 109
Currant-Raisin Bread 110
Millstone Bakery *111*
Swedish Tea Ring 112
Hot Cross Buns 113
Nature's Bakery *114*
Whole Wheat Bread 116
Swedish Rye Bread 117
Buckwheat Bread 118
Sourdough Bread 119
Sourdough Variations 120
Wheat Sprout Crackers 121
Carob Nut Bars 122
Peanut Minus Cookies 123
On the Rise Bakery *124*

Three Seed Bread 125
Daily Bread 126
Corn Muffins 127
Blueberry Muffins 128
Oatmeal Raisin Cookies 129
***Open Harvest Bakery* 130**
Challah 131
Pita 132
Lemon Wedding Cake 133
Banana Muffins 134
Corn Muffins 135
Seven Grain Currant Muffins 136
Sunny Seed Cookies 137
Peanut Butter Crunchies 138
***People's Bakery* 139**
Triticale Sunflower Bread 140
Bran Wheat Germ Bread 141
Hazel's Prune Nut Bread 142
Corn Rye Bread 144
St. John's Bread 145
Irish Soda Bread 146
***People's Company Bakery* 147**
Vegie Bread 148
Cheddar Cheese Bread 149
Scottish Shortbread 150
Ginger Snaps 151
Granola Cookies 151
Cream Cheese Cookies 152
Poppy Seed Cookies 152
Krunch Bars 153
Toasted All Grain Cereal 153
***Rebel Bakers* 154**
Whole Wheat-Rye French Bread 156
Corn-Benne Muffins 157
Bran Muffins 157
Carrot Cake with Tofu Frosting 158
Orange-Oat Cookies 159
Carob Brownies 159
Coco-Almond Cookies 160
Carob-Mint Cookies 160
Raw Fruit Balls 161
Scented Pecan Balls 161
***Rising Star Bakery* 162**
Peasant Bread 163
Apple Kuchen 164
Carob Cake with Carob Icing 165
Honey Cake 166
Fruit Upside-Down Cake 167
Devil's Carob Cake 168
Poppy Seed Loaf 169
Gingerbread Muffins 170
Blueberry Coconut Muffins 171
Eggless Cheesecake 172
Almond Crescents 173
Golden Macaroons 174
Papaya Squares 175
Walnut Shortbread Cookies 176
Lemon Coconut Pie 177
Carob Cream Pie 178
Banana Cream Pie 179
Pumpkin Pie 180
***Slice of Life Bakery* 181**
Christmas Stollen 182
Anadama Bread 183
Cranberry Muffins 184
Spicy Apple Muffins 185
Halvah 186
Marbled Halvah 186
***Small Planet Bakery* 187**
Apple Bread 188
Orange-Date Surprise Bread 189
Sunseed Bread 190
Cashew Date Granola 191
Coconut Almond Granola 191
***Solstice Bakery* 192**
Sprouted Wheat Bread 193
Cinnamon Date Bread 194
Coco Shortbread 195
Date Bars 196
***Somadhara Bakery* 197**
Coconut Macaroons 198
Best Butter Cookie Batter 199
Apricot Almond Bars 199
Tahini-Raisin-Oat Cookies 200
Butter Sesame Cookies 201
Carob Nut Fudge 202
***Summercorn Bakery* 203**
Old World Rye Bread 204
Cinnamon Currant Bread 205
Ozark Barley Bread 206
Peanut Butter Cookies 207
Carob Nut Brownies 207
***Sunflour Bakery* 208**
Rye Bread 209
Onion Crackers 210
Rye Crackers 211
Summer Wheat Bread 212
Raisin Bran Bread 213
Thumbprint Cookies 214
***Sunrise Bakery* 215**
Vickie's Herb Onion Bread 216
Patience' Cracked Wheat Bread 217
Sourdough Whole Wheat Bread 218
Pumpkin Clouds 219
***Grain Dance Bakery* 220**
Pumpcorn Muffins 221
***Uprising Breads Bakery* 222**
Peanut Butter Cookies with Carob Chips or Raisins 223
Sourdough Pumpernickel 224
Bagels 226
***Uprisings Baking Collective* 228**
Raisin Bread 229
Carrot Herb Bread 230
Lemon Sesame Bread 231

Rice Poppy Seed Cake . . . 232
Carrot Cake . . . 233
Coconut Cake and Frosting . . . 234
Auntie Nuke's Nuggets . . . 235
Simple Scones . . . 236
Rich Currant Scone . . . 237
Sesame Crunch Bars . . . 238
Almond Rice Cookies . . . 240
Carob Mint Balls . . . 241
Cream Cheese Carob Chip Cookies . . . 242
Wildflour Community Bakery . . . 243
Seven Grain Bread . . . 245
Date Nut Bread . . . 246
Just Rye . . . 247
Sesame Oat Rolls . . . 248
Onion Rolls . . . 249
Pizza . . . 250
Arepas . . . 252
Date Crunch . . . 255
Pecan-Raisin Essene Rolls . . . 256
Maple Oatmeal Cookies . . . 257
Apple/Apricot-Peach/Date Bars . . . 258
Pecan Sandies . . . 259
Fruit and Nut Drops . . . 260
Carob Coconut Clusters . . . 261
Dream Cookies . . . 262
Wolfmoon Bakery . . . 263
Oatmeal Sunflower Millet Bread . . . 264
Hi-Protein Bread . . . 265
Halvah . . . 266
Carob Halvah . . . 266
Women's Community Bakery . . . 267
Onion Rye Bread . . . 268
Warm Morning Cinnamon Granola Bread . . . 269
Sandwich Rolls—Plain and Onion . . . 270
Breakfast Bran Muffins . . . 271
Dingwall's Delectable Old Country Date Bars . . . 272
Julia's Favorites—Raisin Oatmeal Cookies . . . 273
Yeast West Bakery . . . 274
Buttermilk Dinner Rolls . . . 276
Apple Cake . . . 277
Ginger Cookies . . . 278
Oatmeal Sunflower Cookies . . . 279
Yeast West Familia . . . 280
Starting a Bakery . . . 282
References . . . 283
Index . . . 284
Recipes by Type of Baked Good . . . 286
Recipes by Special Dietary Characteristic . . . 288
Recipes by Major Ingredients . . . 289

Introduction — What's In Uprisings

Uprisings offers you over two hundred recipes, created by past and present bakers in thirty-two whole grain bakeries. Many of these are their most popular and inspired products, made lovingly time and time again to still the cries of disappointed devotees; these come recommended to you by steadfast bands of bakery connoisseurs across the country. Every recipe in *Uprisings* has been reduced to homesize batches. To be sure the scaling-down worked, each recipe has been baked by a volunteer and taste-tested by a group, who rated it, rejecting and retesting when necessary. Most of the comments with the recipes were taken from volunteer tasters.

For several reasons, our recipes are especially good for making at home. Because the bakeries are generally small, with few machines, techniques developed in them are easily transferable to home kitchens. The structure of the bakeries encourages experimentation and innovation, so you'll find many new and creative ideas. Our bakeries always have to ask the question, "Can we make this bread or cookie relatively easily, often, and cheaply, and have it come out good most of the time?". So simplicity and consistency are very important, and that's also good for home bakers.

The baking here isn't hard. Most goodie recipes can be boiled down to: Mix wet ingredients — Mix dry ingredients — Combine them — Bake. Even bread, despite rumors to the contrary, is neither difficult nor complicated. By following a few simple steps, we help along an ancient process which continues to yield that wonderful reward for bakers and friends — fresh, hot bread! Almost all of us working in bakeries were at one time intimidated by the mysteries of that unknown — making bread. Now, thousands of loaves later, we say from personal experience:

Suggestions on how to bake, and what tools and ingredients to use, are here to help you if you need it. You'll also find discussions of the reasons for using whole grains, and of the benefits of working cooperatively. Our concern about these subjects keeps our work stimulating and rewarding; they are linked to many important issues, and this book will talk about what they mean.

Recipes are presented according to their bakery of origin, preceded by an introduction written by the local bakers — often a simple account of the bakery, sometimes a poem, sometimes a polemic. Whenever possible, bread labels and bakery logos are used as illustrations. For easy reference, there is a comprehensive alphabetical index at the end, as well as listings of recipes by type of baked good, by special dietary characteristic, and by major ingredients.

We present recipes bakery by bakery to give a feel for the character and integrity of each one, for each is very different. If you find yourself drawn to the individuality of a particular bakery, consult the map and list of bakery addresses so you can visit if you're in the area. The chances are they'll be baking your favorite bread or cookie, as well as other inspired creations that couldn't be squeezed into *Uprisings*. Our bakeries rely on the interest and support of people who prefer fresh, nutritious food produced by workers who care about each other, their products, and their communities.

Whole Grains — It's Living

There are many reasons for preferring whole grains, and whole foods in general, to white flour and other processed foods. There's how the food tastes, what it does to you, what it implies about the food distribution system, and what it says about the state of the "food industry"—its practices, priorities, and philosophy. The absence of whole grains in most of our readily available food is a grim illustration of the decline in the quality of our diet, and hence the quality of our lives.

Whole Grains — Some Basic Information

Most of this discussion focuses on wheat, since wheat is far and away the dominant grain in our lives. Much of what is said, however, can be applied to other grains. The wheat (or rye, or rice) berry is the fruit of the mature plant, and contains the seed of a new plant. When the dry berries are ground, whole wheat flour, light brown and grainy, is produced. This is what we use in our bakeries and in ***Uprisings***.

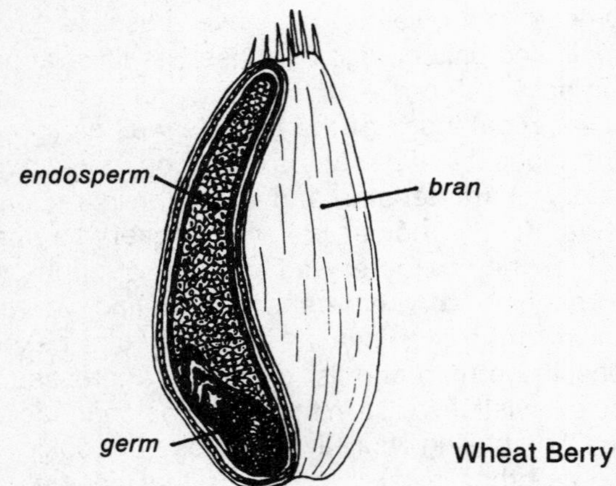

Wheat Berry

Refining the ground berries into white flour involves sifting out the denser, darker particles to obtain a whiter, more powdery and silky-textured product. What gets removed during refining are the bran and the germ of the wheat kernel. The bran, the outer layers of the wheat berry, contains carbohydrates, proteins, vitamins, minerals—especially iron—and fiber. The germ contains a high concentration of vitamin E, B vitamins, iron and other minerals, polyunsaturated fats, proteins, fiber, and carbohydrates. The germ is actually the embryo of the new life that would grow if the seed were germinated, and, appropriately, the nutritional riches are concentrated here.

What is left in white flour is ground-up endosperm, predominantly starch, with a modest amount of protein in the form of gluten and cellulose walls. The endosperm is the high carboydrate food supply for the growing germ at the beginning of its life, and is low in nutrients. Therefore, white flour is devoid of ***over half*** the nutrients available in the wheat berry. A comparison of the nutritional content of whole wheat and white flour reveals dramatic reductions in all vital elements.

Not only are these losses measurable numerically as depletion of nutrients, they also register as loss of flavor. As anyone who has savored its rich nuttiness will attest, whole wheat can stand on its own and doesn't have to be "doctored" (with sugar, salt and other flavorers) to ensure a full-bodied taste. Like other whole foods, in contrast to their refined versions, whole wheat satisfies both our nutritional needs ***and*** our taste buds.

Whole Grains and Health

The removal of most nutrients and almost all fiber from grains creates a severely imbalanced product, which taxes the body during digestion and assimilation. The nutrients in both the bran and germ are needed by the body in order to metabolize the carbohydrate contained in the endosperm. When the pulverized endosperm alone is eaten, the needed nutrients must be pulled from the body tissues as metabolism proceeds. This also occurs when other refined carbohydrates, such as white rice and white sugar, are eaten. They drain, rather than nourish, our bodies.

Composition of Various Wheat Products, *per 100 grams, edible portion*

	Calories	Protein g	Fat g	Carbohydrate g	Fiber g	Ash g	Calcium mg	Phosphorus mg	Iron mg	Sodium mg	Potassium mg	Thiamine mg	Riboflavin mg	Niacin mg
WHOLE WHEAT FLOUR	333	13.3	2.0	71.0	2.3	1.7	41	372	3.3	3	370	.55	.12	4.3
WHITE FLOUR (UNENRICHED)	365	11.8	1.1	74.7	.3	.4	16	95	.9	2	95	.08	.06	1.0
WHEAT GERM	363	26.6	10.9	46.7	2.5	4.3	72	1118	9.4	3	827	2.01	.68	4.2
WHEAT BRAN	213	16.0	4.6	61.9	9.1	6.0	119	1276	14.9	9	1121	.72	.35	21.0

Source: USDA, *Handbook of the Nutritional Contents of Foods*, Table 1.
The figures given are for hard whole wheat flour, unenriched white bread flour, and crude, commercially milled wheat germ and bran

What is more, without the natural fiber, refined foods clog the intestines. Remember what great play-glue white flour and water make? The refined grains interfere with the functioning of the colon, particularly the peristaltic action which keeps everything moving right along and propels wastes from the body. The muscles literally can't get a grip on the gummy paste, and some of it remains to coat and clog the surface and minute folds of the colon. It takes about thirty hours for whole grain bread to move through the intestine, while it takes approximately eighty hours to digest white bread.

White flour and white flour products, in constipating the bowels, are responsible for much ill health. The stagnation of wastes in the digestive tract leads to the development of unhealthy micro-organisms that cause discomfort and disease. In particular, carcinogenic secretions can develop; hence the strong connection between refined carbohydrate intake and cancer of the colon and rectum, now leading killers among the "diseases of civilization". Moreover, many experts believe that changes in the intestinal rhythm have a direct effect on the blood flow, which can lead to varicose veins, hemorrhoids, pulmonary embolus, coronaries and so on—all again related to a diet of white bread and other refined foods.

The changes in the American diet during this century have been directly linked to the changing patterns of disease. A 1977 report by the U.S. Senate Select Committee on Nutrition and Human Needs related the rise in major degenerative diseases to a decrease in complex carbohydrate consumption and increases in fat and refined sugar intake. Whole grains and whole grain products used to be the major source of calories and protein in the American diet—almost 40% of each in 1910; today's consumption of grains is less than half what it was then. More importantly, almost all of the grain eaten in the United States today, including our flours, breads and cereals, is heavily refined—a sharp contrast to the situation earlier in our history. There is no longer any doubt that such rapid changes in eating patterns are directly related to dramatic increases in the incidence of chronic degenerative diseases. We have reached the point where the majority of Americans (including a significant proportion of young people) are afflicted with chronic disease. Similar dietary trends in other advanced countries are rapidly producing the same deterioration in the health of the people. We are literally eating ourselves to death.

Our Diet — Wholeness Is Natural

As we've become more and more "civilized", we've forgotten that we are indeed living organisms like the other species on this planet. A comparison of our physiological make-up with that of other animals shows we all share similar cell structure and processes of cell death and growth. We also share similar needs for elements in our diets to ensure proper health, physical maintenance, and energy supply. Animals, other than humans and their domestic pets, live on a range of unadulterated whole foods, each species having its appropriate diet and eating only what it needs. Animals usually live six times the length of their age of maturity, and die from any of five to ten diseases. Human beings, on the other hand, consider anything we can create from our environment—***anything***—fine for shoveling down our throats. And we live only three to four times our age of maturity, much of that time being spent gradually dying from over two hundred and fifty diseases. We're rapidly inventing new ones, too, at a speed that parallels the degeneration of our food supply.

Whole foods are natural. We are natural beings, though we seem so far from it in our modern way of life. Our digestive system—almost identical to our close relatives, the vegetarian apes—has changed little over thousands of generations. We still need a diet as close to the natural as possible, or else we invite inevitable impairment of our well-being—physical, mental, and spiritual.

Nature isn't just "the rest of the world" (we've already heard too much about "Man and Nature", especially about "Man's Dominion Over Nature"). Nature is the aggregate of all living things, on this planet and beyond. Like it or not, the human species (and that includes both sexes) is a part of nature. And we are at our strongest and happiest when our lives harmonize and are in balance with the natural world. In nature, balance is the prevailing aim of all energy. Human beings have lost sight of the ways to achieve both inner and outer balance, and have forgotten its rewards. But we can rediscover both. We need to start by tuning in to our physical selves and surroundings, becoming aware of all the distress we cause by imbalances in our diet and style of living, and the abuse of our environment. We should recognize the benefits of exercise and good food, work that is pleasurable rather than stressful, loving relationships, and ***responsible*** management of the environment. By doing this, we will be able to discover our real needs, and satisfy them by drawing without greed on the resources in nature, respecting their wholeness and the overall balance of which they, and we, are a part. Only then do we know the feeling of being integrated with the living world, and that brings rewards which are hard to imagine until we experience them.

Bread and Survival

Connect with bread. Feel it and get to know it. It's interesting stuff. It's alive. That's why it's so interesting—you can't exactly predict what it will do next. Bread dough grows, overflows, flattens, and comes creeping back again. It's fun to handle. Without fail, children enjoy working with bread dough—they know a good time when they see it! It's uniquely satisfying to wrap your fingers around some dough and get into it with your wrists, shoulders, back, and mind.

Breadmaking is typical of those activities which are basic, pleasurable, and a part of doing things for yourself. It combines physical and mental activity in a task that connects you to living things and yields a useful end-product. What more satisfying work could there be? It used to be that life consisted of such purposeful and harmonious activities, providing one's needs through one's own creativity. For many people, mostly outside the "developed world", it still does. It is a more natural and truly civilized way of living your life. Let us re-experience the enjoyment of practicing these useful and rewarding survival skills, and regain confidence in our own resourcefulness and respect for the bounty of nature.

How We Got to This Point — A Short History of Bread

For centuries, grain has been regarded as the staff of life. Prehistoric people collected wild grains and ate them just as they found them. With the coming of agriculture to the Fertile Crescent about 9,000 years ago, people began to experiment with the grains they harvested, roasting them over a fire or mixing them with water to form a porridge. A thicker paste, formed into cakes and dried in the sun, became the first loaves. Bread of this kind has been found preserved in Stone Age settlements. Baking the loaves on hot stones was the next step in history.

No one knows for certain who was the first to learn the secrets of fermenting dough—the Chinese or the Egyptians—but well-preserved loaves have been discovered in pyramids dating back 5,000 years. The Chinese style was to steam the bread, much as they do today, but it was the Egyptians who developed and perfected the craft of breadbaking. Their bakers used the yeast produced in brewing beer to ferment and leaven bread doughs, and breweries and bakeries came to be located side by side. It was a mystery to them how fermentation worked; they merely observed that when they baked fermented bread, something different happened. The necessity of baking this bread evenly and in quantity led to the invention of the first ovens. These were made with bricks of Nile clay, and resembled beehives.

Around 600 B.C., Phoenician sailors carried the Egyptian ideas and developments to Greece, where they were refined into an art. The Greeks created many kinds of bread, and their bakers were considered important enough to stand for election as senators. The Greeks in turn passed on their taste for bread to the Romans.

The Romans developed breadmaking still further, with the invention of rotary milling stones. An upper stone revolved on a stationary lower stone as grain was fed through the axle. The resulting flour, made from barley, rye, millet, or wheat—all 100% whole grain—was leavened with brewer's barm, kneaded mechanically, and baked in clay ovens. At the time of Christ, Rome had an average of one mill-bakery for every 2,000 inhabitants.

Originally, milling and baking were twin arts practiced by the same person. The advent of watermills, and later, windmills, led to the formation of two distinct crafts, and by 1,000 A.D. baking and milling were completely separated. Because people's lives depended on bread, the people who controlled its production were extremely powerful. Bakers and millers were among the richest people in any town.

For centuries, stone-ground whole grain flour formed the basis of the bread of both rich and poor. The bread of the poor was coarse, heavy, and brown. The bread of the rich was lighter and more refined, due to sifting techniques in which the ground meal was "bolted" through a silk cloth to remove the coarsest particles. White bread became a status symbol—the whiter the flour, the richer the household. Because of this, bakers used slaked lime, alum, and chalk to whiten flour until well into the eighteenth century—which at least tells us that additives for the sake of profits are not new!

In the 1870's, the invention of a new roller-milling process for flour put white bread within the reach of everybody, rich and poor alike. Roller mills crack the grains between sets of increasingly fine-grooved metal rollers, blowing off the particles of bran and germ in the process. By the end of the century, however, it was evident that people were suffering from this nutritionally deficient flour, and governments began to require the addition of some nutrients in synthetic form, to "enrich" or "fortify" the stripped white flour.

Today's bread market is dominated by the factory-made, wrapped, sliced loaf, the sad result of many years of research by technologists in the food industry. It is designed to have a perfect light-textured white crumb, excellent keeping qualities, and the right shape for toasters and sandwiches and stacking on supermarket shelves. To achieve this miracle of chemical engineering, forty to sixty additives are usually put into commercial loaves; over seven hundred chemicals may be used in baked goods. These include bleaching and improving agents, raising agents, enzyme active preparations, yeast stimulators, preservatives, emulsifiers, stabilizers, anti-oxidants, coloring agents, acids, and diluents. Some of the additives, such as lecithin (an anti-oxidant obtained from soybeans), caramel (a coloring for brown bread, made from burnt white sugar), and chalk (a diluent for other additives), are "natural" substances. The remainder are chemicals, many of which have not been adequately tested, either alone or in combination. Some are believed dangerous, such as BHT (Butylated Hydroxitoluene, an anti-oxidant), which was banned in Sweden and Australia in 1962 after tests showed considerable toxic effects. Quantities of sugar and salt are also added to today's commercial loaf, in an attempt to give the denuded and chemicalized product a semblance of taste to the desensitized palate of the typical processed food eater. By the way, the majority of additives to bread ***do not have to be listed on the label***. You really have no way to find out what you're eating when you consume commercial white bread.

The same warnings must also be made about one of the recent trends in the baking industry—mass-produced "whole wheat" bread. The labels of such breads may reveal an even greater variety of sugars and additives than white breads, and frequently do not list everything contained in the product. Listing white flour as "wheat flour" is a common deception; ***only*** 100% whole wheat flour may be called "whole wheat". To avoid being misled and misfed, the clear alternative is to make your own bread, using simple and wholesome recipes like those in ***Uprisings***, or to buy bread produced by conscientious, small, whole grain bakeries.

What's Happened in the "Food Industry"

At Home . . .

The fate of flour and bread is typical of the way things have been going in the food industry. In America, people now eat more processed than unprocessed food; 75% of Americans' food comes from factories, not farms. At an accelerating pace, products are becoming more refined and adulterated with chemical substances put in to enable cheap, large-scale mechanized production, long-distance shipping, and unnatural endurance capacity (otherwise known as "shelf-life").

One reason for this trend is that the food industry is increasingly dominated and controlled by a small number of giant companies, themselves part of multinational corporations. These companies—it seems almost unnecessary to add—are guided solely by the profit motive, and there is much more profit in processed foods than there is in the unprocessed. Today's food chemists and technologists are meeting this purely economic challenge, in a market saturated with unneeded products, by concentrating on the development of totally artificial "non-foods". Another major development in this onslaught is increasing "vertical integration", in which a corporation controls the entire process of research, growing, transportation, processing, packaging, distribution, and even sale of a given product. By controlling each part of the process, more money is made and greater power is gained over the consumer.

In agriculture, there is a strong emphasis on larger and larger farms, high energy consumption, and manipulation of plant genetics. The biologically weakened, insect-prone hybrid strains require the artificial stimulation of chemical fertilizers (made from natural gas and petrochemicals) and frequent dousing with inorganic pesticides. The very basis of agriculture, the seed industry, has recently undergone many changes, with huge conglomerates that manufacture these pesticides and chemical fertilizers swallowing up the independent seed companies (ITT took over Burpee, and Purex snapped up Ferry-Morse, for example). This trend, along with legislative and judicial decisions affecting the patenting of life forms, makes it possible to impose the domination of hybrid seeds, which cannot reliably reproduce themselves. In other words, the farmer and the gardener in practice ***must buy new seeds each year***. This frightening control over the production of food is being vigorously pursued in both Europe and America, and if this trend continues, diversity may indeed disappear.

Organic growing, which is nothing more than the way it used to be done before chemicals were introduced, recognizes the importance of building the soil, rather than meddling with natural balances. There are many reasons to choose organically grown food, and our bakeries put a priority on using organic flour and other naturally grown ingredients whenever possible. For one thing, organic farming yields crops that are better in flavor and higher in all nutrients than commercially produced crops. (Chemical fertilization drastically reduces the optimum nutritional values of grains, especially vitamins, trace elements, and protein, while excess carbohydrate—starch and cellulose—develops instead.) For another, organic crops are free of the poisonous chemicals, many of which have been used specifically to kill some form of life, which are used on commercial crops. What's more, the miserable end-product of agribusiness, when harvested, is often just at the beginning of a long, polluted journey to somebody's supermarket cart. Once it is taken from the ground, the industry really gets to work on it—heating, pulverizing, deodorizing, homogenizing, hydrogenating, and adding any number of the 3,000 food additives now in use.

With the food industry using over a billion pounds of chemicals a year, it's not surprising that the average American consumes five to ten pounds of additives yearly. Most of these have been inadequately tested or not tested at all. It may seem like only a little per product, but five pounds is a lot of alien chemicals in an organism not equipped to cope with them. Furthermore, each year, this average eater consumes fifteen pounds of salt and one hundred and thirty pounds of sugar and other refined sweeteners. The thirty billion pounds of sweeteners used yearly by the food industry make up over a sixth of the average American diet. Salt and sugar may not be commonly thought of as "additives", but they are highly refined end-products, devoid of nutrition and damaging to health. They are added to give the illusion of taste to a devitalized product, and to satisfy the salt and sugar addictions that are started by our earliest consumption of baby foods and children's snacks.

Finally, as if all this weren't enough, buying commercial foods helps finance a massive propaganda campaign. Over $4 billion a year is spent on advertising by food manufacturers striving to gain the competitive edge over the other 10,000 products in the supermarket. General Foods alone spends $275 million annually, and General Mills $131 million, in the attempt to stimulate our interest in their lifeless products. Over $400 million worth of television ads are aimed each year at young children, and in one year a child sees about 10,000 ads for "food"—mostly candy, beverages, and cereals, loaded with sugar and artificial ingredients.

. . . And Abroad

The food situation on the home front is part of a depressing global picture. The West's—and in particular America's—high-meat, high-technology diet and methods of agriculture are responsible for hunger, disease, and social injustice among many of the world's populations. (This is thoroughly documented in ***Diet for a Small Planet***, ***Food First***, and other publications of the Institute for Food and Development Policy.) The massive and unequal consumption of resources by America's food industry has been brought to people's attention in recent years by figures such as:

- Each American citizen consumes, on the average, 2000 pounds of grain yearly, compared to 400 pounds per person in poor countries (Americans consume most of theirs indirectly as meat and dairy products).
- One pound of steer sold as edible meat represents sixteen pounds of soy and grains—an energy wastage of more than 90%.
- Over 50% of the total harvested acreage in the U.S. (including 90% or more of corn, oats, barley, sorghum, and soybeans) is fed to livestock.
- In 1910, the American food system consumed less energy (in calories) than it produced as food calories; by 1970, it used nine calories of energy to produce each single calorie of food.
- For every unit of energy expended in on-farm production, three more units are used in processing and distributing thousands of food products.

Meanwhile, Western agribusiness has had a disastrous effect on the economies and political conditions in many Third World countries (see ***Food First*** for details of this role). It has disrupted local ecologies and created hunger in poorer nations by imposing a single export crop economy in the place of the diversified agriculture which previously grew the local food supply. In some places, a completely unfamiliar luxury crop, such as strawberries or asparagus, may be introduced, while in others, the numerous local varieties of a traditional crop are supplanted by a weak hybrid strain necessitating the use of chemical fertilizers and pesticides (including very toxic ones banned in the U.S., such as DDT). Gassing, bleaching, dyeing, spraying, and other chemical treatments follow harvesting, in order to store, preserve, and transport the crop. Most of this is done with complete disregard for workers' safety.

There are many aspects of the world food situation that we don't even touch on here. One, for example, is the domination of wheat in world grain consumption, a development encouraged by the big wheat brokers of North America to enlarge their market and their power. Increasingly, too, the food manufacturers are boosting sales and profits by marketing their most processed products abroad. This is done even to the point of bringing malnutrition and death to the new consumers as, for instance, in the promotion of infant formula to replace breast milk in poorer, less literate cultures abroad (again, see ***Food First*** for details of this kind of exploitation).

Our global responsibility comes home to us in baking because there are several common ingredients produced only by agribusiness in Third World countries. Many bakeries have raised the question whether or not to continue to use products such as cashews, coconut, and bananas, all of which are treated with chemicals by native workers who have no protection from these questionable substances. As a matter of course, most of our bakeries have never used coffee, cocoa, and sugar—prime products of multinational agribusiness. We never recommend the use of these non-foods. As for the use of Third World crops in your own baking, you'll have to make those decisions yourself.

Whole Grains — For Life

Looking at the question of whole grains versus processed foods leads us to many issues, as we've seen in the preceding sections. Proceeding from taste, to health, to harmony with the environment, we finally reach national and global levels of concern and responsibility. As we begin to see our present food system for what it really is, it becomes more and more of a pleasure to detach from it. At the most basic level, despite a lifetime of conditioning about the great taste and superiority of processed, packaged foods like white bread, an increasing number of people are realizing that the darn stuff doesn't even taste good or—somehow—make you feel too well.

Because of all this, many of us are gradually disengaging from the "big business" food industry. In its place, we are linking up with local networks of conscientious farmers, small independent mills, and suppliers such as cooperative warehouses and stores. These regional networks have begun to mesh across larger areas, even nationally, through coops and organizations like the Cooperative Whole Grain Educational Association. As this alternative system stresses involving and serving people rather than exploiting and making money from them, we begin to lose that feeling of being the powerless consumer dangling at the end of a long chain which exists only to make a profit for all of its links.

Because the issue of nutrition is inextricably tied to the economic and political aspects of whole grains, choosing whole grains is in itself a political statement. It is a rejection of the prevailing system of supplying food to make money, regardless of the damage to people and to the earth. Moreover, it is an assertion of concern for health and well-being, and of our place in society and nature. Let us recognize that we are living parts of an organic whole, and begin to be conscious of our responsibility to ourselves, to other people, and to the natural forces that are the driving energy of our world.

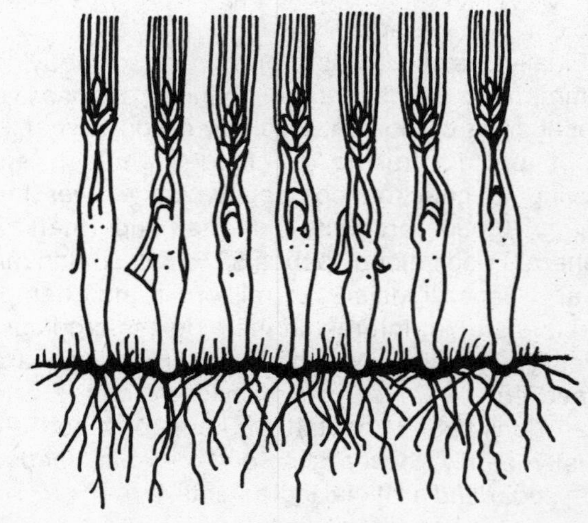

Cooperation — It's Working

Many people aren't at all sure what a cooperative is — it's not surprising in our competitive society that there are widespread misconceptions about doing things collectively. Yet cooperatives are a part of our history, spanning many areas of economic endeavor that include agriculture, housing, production, finance, and the distribution of goods and services. In recent years, cooperatives — enterprises organized and operated for mutual benefit — have enjoyed renewed interest. Coop food stores can now be found in most population centers and in many rural areas as well; they are usually open to everyone, whether or not a member.

Collectives, another term for cooperative enterprises or the people working in them, can vary considerably. Certainly there are many differences among our bakeries. But there are common principles we all share as collectives, and these are basic to their success and to the satisfaction of working in them.

Collectives as an Alternative

Most small businesses have an owner whose primary goal is personal profit. This owner hires people to work for wages. Everyone employed has a supervisor or boss, and that person probably has someone above them — and so on and so on, the complexity of the hierarchy depending on the size of the operation. The owner gets to shoulder both the burdens and the benefits of ownership, taking on the headaches and decision-making as well as taking home the extra money made by paying less in total expenses (rent, wages, ingredients, etc.) than comes in from sales — the profit.

In contrast, a typical collective has these features:

- All the work is shared among the people operating the business.
- No-one is anyone else's boss.
- Decisions in the running of the business are made by the whole group, by consensus decision-making. Problems or issues are worked on until a decision is made to which everyone can give their consent.
- In general, collective members are familiar with all, or most, aspects of the work and participate in them in varying degrees. Some collectives do rely more heavily on separation of tasks and specialization by workers, usually citing reasons of convenience and efficiency. But most collectives hold non-specialization as an ideal and all tasks are shared, sometimes being rotated over periods of months.

These characteristics offer benefits for both the enterprise and the individuals in it. For the business, it means increased versatility as well as freedom from purely managerial costs — since everyone who works also manages. For the individual, this all-round competence and total involvement helps remove the feeling of being alienated from your work, of being limited, exploited, or just plain bored by having to do it. Working cooperatively with others and learning to be responsible to them and to yourself is an empowering experience. It's fun too — people working as a group can accomplish tremendous things. There are few things as pleasant or satisfying as solving a problem or completing a task — together. We think everyone should have the opportunity to work this way, instead of the present system of working in competition with people, afraid of your supervisor's power, and frequently taking out your frustrations on the people under you. This only seems to create anxiety, bad feelings, and poor work.

In collectives, one priority is to act in such a way that you are working as harmoniously as possible with other people, providing and receiving support, encouragement, constructive feedback, and kindness. This involves being conscious of how you relate to people so you can be both more honest and more constructive. Because of this emphasis on understanding your own behavior and the dynamics between people, working in a collective is usually very stimulating towards personal growth and change. It's hard to stagnate with constant opportunities to evaluate, learn, and innovate in areas of both practical concern and personal dynamics. Thus it's exciting and meaningful work.

As you'll no doubt have noticed, businesses run by collectives are in quite a minority! The predominant competitive business ideas are too strongly entrenched in our society at present for collectives to make much headway against the power of the profit motive and private property. We've been brought up to believe unquestioningly that being in competition with other people for ownership privileges, or, for most people, even a decent job (i.e., the chance to be somebody's subordinate), is the natural way of things. The heart of the competitive system is the motivation to gain for oneself more wealth than others have, by being in control of some resource or operation and being able to employ other people and pay them ***less*** than their work is really ***worth***.

Most collective bakeries realize little or no profit, and a number are deliberately non-profit-making. Functioning as a non-profit business means that you don't figure in an extra slice that's yours just for being the owner. Instead you add up your expenses, and charge enough on your products to cover your overhead, labor, and ingredients. Everyone involved makes a living, the product is produced, and the people buying it do not pay an extra percentage to enrich an individual. It's that simple.

Since cooperative businesses grab money neither from those doing the work nor from those buying the product, being involved in one feels different from being in a regular business. We find it very enlightening to stop viewing people in terms of the money you can make from them. The nature of your work begins to feel different and your relationships with your fellow workers and with your customers change. You realize how strongly such things influence how you feel about yourself and how you're spending your life.

The Success of Collectives

Working in a collective is not always easy. In the distinctively hostile environment of our competitive business system, survival of a cooperative enterprise is often a struggle. Landlords, banks, and local authorities are rarely supportive, and frequently quite the opposite. Some collective bakers have gone without pay when the business needed it, particularly when trying to get a new bakery off the ground. But the other rewards were compensation enough at such times.

Above all, we want people to know that coops and collectives ***work***. Most of our bakeries are successful businesses of several years' duration. Our bakers are both paid and happy! And we wouldn't trade the challenges and joys of working collectively for anything. Collectives are effective, responsible businesses and exciting, humane workplaces. Although we are surrounded in our present society by traditionally competitive institutions and beliefs, we are quite sure that the future belongs to people working together. Cooperative, collective workplaces will be the nuclei of future communities in a society that brings respect, fulfillment, and peace to all.

Bread and Nutrition

Nutrition is undoubtedly one of today's "hot" topics. Concern about the effects of what we eat is a major part of the growing interest in health that is evident these days. Dietary theories are iterated by the hundreds, ranging from the conventional approach of the four basic food groups to more esoteric macrobiotic diets and beyond. Diet regimens of many kinds flood our bookstores, each claiming discovery of the secrets of weight loss and optimal nutrition. Countless millions of people substitute margarine for butter, stuff their sandwiches with sprouts, snack on carob-yogurt chews, and gobble vitamin supplements. In this complicated melange of conflicting claims and ideas, where does one turn for responsible information and advice?

The questions regarding nutrition asked by most people are basic ones: what are the nutritional requirements for good health?; how can these needs be met?; and what difference does it make anyway? In attempting to answer these questions, modern nutritional science has painstakingly searched for, discovered, and classified many of the individual components. Thus, most modern writings on nutrition concentrate on identifying and defining the nature of proteins, fats, carbohydrates, vitamins, and minerals, and describing the individual role of each in nutrition. Further, science continues to test and document the effects of various diets on the incidence of disease and life expectancy.

Initially, however, we should understand that nutrition, much like modern medicine, is an infant science. Elementary facts we accept as gospel were unknown well into the twentieth century; for example, the molecular structures of vitamins A, B-1, and C were not discovered until the 1930s, the word "vitamin" having been coined only two decades previously. The effect on the body of food and its individual components is by no means fully understood, much less set in stone. Facts remain to be discovered, theories to be tested and re-evaluated, delicate relationships and interactions to be explored. In all probability, what we don't know about nutrition will prove even more important than what we do now know.

A good example of the type of knowledge presently provided through modern nutritional research are the Recommended Daily Allowances (RDAs) of some individual components of our food supply. The tendency of most people—whether expert or layperson—is to accept these figures as an absolute standard or goal and to be satisfied if their diet meets these requirements. But this blind faith gives potentially dangerous credence to a scientific approach which is fraught with weakness. Among other problems, the RDAs are generalized estimates based on averages; hence the entire range of individual variation, whether among people or for the same person in different circumstances, is not taken into account. Moreover, as the continual updating of the figures shows, they reflect only the current state of nutritional knowledge, which is widely acknowledged to be partial and fragmented.

Further, the RDAs only make sense if we know how much of each nutrient is present in our daily food intake. But the tables giving the nutrients in common foods (another achievement of modern nutritional science) have huge weaknesses of their own. They are only averages of the nutrients found in a limited number of laboratory samples of a particular food. In reality, there is enormous variation in the nutrient content of different samples of the same foodstuff. Such factors as climate, type of soil, and agricultural methods have a major impact on nutrient content. (For example, the nutrient tables credit broccoli as a good source of iron. But if the soil where ***your*** broccoli was grown is deficient in iron, your broccoli may be similarly lacking.) Another source of variation lies in the length and kind of storage and/or processing. The effect of cooking is a further gray area (many tables give figures only for raw foods). It depends on the method and length of cooking, and the amount of heat applied.

But significant changes do occur, and all of them for the worse. Finally, whether from acquired allergy, genetic limitation, or general state of health, your body may not assimilate a nutrient as well from one food as it can from another. Inevitably, then, individual variation in response to food undermines the attempt to "eat by numbers".

If we match the RDAs against our food intake and discover a deficiency, many of us are tempted to take a food supplement. But are synthesized vitamins the exact nutritional equivalents of the vitamins consumed in whole foods? Remember how little we really know, scientifically, about nutrition. And remember too that the RDAs are for the most part only the amounts necessary to prevent clinically identifiable disease. But the difference between the amount needed to prevent disease and the amount required for optimal health may be significant.

Nonetheless, despite the shortcomings of the scientific approach to nutrition, it is becoming increasingly evident that the numerous scientific advances are together pointing to a larger picture concerning our health and what we eat. This larger picture is also suggested by a common-sense appraisal and understanding of who and what we are, and where we have come from. Let's examine a few fundamental concepts.

First and foremost, we know that whether one favors the creationist or evolutionary explanation of our origins, the human species has been molded by evolution. Each person is the product of a complicated genetic code, passed to us by our parents from a long series of ancestors stretching back for thousands of generations. And in turn, this genetic code was (and continues to be) determined by the environmental conditions humans faced; the climate they lived in, the lifestyle they adopted, the dangers they faced, and the food they ate.

There is no question that for the vast majority of human history, our species lived a simple, energetic life and ate a simple diet. When hunger was felt, food was eaten until the hunger was satisfied; if there was no hunger, the human didn't eat. And what was eaten was usually freshly picked or caught. "Refining", "processing", "pasteurization", and "preservatives" were unknown concepts, and even simple cooking was a relatively new development. The human existence was an active, sometimes strenuous one; great distances might be traveled in search of food, and humans were naturally endurance athletes.

As could be expected, the human body adapted to dealing with and thriving on this type of diet and lifestyle. Some members of the species tolerated these conditions poorly, and failed to survive. Others succeeded, and produced offspring with similar genetic characteristics. After eons of this natural selection process, the human being entered the modern era (defined as the last two or three thousand years) firmly tied by evolution to this ancient and relatively constant diet and vigorous lifestyle.

In the modern era, however, and particularly in the last century, we have greatly altered the environment in which we must exist. Today we deal with physical and psychological stresses never encountered by early humans: environmental pollutants, pressures in the modern workplace, the pursuit of material wealth, the threat of nuclear annihilation, a sedentary lifestyle, and perhaps most importantly, a diet which is highly processed, refined, and chemically altered.

The modern human eats too much food, and too much of the wrong kind of food. The results of this unplanned experiment are becoming obvious: our bodies, having evolved to thrive on an entirely different diet, are breaking down in vast and increasing numbers. Research tells us that the plagues of modern society are creatures of our present lifestyle. Our high fat diet directly affects the rate of heart disease, our low fiber diet and environmental pollutants (including food additives) produce huge increases in human cancers, our diet replete with highly refined foods is directly related to the incidence of diabetes, and our sedentary ways lead to obesity and severe stress on a body begging for exercise. We are simply asking ourselves to do the impossible; the process of evolution does not produce such rapid changes.

So what are we to eat? Fortunately, it's not as difficult as it might seem. By understanding our origins and paying attention to our needs, we find that we thrive on a simple diet of fresh, whole foods, grown in naturally composted, nutrient-rich soils. If we treat our bodies to a nourishing, organically raised, whole foods diet ***and*** really pay heed to our reaction to this diet, the chances are good that we will be getting just what we need.

How do processed foods fit into this picture? Of course, the term "processing" has an extremely broad meaning, encompassing lightly-handled foods like frozen blueberries to items more appropriate to a science fiction novel (Question: What product contains sugar, dextrose, cornstarch, modified cornstarch, salt, calcium carageenan, polysorbate 60, artificial flavor, natural flavor, artificial color, including FD&C Yellow? Answer: Banana Cream Jell-O Pudding! Question: Where are the bananas? Or the cream, for that matter?). Some processing may in fact be unavoidable in our modern, complex society. But the question of high technology food processing (heating, refining, preservatives, coloring, long storage, strange chemical combinations, and so on) and its effects on our health is one we cannot afford to overlook.

Here the broader evolutionary perspective helps us understand the facts. From time immemorial, the diet of humans had ***no*** processed food of any kind. Only fresh, whole foods were eaten, and eaten immediately after harvest. Our bodies are simply not prepared to deal with the radically different diet of the last few decades —hence the epidemics of degenerative diseases. And this observation is reinforced by health statistics from the few modern-day societies which still eat a simple, non-processed diet; the people in them are virtually free of these diseases. Even more telling, when such "primitive" people are transplanted to the "civilized" world and adopt a modern diet, they too become prey to heart disease, cancer, and other "diseases of progress".

The present controversies over salt and refined sugar relate closely to the question of processing food and its impact on mental and physical health. If one's diet consists entirely of fresh, whole foods, one's daily intake of sodium chloride will usually average between 500 and 1000 milligrams, and that amount is of course what our bodies are adapted to accept. However, the average American, eating a diet replete with processed foods, consumes twelve to thirty times this needed amount. The results are entirely predictable: massive overload on the system, and an epidemic of hypertension (high blood pressure).

Refined sugar is a highly processed, nutrient-free substance, consisting entirely of simple carbohydrates. The average American eats 130 pounds of the stuff each year. This amounts to over 600 calories per day—or 20% to 35% of the total diet. Our human ancestors did in fact eat substantial amounts of simple carbohydrates—in the form of fruit. But the simple carbohydrates in raw, whole fruit come complete with all sorts of vitamins, minerals, enzymes, and fiber (as well as any as yet undiscovered essentials), and our bodies are adapted to need all of these nutrients along with the carbohydrate. That's one of the subtle and insidious dangers of refined sweeteners; the body has to find all of these nutrients somewhere to help assimilate such massive doses of sugar. If these nutrients do not come with the food being eaten—and they decidedly do not with refined sugar—the body must provide them itself from its tissues. This constant sacrifice by the body is a severe strain upon its health—for those sacrificed nutrients are needed elsewhere for crucial body functions.

Another example of our diets evolving faster than our bodies is evidenced by an examination of fat consumption. Forty percent of the total calories in the average American's diet comes from fat, and this is primarily saturated fat from animal sources. This represents an enormous increase in dietary fat during the last 150 years, and is three to four times more than the amount of fat consumed by our ancestors. The results, documented by decades of increasingly compelling research, are epidemics of heart disease, obesity, and cancers of the breast and digestive system. (A further implication of our society's "steak religion" is the vastly increased consumption of protein, along with the belief that we need huge amounts to function; overconsumption of protein has been linked to many maladies, especially cancer.) In 1977, the Senate Select Committee on Nutrition and Human Needs took heed of this evidence and urged a drastic revision in America's dietary habits: less total fat, less saturated fat, less salt, more complex carbohydrates. The meat, dairy and egg industries have mounted a vehement counterattack, defending fat (and their pocketbooks), and producing at least the appearance of scientific controversy. What is the interested, sensible, and justifiably confused consumer to do?

Again considering our origins and evolutionary history helps us find the answer. The diets of our ancestors were comprised of fruits, vegetables, nuts and seeds—all fresh—and occasionally the flesh of fish and wild animals. Almost all fruits and vegetables have little or no fat. Nuts and seeds are generally high in fats, but these are largely unsaturated; moreover, because each nut was solidly encased in a frustratingly hard-to-open casing, levels of consumption were naturally controlled. Almost all fish are very low in fat. And even though the wild animals that may have been consumed did have saturated fat (all animal fat is saturated), there were at least two limiting factors: (1) wild animals have considerably less fat than the sedentary feedlot beasts of the modern era; and (2) chasing an antelope with a stone axe did not guarantee meat at every meal! Moreover, the highly active life both burned more calories and helped eliminate waste products from the body at a much higher rate than our typical low-energy existences.

Once we begin to see our place in the natural scheme of things, as a species developing along with all other forms of life, our characteristics and physiology strongly determined by the marvelous processes of evolution, we can begin to choose and act more wisely. We don't have to become neanderthals again to respect and re-assume many of the practices that have assured our health and vigor throughout our evolutionary development. We can orient our diet towards the whole, the raw, and the fresh, growing our own food where possible, and growing it organically. We can decrease our level of food consumption overall and adopt a more active lifestyle. Do more things ourselves, enjoy being energetic, adopt a regular program of vigorous exercise—walking, running, cycling, swimming. We should educate ourselves as to the modern food industry, understanding the possible effects of certain processes and additives. We must avoid processed foods whenever we can (and we usually can), or at least scrutinize the labels if we can't. We must listen to our bodies, and eat the foods that we really demand—rather than habitually eating those products urged upon us by the ubiquitous advertisements of the corporate food industry. In other words, we can personally take charge of our own diets and lifestyles, and make them as simple and "time-honored" as possible.

It is in doing this that we will discover our greatest resource in the move towards optimal nutrition and greatest health—ourselves. For it can be argued that just as science does not give the whole picture, neither does slavishly following the rules of the past. For our ancestors were highly diversified, over time and space, and we cannot determine with precision what is the biologically perfect human diet from studying their ways. Moreover, evolution is not a thing of the past! It is an integral and ongoing process of life itself. Our own lives are themselves experiments in newness. Hence it is primarily through taking charge and experiencing our lives that we can best learn what is right for us. Our greatest source of knowledge about what we should eat and how we should live is, therefore, personal experience.

Our society has taught us to depend upon experts and outside sources of information for the truth about even the most personal and intimate parts of our lives, such as how we feel physically, mentally, and emotionally. Moreover, our upbringing has usually habituated us to desiring and consuming foods which put a strain on our systems[1] and ultimately lead to breakdowns. Nonetheless, it's true that we (our bodies/our minds) can discover and prefer what is best for us. We can make this highly functional sense come through more and more clearly as we take steps to improve our diet and lifestyle, so that after a while we can begin to rely on our regained nutritional instinct.

This process of rediscovery isn't an instant one, though. We won't be able to trust our instinct about what is best for us for some time at least, since we've confused things with a lot of habits and addictions that give false promptings of our desires and dislikes. We have to work on understanding and facing these, part of which involves undoing a lifetime of programming about what we should and should not eat. Nutritional information and awareness of our species' history help us to eat wisely while we're developing a reliable and accurate ***inner*** nutritional sense.

While both modern science and human evolution point to the appropriateness of a simple, fresh, whole foods diet, the real test—what will most deeply convince us—is how it feels. No matter how persuasive the arguments, we humans demand the ultimate proof of personal experience. And even though at first when we "listen to our bodies", we may not hear much, increasingly the channels will clear and new awarenesses set in. With increased sensitivity and unity of body, mind, and spirit, the deleterious or beneficial effects of consuming a given food will be quite apparent to us. Health comes to be felt as something considerably greater than mere absence of disease, and the new experiences of feeling really good promote us to choose more and more those foods and behaviors that add to our well-being and new-found vitality. But—don't take our word for it! This is an experience that is within the power of each one of us to realize. Take control of your life—it is your unique opportunity to affect the conditions of your own existence and, however minutely, contribute to the exciting evolution of the human species, and of all life.

Bread and the Healthy Diet

Where does bread fit into this picture? Is it part of the problem, and therefore to be avoided? Or is it part of the solution, and therefore to be encouraged? The answer is "it depends"—depends on what goes into that bread.

The modern commercial loaf is in many ways an almost perfect mirror image of our present dietary problems. It is made primarily from highly-refined wheat flour, denuded of the nutrient-rich bran and germ. It is frequently doused with quantities of both salt and sugar (the latter coming under a wide variety of names: sucrose, dextrose, glucose, fructose, maltose, brown sugar, corn syrup). It is replete with chemical extenders, conditioners, emulsifiers, preservatives, flavoring and coloring agents. It frequently contains significant amounts of saturated fats—in the form of lard, palm oil, or coconut oil. And if we slather each slice with salty butter—to give it a semblance of taste—the nutritional disaster is complete.

On the other hand, the home-baked, whole grain loaf can be a real nutritional plus. A simple loaf made from freshly ground, whole wheat flour, yeast, and water contains plenty of vitamins and minerals, no added sugar or salt, lots of complex carbohydrates and protein, and no chemicals or saturated fats. And when you are doing the baking, you can control the quality and type of ingredients that go into the loaf. For a sweeter loaf, you can add honey, malt syrup, or fruit instead of refined sugar. For a sharper taste, you can add herbs instead of salt. For a moist rich crumb, you can add cold-pressed safflower oil instead of lard. And to extend the loaf's keeping qualities, you can add a tablespoon of vinegar instead of BHT.

The simple whole grain loaf was in fact a part of the diet of our evolutionary forerunners, at least in their later stages. But you must keep bread in its proper perspective. As bakers, we are well aware of some less positive aspects of consuming baked goods—especially in excess! Bread and other baked goods are definitely a heavy. A baked treat—even whole grain and natural—is often a complex blend of ground or semi-"refined" ingredients (flour, oils, nut butters, molasses, for example). Moreover, the baking process requires extended exposure to high heat, and we know that heat destroys many vital elements in foods. For these reasons, the primary dietary emphasis should still be on fresh, raw, whole foods. Even more importantly, though, our ancestors ate a wide variety of foods, and a diet based largely on bread would miss that necessary range and diversity. Maintain a sense of balance, and be attentive to your body's real needs. Enjoy home-baked bread made from fresh, whole ingredients—but enjoy it in moderation.

Foods for Whole Grain Baking

Understanding the variety and properties of ingredients, and choosing them carefully, is basic to successful baking. Using poor quality ingredients or combining the wrong proportions will give the baker disappointing results. In this chapter, we provide a review of the foods used most often in baking.

A good general guideline is to buy your ingredients as "whole" and fresh as possible, obtaining organically grown products if you can. If possible, buy whole grain flours which have been stone-ground. Look for unfiltered, uncooked honey and unrefined, unbleached oils. Keep whole grain flours, oils, seeds, and nuts refrigerated in sealed containers to preserve freshness, and use them within a short period of time.

In making bread, there are actually only two ingredients which are absolutely essential—grain and liquid. Historically, bread began as a simple, unleavened loaf. Roughly ground grain was mixed with water, shaped, and baked in the sun. Try making it this simple sometime.

Grains

Many kinds of grains are used in baking throughout the world. The North American perspective is inevitably wheat-centered, and thus we tend to see other grains as additions to wheat bread rather than the central grain in the loaf. However, there is a wide variety of grains, ranging from the more subtle oat, millet, and rice to the uniquely-flavored buckwheat, sorghum, barley, and corn. All of these grains, and others even less familiar to us, have been, and still are, staple foods in other civilizations and cultures.

Grains are seeds and can be used in many different ways: whole, sprouted, cooked, roughly milled or cracked, rolled into flakes, or ground into meal or flour. Grains are highly nutritious, being excellent sources of protein, carbohydrates, fats, vitamins, minerals, trace elements, and fiber. Loss of nutrients occurs when grains are refined in any way, so make sure the grain products you are buying are 100% whole.

Grains have several key functions in bread. The complex carbohydrate in all grains provides food for the yeast organisms (whether added by the baker, or incorporated from the air), allowing them to grow and multiply rapidly. In growing, yeast converts sugars and oxygen into carbon dioxide and alcohol, the first of which causes the bread to rise and the latter contributing to the bread's flavor.

The flours of some grains contain gluten, a protein consisting of gliadin and glutenin. When bread dough is kneaded, these two stick together to form an elastic network which traps the carbon dioxide released by the yeast. This causes the bread both to rise and to keep its shape during baking. Wheat is highest in gluten, while rye and triticale contain some (mostly the stickier gliadin). Oats and barley contain a little, and other grains none; thus only small amounts should be used in combination with mostly wheat flour if you want your bread to rise well.

Gluten, especially wheat gluten, causes adverse (or "allergic") reactions in some people. However, many of these people can tolerate other grains, including rye, and even wheat if it has been sprouted. Essene bread is a very ancient bread, made only of sprouted grains (usually wheat), ground, shaped, and then baked at low temperatures. If you are "allergic" to wheat flour, you might try essene bread instead.

Grains in all their different forms provide an exciting variety of tastes and textures in bread. Without demeaning basic whole wheat bread, the same loaf undergoes remarkable changes of flavor and texture when stone-ground cornmeal is added (or try some cracked wheat, oats, barley flakes, cooked rice, sprouted wheat, or whole millet). Multi-grain blends of flours can be extremely delicious. Grain flours other than wheat can work very well in muffins, cakes, and cookies, while oats and other flakes provide the basis for granolas, bars, and many cookies.

To guide you in your choice of grains for baking, we offer the following review of whole grain terminology.

Amaranth

Although not widely used in our culture at present, this ancient grain is expected to become more available in the near future. It is exceptionally high in protein, especially the rarer lysine and sulfur-containing amino acids. Amaranth was cultivated on this continent thousands of years ago, and was a staple in Aztec culture before its eradication by Cortez. Reportedly, the small grains can be popped and used in cereal or confections, while amaranth flour can be added to whole wheat to enhance the flavor and nutrition.

Barley

Extremely hardy, barley flourishes from the Arctic Circle to subtropical climates. It is believed to have been the first grain cultivated by humans, and is still today a dietary staple in many parts of the world. Barley has been largely forgotten in the West, however, where most of the crop is fed to livestock. Sprouted barley is used to make malt and beer.

Most of the barley commonly available is "pearled", which means it has been refined to remove the bran and the germ, and hence much of the flavor and nutrition. Try to find natural brown barley, which has only been hulled. Grind it yourself into fresh flour, or buy this ready-ground. Adding this mild-flavored, low-gluten flour in small amounts to a yeasted wheat bread (lightly pretoasting it, if you like) gives a moist, sweet, cake-like texture. Barley flour in combination with whole wheat flour creates a delicious, chewy unyeasted loaf. Used alone in cookies, barley flour yields a tasty, light-colored, slightly pasty product. Cooked barley and rolled barley flakes can also be added to bread.

Berry

The berry is the whole grain, before it is hulled, cracked, milled, or processed in any way. It contains bran, germ, and endosperm (see diagram, p. 2). Buy berries to sprout, or to grind into flour yourself for maximum freshness. Soaked, cooked, or sprouted berries give a nice chewy texture to yeasted breads.

Bran

Usually, we associate this term with the partially ground husk of the wheat berry, and any product just called "bran" is almost certainly wheat. However, the term properly refers to the husk layers surrounding any grain. These layers have some protein, vitamins and minerals, and lots of fiber, all of which are lost when milled grains are refined. Adding extra bran to your breads (and goodies) makes them high in fiber and darkly-flecked, although bran is naturally present, of course, in whole grain flours. Warm bran muffins are unrivaled for breakfast!

Buckwheat

Probably first cultivated in ancient China, it was spread to Europe by migrating tribes. A refined version of buckwheat flour was farinha, which became a staple around the Mediterranean. ("Farina" today is usually degermed wheat.) Buckwheat is still an important foodstuff in Eastern Europe and Russia, where the groats are roasted and cooked as a gruel, called kasha.

Buckwheat in the United States is mostly fed to animals, or plowed under as green manure. However, buckwheat flour and groats (hulled whole berries) are available, and may be used in baking. (Fresh flour can be ground from groats in a blender.) Buckwheat has a nutritional value similar to wheat, and is outstandingly high in lysine.

Buckwheat has a distinct and unusual flavor, which can easily dominate a bread. Experiment with it judiciously to see if you like the taste. Try adding some cooked groats or substitute ½ cup buckwheat flour in a two-loaf batch of whole wheat bread. It will come out somewhat heavier and more fully-flavored. A terrific unyeasted bread can be made using cooked buckwheat and buckwheat flour, with some whole wheat added for gluten (see Index).

Corn

A grain which probably originated in Mexico, corn was first cultivated by the earliest inhabitants of North and South America. Literally hundreds of varieties exist, many grown only in isolated South American communities. Corn is very nutritious, and is the only grain high in carotene, which produces vitamin A.

Yellow cornmeal is most commonly used in baking, giving a crumbly, slightly crunchy sweetness and golden color to whole wheat products. It makes a nice addition to yeasted breads, and is delicious in corn muffins and quick breads. Since cornmeal is often "degermed", make sure you are buying whole cornmeal, preferably stone-ground. Cornmeal is also used to dust the baking sheet to prevent sticking of round loaves, pita bread, or pizza. Dried whole kernels of corn can be cooked till soft and added to yeasted bread for a chewy surprise, or cooked, ground, and shaped into patties, to bake a popular Venezuelan staple called arepas (see Index).

Cracked Grains

Whole grains are broken into several rough pieces by coarse milling to produce cracked grains. Cracked wheat, the most common, gives a nice texture when added in small amounts to whole wheat bread.

Endosperm

The starchy inner part of the cereal grain, the endosperm contains carbohydrates and occasionally, as in wheat, some protein. It is low in vitamins and minerals, and entirely lacking in fiber. White flour is made up of ground endosperm alone.

Germ

An inner part of the grain berry, containing the embryo of the new plant, the germ is naturally high in food value. Wheat germ is most commonly available (see "Wheat" below), and makes a rich, flavorful addition to breads, muffins and cookies.

Meal

Meal usually refers to coarsely ground flour. But in England and Australia, for example, "wholemeal" flour means "whole wheat" flour. The addition of some meal to bread gives it a grainier texture.

Millet

One of the most ancient of grains, millet was a staple in China long before rice. Millet flour is much used in Africa, and is the basis of the national bread of Ethiopia (injera), the flat cakes of India (roti), and is a staple of the Hunzas. It has a very high quality protein (though it lacks gluten), is particularly high in minerals, and is said to be the most digestible of grains.

The tiny, delicately-flavored grains have usually been hulled before reaching the stores. You can grind these into flour in a blender, and use in baked goods for a light crunchiness and sweet richness of flavor. Toasting it first enhances the sweet, nut-like taste. ½ cup in a two-loaf batch of whole wheat is a good rule of thumb. Small quantities of whole, uncooked millet add a gentle crunch and pretty white-flecked appearance to breads. You can also cook the grains and use a little in bread for a moist sweetness. And a successful wheatless cookie can be based on cooked millet (see Peanut Minus Cookies in the Index).

Oats

A relative newcomer among cultivated grains, oats were apparently first used extensively by the Roman Empire. Oats grow worldwide, flourishing in climates that are too cold for wheat.

Oats are available in several forms: whole groats, generally hulled; thick-cut and regular rolled oats (sometimes misleadingly called oatmeal), which are made by rolling whole groats; instant rolled oats (made by cutting the whole groats into pieces, precooking the pieces, and then rolling them super-thin); steel-cut oats (groats cut lengthwise with sharp blades); and oat flour (groats or rolled oats ground to a fine meal). You can grind your own flour in a blender.

Oats make a delicious and nutritious addition to baked goods, and because they contain a natural anti-oxidant, they extend the keeping quality of breads. Oat flour contributes a moist sweetness to bread; use about one cup of the low-gluten oat flour to four cups of whole wheat. Cooked oats in bread produce a sticky dough and a moist, sweet loaf. Rolled oats appear as pale flecks and make the bread chewy; they'll absorb some water during kneading and rising, so make the dough a little wetter than usual.

Rolled oats produce a nice flavor and great chewy texture in cookies, and are the mainstay of bar crusts. They also make excellent cereals, whether left raw, as in muesli, or mixed with other ingredients and baked, as in granola.

Rice

Rice is an oriental grain that has been grown in India and China for over 4,000 years. Its cultivation was not adopted in Europe until the 15th century and in America until the late 17th century. Today, rice is the staple food for over one half of the world's population.

In its whole state, as brown rice, this grain is very nutritious and high in B vitamins. Refinement into white rice by removal of the bran and germ greatly depletes the flavor, texture, and food value. Rice can add an exciting variety of tastes and textures to your baked goods. A couple of points about buying rice: firstly, it is susceptible to many field diseases, so commercial rice products are high in pesticide residues. Buy organically grown brown rice if at all possible. And secondly, the rice flour that is most commonly available is made from white rice, with all the same nutritional deficiencies, so look for brown rice flour, or grind your own from whole brown rice.

Sample the sweet graininess of brown rice flour in your recipes, pretoasting it lightly if you like. Breads with some rice flour tend to come out moist, dense, and smooth. It holds up well alone in a wheatless cake, creating a close but delicately-textured crumb and a subtle sweetness. A soft, close texture is obtained when rice flour is used alone in cookies; ground rice, coarser than flour, gives a soft sandiness when blended with whole wheat flour in shortbreads.

Cooked brown rice gives yeasted breads a moist, chewy character, and long-cooked rice gruel is the basis for a delicious unyeasted bread called Grandpa's Farm Bread (see Index). Coarsely ground rice grits add crunch. Rice polishings (the inner bran layers) and rice bran (the outer layers) are by-products of the refining process, and can be used like wheat bran or wheat germ in baked goods. They are, of course, high in fiber, as well as B vitamins, calcium, phosphorus, and potassium.

Rye

Another of the newcomers to the cultivated cereal family, rye was apparently first grown during the Roman Empire. Its moderate gluten content and distinctive hearty flavor have made it a staple bread flour in northern regions where wheat cannot subsist. Black rye bread, sweetened with molasses, is popular in Eastern Europe and Russia, sourdough rye and pumpernickel are German favorites, and a lighter rye bread, made with honey, and, often, orange, is common in Scandinavia.

Rye is a soft grain, nutritionally very similar to wheat; it is high in minerals and B vitamins, particularly potassium and riboflavin. When buying flour, make sure you get the dark variety; "light" rye flour has had some of the bran removed. Whole rye berries can be readily ground into flour at home.

A yeasted loaf made entirely of rye flour will be fine-textured, moist and compact, with a unique, rich, slightly sour flavor. Rye flour produces a sticky dough, not as smooth as whole wheat dough. But if you avoid the temptation to keep adding flour, you can get a nice rise and reasonably light texture even in 100% rye bread.

Perhaps the most delicious "rye bread" is made from equal amounts of rye and whole wheat flour. This bread has a dark color, rich aroma, and distinctive rye taste, and is still buoyant and light-textured. Caraway seeds and molasses complement the flavor of rye, while a touch of anise is another popular flavoring. Rye flour used alone can make a decent wheatless muffin, with currants as a nice addition. Rye meal can be added to whole wheat breads, too. Rolled rye flakes may be used in baked goods, though they are tougher than rolled oats. They are often combined in small quantities with oats in granolas and cereals. Finally, an unexpectedly delicious way to prepare rye is to sprout the whole berries, grind, shape, and bake the loaves at low temperatures; it produces a rich, dark, sweet essene bread.

Sorghum

A food staple in Africa and Asia, sorghum is third only to wheat and rice in worldwide consumption. It is a relative of millet and somewhat similar to corn nutritionally. Until recently, it was widely grown and eaten—especially the sweet syrup extract—in the southern United States. You may be able to find the grain at feed stores and elevators, and it is very inexpensive. Whole sorghum can be cooked or ground into flour (which is very low in gluten). This is a grain we haven't worked with much, but it is said to make a tasty addition to bread.

Triticale

A cross between wheat and rye, triticale is a monument to modern agricultural research. It reputedly combines some of the best qualities of each grain; the high-protein, high-gluten content of wheat and the high yield and ruggedness of rye. You can buy triticale as whole berries, rolled flakes, or flour. The grain has a subtle yet distinct flavor which many find delicious.

An excellent loaf of yeasted bread can be made using 100% triticale flour, but the technique is somewhat different. The gluten in triticale is quite soft and must be treated gently. Gentle rather than vigorous kneading, and allowing only one rising of the dough rather than two or three, preserves the elasticity of triticale gluten. However, we haven't worked extensively with a 100% triticale loaf, and the flour is usually combined with wheat to ensure strength and shape. Rolled triticale flakes can be added to breads, cookies, and granolas. Whole berries may be sprouted for essene bread, but the sprouts tend to spoil easily.

Wheat

Wheat is thought to have originated in the Middle East, possibly Turkey, and competes with barley for being the oldest cultivated grain. A hardy, rugged plant which grows almost anywhere if it has fertile ground and water, wheat has been a food staple of many ancient civilizations. Containing the highest amount of gluten of all grains, it is today widely considered in the Western world as being almost synonymous with bread.

Wheat is extremely nutritious, containing most of the elements needed for human nourishment. The whole grains are rich in magnesium, iron, phosphorus, vitamins B and E, carbohydrates, protein, and numerous trace minerals. (See pp. 2-3 for diagram and more detail about the constituents of the wheat berry.) When the grains are ground, the natural fats begin to go rancid, so grind or buy your whole wheat flour as fresh as possible, use quickly, and refrigerate if necessary. Any wheat flours other than ***100% whole wheat*** have been refined and therefore have less nutrients and flavor. That includes "unbleached white flour", which though lacking chemical bleaches and sometimes preservatives, is still devoid of the most nutritious parts of the grain: the bran and the germ.

Try to buy your whole wheat flour stone-ground. Stone-grinding, as opposed to conventional high-speed milling, does not overheat the grain and cause serious deterioration in nutrients and flavor. Grinding your own berries is best of all, of course.

There are two distinct types of whole wheat flour used in baking, and it is important to understand their properties and uses.

Hard Whole Wheat Flour, or ***Whole Wheat Bread Flour*** should be used in breads, or the gluten network will not be fully formed and the bread won't rise well. Hard whole wheat flour is milled from hard red spring wheat or hard red winter wheat, both of which are high in gluten. It is desirable for bread flour to contain about 14-15% gluten. A flour significantly deficient in gluten may give you rather flat bread.

Whole Wheat Pastry Flour or ***Soft Whole Wheat Flour*** is usually used in cookies, cakes, muffins, piecrusts, and so on. It is much lower in gluten than hard whole wheat flour, and produces tender, finely-textured goodies. It is milled from soft winter wheat.

Additional points about the use of these two kinds of wheat are:

1. Hard whole wheat flour ***can*** be used in cookies, bars, and brownies, either alone or combined with pastry flour. The texture will be less fine and delicate. It's not recommended for cakes and muffins, though. If a goodie recipe doesn't specify whole wheat pastry flour, you can use either kind, bearing in mind the slight differences in your results.
2. Whole wheat pastry flour can be added to breads, but use plenty of hard whole wheat too, or the bread may turn out heavy and flat.
3. Some yeasted sweet rolls and desserts use all whole wheat pastry flour. The yeast will still produce a rise in the dough, but the texture will be more soft and cakey, rather than firm and elastic.

4. Sometimes a hard wheat crop may be too low in gluten to produce a well-risen yeasted bread. If you're really unable to get hold of flour with adequate gluten content, you may want to consider using additional gluten flour as a last resort (see below for definition and caveats).
5. For sprouting whole berries to make essene bread, use hard whole wheat for a more cohesive texture. Pastry wheat sprouts produce a softer, more crumbly dough, and tend to spoil more quickly.

Other Wheat Products:

Cracked Wheat is whole wheat berries, usually the hard red variety, which have been coarsely cracked into small pieces. A small amount adds a crunchy texture to yeasted breads. Bulgur, which has been cooked and parched before cracking, can be used similarly.

Wheat Bran, the outer layers of the whole wheat berry, is a by-product of refining white flour. High in vitamins and minerals, it adds nutrition, texture, and fiber to baked goods. Remember, too, that whole wheat flour already contains its own bran.

Wheat Germ is another by-product of the refining process. It is the nutrient-rich embryo of the wheat plant, containing a high concentration of B vitamins, vitamin E, iron, and protein. Because of the high oil content (wheat germ is high in unsaturated fat), raw wheat germ goes rancid very easily. There is evidence that rancid foods draw nutrients from the body during digestion. If wheat germ hasn't been refrigerated and smells somewhat strong, it is probably rancid and not worth eating. Toasted wheat germ has a pleasant nutty taste and keeps somewhat longer than raw if refrigerated; however, the toasting destroys many of the nutrients. Wheat germ makes a healthful addition to breads and goodies, giving richness, fiber, and a nice flavor to baked goods.

Wheat Flours not explicitly labeled ***100% whole wheat*** have been processed to remove some or all of the bran and germ of the whole berry, thereby reducing the flavor, texture, and nutrition. In addition, most commercial flours have been treated with chemicals and preservatives. We do not recommend any refined flours. There is no need to use ***any*** white flour in baking to produce well-risen loaves and delicate cakes and pastries.

Gluten Flour, also called ***High Gluten Flour*** or just ***Gluten***, is a highly refined mixture of white flour and additional gluten; gluten itself is refined from white flour. If you seem unable by any other means to make your bread rise, and know that the hard whole wheat flour you can obtain has a low natural gluten content, then you might consider adding gluten flour in very small amounts. This product, like all highly refined foods, is difficult to digest and many people suffer strong reactions to it. Our bakeries prefer not to use it and we don't recommend its use. It is occasionally added by a few bakeries, however, to boost a low-gluten whole wheat flour.

Liquids

Liquids are the other indispensable ingredient for bakers. They combine the dry grains into a workable dough, allowing you to shape an endless variety of loaves and rolls (or in the case of essene bread, cause the grains to sprout and grow into a dough). Liquids serve as a vital catalyst in the leavening of baked goods, providing the moist environment in which bread yeasts can multiply and chemical leaveners react. Lastly, liquids can add flavor, nutrients, and texture to breads and baked goods.

Water

The common denominator, and the one indispensable element, of all liquids. Water is all you ever really need in breadbaking—it's also the cheapest and most available. Many people in bakeries are concerned about the quality of municipal water, and look for more healthful alternatives.

Milk (see also "Dairy Products" below)

The use of milk in yeasted doughs adds flavor and protein, increases the browning, produces a softer, smoother crumb, and is somewhat more preservative than water. Whole milk is most often used in sweet, rich doughs, like tea rings or sweet rolls. The fat in whole dairy milk tends to coat the flour particles and somewhat inhibit the formation of gluten. For this reason, as well as to avoid saturated animal fats, many people prefer to use skim or non-fat milk.

Non-fat dry milk, either made liquid with water or added dry with adjustment in the liquid, is used in our bakeries to make a sweeter, richer bread that appeals to people trying to move away from white bread. Milk and milk powder give richness and cohesive texture to cakes, muffins, and cookies.

Buttermilk (see also "Dairy Products" below)

Buttermilk adds nutrients and a cheesy flavor to bread, plus a more finely textured dough and less fat than whole milk. Unfortunately the buttermilk of today is produced chemically, not naturally. Buttermilk powder has recently become available. Like other cultured products, such as yogurt (which can also be used in breads), buttermilk gives a delightful rich tang to cakes and biscuits.

Fruit Juice (see also "Sweeteners" below)

It's nice to make your breads using warm fruit juice. Cider or the juice in which dried fruits have been soaking are most common. Fruit juices add nutrients as well as sweetness and distinctive flavor to baked goods; you can reduce or eliminate the concentrated sweetener in the recipe by using them.

Potato Water

Made from steeping raw grated potatoes, potato water is thought to aid the rising of dough by encouraging yeast activity. It also contributes nutrients and flavor.

Beer

Beer provides an interesting flavor, not unlike some sourdough breads. Not widely used, however, at least in the actual baking.

Leaveners

Leaveners cause doughs and batters to rise, making them light and porous. There are really only two types, both producing carbon dioxide, but in different ways; the live variety (yeast, sourdough), which gives off the gas as it lives and multiplies in the dough; and the chemical versions (baking powder, baking soda), which leaven through the reaction of acid and alkaline substances.

Yeast

Yeast is a microscopic fungus which reproduces rapidly by budding when provided with a warm, moist environment and carbohydrates to feed on. Enzymes break down carbohydrates into sugars which the yeast ferments into carbon dioxide (CO_2) and alcohol. The alcohol contributes to the flavor of the bread, while the CO_2 is trapped by the elastic network of gluten formed in the flour by kneading of the dough. As the yeast organisms continue to multiply, more CO_2 is formed and the dough rises.

It is important to keep these two by-products in balance. Too much yeast, or over-rising of the dough, results in excessive production of alcohol, and the finished loaf may well taste disagreeably "yeasty". (This may happen more quickly when the bread is unsalted.) Although you can eliminate a surplus of CO_2 by simply punching down the dough, the dough may have expanded beyond the elasticity of the gluten bonds. This would result in tearing of these bonds and a heavier, more coarsely-textured loaf.

Baking yeast (not to be confused with brewer's or nutritional yeast) comes to you alive, but inactive. Dry yeast is inactive because it lacks moisture. Fresh or cake yeast is inactive because it is kept cold. Yeast organisms need warmth to become active, but begin to die at about 120° F and are useless at 140° F. To activate dry yeast, dissolve in lukewarm liquid in the range of 95° F-115° F. Fresh yeast likes it cooler, 80°-105° F. The liquid should feel slightly warm or neutral to the fingers, but not hot. Yeast will come alive, but more slowly, at cooler temperatures.

All of the recipes in this book use dry yeast, as do the majority of bakeries. Dry yeast can safely be stored for months in a sealed container in a cool, dry place. Fresh yeast should be refrigerated and used within one to two weeks. It can conveniently be frozen, in one batch blocks, for several months. Use immediately upon thawing.

The equivalent for using the two types of yeast is:

1 Tbl. dry yeast = 1 oz. fresh yeast

If you are uncertain of the quality or freshness of your yeast, you may want to test or "proof" it. For this method, see "Making the Sponge" in "How to Bake—Yeasted Breads". To activate yeast, it is not essential to use a simple carbohydrate—some form of sugar—since the organisms will come alive in warm water alone, and can break down the carbohydrate in flour to feed on. The process will take a little longer though.

Sourdough

This leavener is actually just one special way of introducing yeast organisms into bread dough and produces a distinctive sour taste, which can be delicious. A mixture of flour and liquid is left in a warm place to "ferment", during which time natural yeasts in the air and flour are trapped in the dough. (This is the means by which all unyeasted breads rise.) The sourdough "starter" is kept inactivated by refrigeration, like fresh yeast. It comes to life in a warm, moist environment, when left out to warm up to room temperature and then mixed with other ingredients. For details of how to make and use sourdough, see "How to Bake—Sourdough Breads" and recipes in the Index.

Baking Powder and Baking Soda

These chemical leaveners are commonly used in many types of baked goods. Their action relies on the chemical reaction of acid and alkali, which gives off carbon dioxide. ***Baking soda***, sodium bicarbonate, is an alkali which reacts with acidic ingredients such as honey, vinegar, fruit juice, buttermilk, etc. ***Baking powder*** contains sodium bicarbonate and its own acid agent, as well as starch. It reacts when moistened. Commercial baking powder usually contains calcium acid phosphate (as its acid ingredient) and cornstarch. For a better home-made blend, using cream of tartar (potassium bitartrate) and arrowroot powder, see "How to Bake—Substituting Ingredients". Be aware that baking soda is very high in sodium. By making your own baking powder, you eliminate some of that sodium and all of the toxic aluminum compounds that are frequently added to commercial brands.

Both baking powder and baking soda work quickly; in fact, they generally require a minimum of mixing and speedy dispatch into the oven, or they'll begin to puff up the batter prematurely. They successfully leaven flours with no gluten content, and thus open up a wide range of possibilities for quick breads, muffins, brownies, and cakes. Baking soda used alone produces a very tender crumb. They can also be used in cookies to give a more porous texture.

Sweeteners

All sweeteners are a form of sugar. Often confused, there are two very distinct definitions of the word "sugar". The ***chemical*** definition refers to all simple carbohydrates—including those found naturally in fruits and vegetables as well as those known as sweeteners, such as honey, maple syrup, and table sugar. Within this chemical definition, there are several named varieties of "sugar" based on chemical structure. Fructose, sucrose, maltose, and glucose are examples.

The ***common*** definition of sugar refers only to the refined products of the sugar cane or beet. This includes white (granulated) sugar, confectioner's (or powdered) sugar, brown sugar, and raw or turbinado sugar. We do not use or recommend ***any*** of these sugars. They are highly imbalanced products which are absorbed too rapidly into the bloodstream and put considerable strain on the body. The consumption of refined sugars has been shown to be responsible for many health problems. Other refined sugars to avoid are corn syrup and commercial fructose.

The major sweeteners used in whole grain baking are honey, malt, and molasses. As previously mentioned, sweeteners hasten the action of yeast and add sweetness and flavor to baked goods. Here we briefly review various sweeteners, but bear in mind that most sweeteners are almost totally lacking in food value other than calories. We're so fond of them because we've been raised on sugary foods. But reducing sweeteners in your baking will bring an appreciation of the flavorful sweetness in grains and other natural foods. In particular, remember that sweeteners are ***not*** essential to a successful loaf of bread, and many people find they prefer the full grainy flavor of unsweetened bread.

Honey

Many people ascribe a wide variety of health-giving properties to honey. Moreover, it is the sole source of nutrition for a very active and industrious animal — the bee — and as far as we know, white sugar alone will not sustain any form of life. So, although analysis indicates that honey has a similar chemical structure to white sugar, perhaps science does not yet know everything....! Always try and buy raw honey; the others have been pasteurized and this heating does no good for honey's nutritive benefits.

There are many different honeys, from light-colored and mild to dark, strong-flavored ones, such as buckwheat. Most of our baked goods call for a mild honey. Honey gives a nice golden color and a delicious aroma and flavor to whole wheat products. In its uncooked, undiluted, and unfiltered form, it seems to have a preservative effect. Honey has an acidic quality and thus can be used to catalyze baking soda.

Malt

Available in either powdered or very sticky liquid form, malt is made by sprouting wheat, barley, or corn, lightly toasting the sprouts, grinding them to a powder, and then filtering out the solids. Malt is 65% maltose and contains moderate amounts of minerals and vitamins. It is, perhaps, the best of all sweeteners and is preferred by a number of bakeries for its more subtle sweetness and greater nutrition. It works well in all kinds of baked goods.

One tip about using malt syrup: to avoid having sticky strands everywhere, coat your measuring cup or spoon with oil before dipping it into the malt.

Maple Syrup

This comes from the sap of the sugar maple tree, which is boiled to produce the very sweet, delicately-flavored, and expensive syrup. It is a simple sugar, about 60% sucrose, and many of the nutrients are destroyed in the refining process. Many of the larger producers use formaldehyde in the extraction of the sap (a practice permitted by the USDA), and add flavoring and antifoaming agents. Try to buy pure maple syrup, and keep it refrigerated to avoid fermenting.

Molasses

Most molasses is a by-product of the refinement of white sugar. In this process, the cane or beet is crushed and then flushed with water to extract a syrup (molasses). The degree of sweetness in different types of molasses is determined by the number of sugar crystals that are removed from the syrup in the refining process. Molasses contains vitamins and trace minerals like iron, calcium, zinc, copper, and chromium. Blackstrap molasses is the residue of the third and last extraction. It is about 35% sucrose and has the highest concentration of minerals — and also, unfortunately, of pesticides and residues of the refining process.

Molasses has a strong flavor, particularly suited to dark rye breads and gingery cakes and cookies. It is used sparingly, often in combination with malt or honey.

Fruits

Don't overlook fresh fruits, fruit juices, and dried fruits as sources of sweetness. They avoid the intensity of the concentrated syrups and also contain other balancing nutrients and fiber. Juices, including water in which dried fruit has soaked, are good liquids for sponging breads or binding cookies and muffins. Soaking raisins or dates is most common, while figs or apricots add a unique flavor. Well-soaked dried fruits can be blended, ground, or mashed into a paste or butter and then, for example, substituted for honey in a recipe. Dates give the smoothest butter and a very sweet, wonderfully rich flavor. They are high in natural sugar (about 70%) and rich in minerals and B vitamins. ***Date sugar***, usually ground dried dates, is a dark, granulated sweetener sometimes used in cakes.

During the drying process, dates and other fruits are often treated with sulphuric acid. Apples, peaches, and apricots dried commercially are frequently bleached, and sorbic acid is usually added as a preservative. Try to obtain unsulphured, organic dried fruits if possible.

Among fresh fruits, mashed bananas, chopped apple, and applesauce give a moist richness to quickbreads, muffins, and cookies. Don't forget the appeal of a handful of blueberries, cranberries, cherries, or chopped peaches in cakes and muffins. Grated citrus rind and juice give a flavorful zing to doughs and batters, orange goes nicely in fruity breads, and lemon brings a fresh flavor to goodie recipes. Finally, fruits can be used to make cake fillings, frostings, and toppings; pureed soaked dried fruits, mashed bananas, or raspberries cooked to a gel with arrowroot are just some of the ways to give a wonderful fruity sweetness to a special cake or dessert.

Sorghum Molasses (or Sorghum Syrup)

Derived from the stalks of sorghum, a relative of millet, sorghum molasses was a staple sweetener in the Southern United States until sugar began to dominate the market. It contains mostly levulose sugar (fructose) found in certain fruits and honey and is quite high in minerals. It is milder than molasses, but can be substituted for it, or for malt, or used in combination with other sweeteners.

Rice Syrup

Made from rice, this is one of the mildest sweeteners, but rarely used in baking.

Refined Commercial Sweeteners

Raw or ***Turbinado Sugar*** is the light brown crystalline substance that is separated from molasses in the first step of the sugar refining process. It is a highly processed product, having gone through all but the final filtration of the refinement process. It contains 96% sucrose, and almost no nutrients—only calories.

White (Granulated) Sugar is produced by further refining turbinado sugar. After being washed and clarified with lime or phosphoric acid, the sugar is filtered through charcoal to whiten it and remove any calcium and magnesium salts. White sugar is 99.9% sucrose—it is nutrient-free, a veritable non-food.

Confectioner's (Powdered) Sugar is made by pulverizing white sugar into a powder.

Brown Sugar is simply granulated white sugar, colored with a small amount of molasses or burnt white sugar.

Corn Syrup, frequently seen on grocery shelves by the brand name "Karo", is nothing more than corn sugar in a liquid state. It is mostly glucose and is a highly refined, nutrient-empty product.

Fructose is a type of simple sugar, found naturally in most fruits and in honey. Commercially available fructose, however, is highly refined from corn and comes in liquid or white granulated form. It is the sweetest of all sugars, only a marginal improvement on regular white sugar, and a lot more expensive.

Salt

Salt has been used in breadbaking primarily for its taste and preservative qualities. It also slows and regulates yeast growth, and should not be added to doughs until the yeast has had a good start. Salt-free bread tends to rise faster and should be watched to avoid over-proofing and development of too yeasty a flavor. It may have a somewhat coarser texture than salted bread.

However, we want to stress that salt is not essential to breadbaking. You can make a great-tasting loaf without any salt, and yeast activity can easily be controlled by other methods. The addition of salt to cakes and cookies is just habitual and completely unnecessary. It can even be unpleasant when a soda taste is already present from baking soda or powder.

Salt is a ubiquitous taste that we encounter continually from birth. Almost all processed foods, from baby foods through pot pies and sweet snacks to soups and beverages, are loaded with salt. Our palates become habituated, and food without salt seems "tasteless". In fact, so much salt (and sugar) is put into processed foods in order to conceal the fact that they have been completely denuded of all taste! Meanwhile, modern science continues to uncover evidence of salt as a serious health risk. So why eat it if you don't need it?

Many people aren't aware that commercial or table salt is refined by applying great pressure and temperatures to 1200°F, and then flash-cooling the salt solution. This strips away the many minerals and trace elements naturally present (though in minute quantities) in unrefined salt. The resulting crystals—99.9% pure sodium chloride—are very small, with a tighter molecular bond than occurs during natural crystallization. According to several authorities, this makes refined salt not completely soluble and harder for our bodies to digest.

Moreover, a number of chemical substances are added to commercial salt: potassium iodide (supposedly as a health measure); dextrose (sugar) to keep the iodine from oxidizing; sodium bicarbonate to prevent the iodine turning the salt purple; sodium silico aluminate or magnesium carbonate to coat each crystal and prevent moisture absorption; silicon dioxide, yellow prussiate of soda (sodium ferrocyanide) and green ferric ammonium citrate—all permitted additives to promote free flow. Needless to say, none of these additives (including iodine) is necessary. So if you thought that—even if it was bad for you—at least salt was "pure", now you know! Just remember to say, "Pass the sodium ferrocyanide, please . . . ."

Commercial salt is generally made from inland salt deposits (originally left by oceans millions of years ago). Sea salt, available in coops and many groceries now, is richer in trace minerals than inland salt and our bakeries generally prefer it. The primary emphasis, however, is on using as little of this highly concentrated substance as possible—even when unrefined or "whole".

When you use whole grain and natural products, you will find your baked goods have a much more hearty and varied range of flavors than anything you ever bought at the supermarket. Enjoy these new and delightful tastes, and don't mask them with salt! All foods, including grains, naturally contain some sodium along with other minerals. If you feel initially that your bread is lacking in flavor, experiment with gradually reducing the salt, or use a substitute. Try any one or a combination of the almost endless variety of herbs and spices: basil, oregano, dill, thyme, tarragon, onion, garlic, caraway, poppy seeds, cumin, coriander, cinnamon, ginger, nutmeg, to name just a few. While making a transition to unsalted bread, some people use a more nutritious salty substance such as seaweed (powdered kelp, for example), nutritional yeast, or fermented soybean products like tamari and miso.

The recipes in ***Uprisings*** omit salt from cakes, cookies, muffins, granolas, and bars, since we have found its presence there to be unnecessary and even distasteful. In the bread recipes, two loaves rarely call for more than a teaspoon of salt. We encourage you to reduce or eliminate even this amount. Most of our bakeries offer salt-free breads, although the majority of loaves still contain it. Unyeasted breads work especially well without salt.

Fats and Oils

Fats and oils give richness, flavor, moistness, and calories to baked goods. They act as tenderizers in doughs by coating flour particles and inhibiting gluten formation. There are two main categories of fats: animal and vegetable. Animal fats include butter, egg yolks, cheeses, cream, and lard. They are very high in both saturated fat and cholesterol. Since all modern scientific research indicates that our diets are too high in these substances, many people avoid animal fats whenever possible. Environmental pollutants also concentrate in the fats of animals.

Vegetable fats include margarine, avocado, and many oils: olive, peanut, corn, safflower, sesame, sunflower, coconut, palm, and soybean, for example. Most of these are polyunsaturated fats, at least in their natural state. However, coconut and palm oils are high in saturated fats, and by hydrogenating any oil to make margarine or shortening, for example, the food processors turn them into saturated fats. You can cut out saturated fats by avoiding any fat that is solid at room temperature.

One serious problem with fats is their potential for rancidity. Any oil begins to oxidize, or go rancid, upon contact with air. Oxidation goes on even inside the body after oil has been consumed, and nutrients are taken from body tissues in order to try to digest and eliminate the undesired substances. In solid fats like butter or margarine, salt is often added to conceal the rancid taste and to act as a preservative. The process of oxidation in extracted oils can be slowed if they are kept tightly capped and refrigerated, but cannot be stopped altogether.

Common oil extraction methods involve heating and the addition of petroleum-based solvents. "Mechanically pressed" oils are superior since crushing, and not chemicals, is used; these are sometimes referred to as "cold-pressed", although temperatures may reach 150° during processing. In addition, unrefined oils still contain nutrients, especially Vitamin E (an anti-oxidant which helps preserve the oil), lecithin, and some particles of germ. In contrast, refined oils have been bleached and deodorized, are pale and bland, and often disguise the fact that they are rancid.

The oil most commonly used in our bakeries is safflower (the oil highest in unsaturated fats). If a recipe just says "oil", it's probably safflower. Corn and soy oils are stronger flavored and are sometimes used in breads. Oil is usually put in bread recipes, but it can be omitted. Oil can often be reduced in goodies, if you allow for the reduction of liquid. Oil works well in cookies, cakes, and pie crusts, although solid fats tend to produce a flakier dough.

Dairy Products

Dairy products add richness, texture, flavor, and nutrients to baked goods. Milk, the most common ingredient, produces a softer crumb and has a browning effect. It also retards staling better than water. However, with the exception of nonfat products (nonfat dry milk, nonfat yogurt, whey, and traditional buttermilk), dairy foods add lots of saturated fats and cholesterol to our diets. They also contain high levels of pesticide and pollutant residues, and additives such as hormones, which concentrate in the fat. Many people connected with our bakeries have come to feel that cow's milk, especially when pasteurized, may produce undesirable health effects (such as respiratory and digestive problems), so use dairy products with care.

Remember, too, that most cheeses are loaded with salt, though the unsalted versions are increasingly available. Dairy products are naturally high in sodium, so when using milk powder, many bakers reduce or cut out the salt. For other functions of milk and buttermilk in baked goods, see "Liquids" in this chapter. For suggestions on dairyless baking, see "How To Bake—Substituting Ingredients". Despite our warnings, however, we can't pretend there's anything quite as rich and melt-in-the-mouth as a buttery cake or cream cheese frosting!

Eggs

Eggs contribute richness, nutrients, lightness, and a golden color to baked goods. The egg's protein coagulates during baking, adding to the structure of the crumb, while the lecithin serves as an emulsifier and the liquidity increases the moisture content. When beaten, eggs incorporate air and give batters a light airy texture. The whites alone can be beaten into a stiff, air-filled mass, and give a special lightness to cakes when folded in last of all ingredients. The yolks are very high in saturated fat and cholesterol, and give a thick richness to baked products.

Many people do not eat eggs because of the methods of their production, their contaminant content, and their high fat content. They produce congestion and allergic reactions in many individuals. They are not essential in baking, since lightness and richness can be introduced by other means (see "How to Bake—Substituting Ingredients). It is best to use eggs as fresh as possible, and at room temperature. Look for "free-range" and fertilized eggs for a more natural product.

Other Ingredients

Legumes

Beans, peas, lentils, and peanuts are legumes (or pulses), the fruits of leguminous plants. They have been eaten for thousands of years and today are food staples in many cultures; for example, lentils and chickpeas (garbanzo beans) in the Middle East and India, beans in the Americas, peanuts in Africa, and soybeans in the Far East. However, they are largely, and sadly, overlooked in the Western World.

Legumes are high in complex carbohydrates, vitamins, minerals, fiber, and protein (which complements the protein in grains). They are low in fat, and contain no cholesterol. Most of the nutrients are increased by sprouting.

Legumes can add flavor, texture, and nourishment to baked goods. Soybeans are most often used, generally as soy flour, which adds protein and helps bind in breads and goodies. Garbanzo flour can also be useful and makes an egg substitute. Soy oil, soy grits, and sometimes soy curd (tofu) are also used; tofu can be pureed into an egg substitute, or beaten smooth for frostings and cheesecakes. Peanuts and peanut butter are favorite baking ingredients, and make classic cookies. They can go rancid easily, however, and develop a toxic mold called aflatoxin, which survives roasting. Check your source. And look for peanut butter without added oil, salt, sugar or stabilizers.

Nuts and Seeds

There is a large variety of nuts and seeds, including almonds, walnuts, pecans, cashews, filberts or hazelnuts, Brazil nuts, coconut, sunflower seeds, sesame seeds, pumpkin seeds, poppy seeds, and caraway seeds, to name just a few. They can make very positive additions to the taste, texture, and nutrition of baked goods. Most are high in fat, though largely unsaturated, so use with discretion. Seeds and some nuts can be sprouted, or at least soaked, for greater digestibility.

Use nuts and seeds raw or toast them lightly for a stronger flavor. They can be ground into meal, toasted if you like, and added to baked goods for richness of texture, or first ground and then beaten at length (producing smooth nut butters). Nut butters made from almonds, pecans, walnuts, cashews, or sunflower seeds can make wondrously rich cookies and candies. For a dairyless frosting, cashews may be blended to a powder and mixed with liquid into a creamy paste. Nut and seed milks can replace dairy milk in recipes; simply soak almonds or cashews in water, strain, and blend with fresh water. You can filter out any solids if you prefer. Sunflower and sesame milk can be made the same way; the former is mild, while sesame milk has a strong, very rich flavor.

Coconut is usually finely shredded or in flakes, strips, or chips. It adds richness (it is high in saturated fats), flavor, and a pleasing texture to cakes, cookies, and candies. Shredded coconut can be lightly toasted before use. Fresh coconut can be used to produce vastly superior grated coconut, or coconut milk (blend grated flesh with water and strain), a very rich addition to cakes.

Nuts have the best flavor and food value when bought in the shell and shelled at home. In any case, refrigerate shelled nuts and don't buy them if they have a strong or rancid smell.

Sprouts

On all parts of this earth, seeds have been an object of reverence and awe throughout history. And well they should be, for a seed contains both the potential to become a plant and the elements necessary to sustain it through its early stages of life. Seeds are thus one of the richest foodstuffs for both humans and animals. But nutritious as the dry seeds are, their vitamin, fat, protein, and mineral content becomes even higher and more digestible when they are sprouted. Sprouts of all kinds are sufficient to sustain life, and are believed to have a cleansing and rejuvenating effect on our bodies.

Sprouts can make a great addition to breads, adding flavor, texture, crunch, and lots of nutrition. Wheat sprouts give a chewy sweetness to yeasted breads, and of course can be used alone in essene breads and goodies (see "How To Bake—Essene Bread"). Rye and other grains can be sprouted for this purpose. Other sprouts that go nicely in yeasted breads include alfalfa, mung, lentil, sunflower, and chickpea. Experiment and find your favorites. Buy organic seeds and sprout at home—it's easy, inexpensive, and fun!

Fruits and Vegetables

These can add a great variety of tastes, textures, sweetness, fiber, and nutrients to your baking. We talked about fruits in "Sweeteners", further back in this chapter. They can be used fresh (in chunks, purees, sauces, or juices) and dried (whole, chopped, soaked, pureed, or ground). Soaking in apple cider or brandy adds a distinctive flavor to festive breads or cakes.

Vegetables can be incorporated into bread in chunks, grated, or pureed. Puree of winter squash will give you a delightfully golden loaf with a subtly delicious flavor and soft, moist texture. Mashed or grated potatoes add texture and flavor (potato water is sometimes used to aid rising). Finely chopped or grated vegetables give wonderful flavor and aroma to breads; onion rolls are a classic, while a mixture of carrots, celery, onions, and green pepper makes a delicious Vegie Bread. Tomatoes worked into your dough give a nice hint of color and fresh zesty flavor.

Kneading dough containing fresh fruits or vegetables will squeeze out juice and make it somewhat sticky. It is therefore easier to add them after some mixing, unless you want the flavors to permeate the bread. If so, be prepared to knead gently and perhaps add extra flour.

Herbs and Spices

These can add a wide variety of flavors, textures, and appearances to baked goods, and your lightly flecked dough will give off tantalizing aromas. Try one or two of your favorite herbs, but use discretion. Two herbs, each with a distinctive character, may taste odd when combined. Dried herbs are usually used, but try fresh for extra zip. Herbs are a good way to make a very flavorful bread in the absence of salt. Vegetables and Italian herbs added together to a loaf come out smelling like pizza!

Spices have their best flavor if used fresh; for instance, grind up cinnamon sticks, grate nutmeg or gingerroot, or lightly roast whole seeds and grind just before using. However, powdered spices will work fine. Use a little less of a spice if using fresh, as the flavor will be stronger. Keep herbs and spices in tightly capped containers to retain freshness.

Whole, Cracked, or Rolled Grains

Although we covered grains in some detail earlier in this chapter, it is worth noting here that grains in all forms make excellent additions to breads and goodies. If using the whole berries, presoak or sprout them. Cracked grains, grits, flakes, or meals add a nice variation of texture and taste.

Carob Powder

Carob powder or flour is ground from the carob pod or locust bean. (It is believed to have been the staple of St. John the Baptist's diet in the wilderness—hence the name St. John's Bread, often applied to carob.) Carob is a balanced product, naturally sweet, high in complex carbohydrates and nutrients, low in fat, and completely lacking in caffeine. These characteristics, along with its dark brown color and chocolatey flavor, have made it a popular replacement for cocoa products in baking. It can be used in small amounts for a subtle sweetness, or added generously for dark, aromatic products. The powder is available both raw and roasted, the latter being darker and perhaps more richly-flavored.

The ability to make carob chips using carob powder and a few other ingredients has given us a wide range of delicious chip cookies, just like the old days . . . . ! Look for carob chips containing no additional sweetener, but be aware that they contain hydrogenated fats, such as palm oil, and sometimes milk powder.

Vinegar

Vinegar can be used for a variety of purposes in baking and derives from a variety of sources. Sugar vinegar comes from molasses, malt vinegar from grains or potatoes, wine vinegar from wine, and apple cider vinegar—most common in our bakeries—from apples. One tablespoon of vinegar in a loaf of bread is an effective preservative and mold retardant. In quick breads and cakes, vinegar's acidic quality reacts with baking soda to produce carbon dioxide and a very light texture.

Flavorings, Colorings, Trimmings

A few drops of flavoring essence or oil give great versatility to your baking. You can vary a basic butter cookie or cake recipe, for instance, by reaching for the vanilla, almond essence, orange or peppermint oil, to name a few. Vanilla essence finds its way into almost all goodie recipes—the flavor seems to complement others (it makes carob taste more chocolatey), and stands fragrantly on its own. Pure vanilla is made from beans (which you can buy and soak), and usually contains alcohol, which evaporates during baking. Even though expensive, it's vastly superior to synthetic vanillin, which is widely available. Look for flavorings labeled "natural". Even some of those we're not sure about, so buy and use them with awareness. With all the other good stuff going into your baking, it's worth keeping the dreadful artificial flavoring chemicals out of your kitchen.

Another chemical horror to avoid are the little bottles of coloring; artificial coloring agents are frequently carcinogenic. We've found several ways to color naturally for special occasion frostings, and there are probably many more plant-based dyes that haven't been explored. These natural juices tend to fade and separate after a period of time, so make and eat frostings fresh. Some suggestions:

red and pink: beet juice (which will also produce a light pink in baked batters), hibiscus, concentrated red fruit juices
green: parsley juice, any high chlorophyll juice (such as wheat grass)
orange: carrot juice, orange juice
yellow: turmeric (watch the quantity and flavor!), saffron
purple: blueberry juice
brown: carob powder

Let us know if you discover other safe and natural colorings.

Finally, for those finishing touches, avoid the bright-colored crystallized fruits and molded sugar decorations that are often used on cakes. Instead, create your own delightful patterns with fresh fruits, leaves, and flowers. These can be edible (mint leaves and violets are favorites), or can be removed before eating. For obvious reasons, these natural creations should be put together just before the big occasion.

How to Bake

This chapter contains suggestions on how to make bread and other baked goods. We want to do away with the mystique that surrounds baking; neither inborn talents nor lists of complicated directions are needed to bake well. In fact, rather than gritting your teeth and following instructions, it's better to understand the simple processes that you initiate and help along when you bake. In the guidelines that follow, we describe what's happening in the dough as we set out methods. The more you bake, the more you will understand what's going on and why, and the results of your efforts will reflect your learning. That's why baking—bread, especially—is never simply repetitive. You learn something from how every batch behaves!

Nevertheless, don't feel too much trepidation about how doughs will act. There's actually a great deal of leeway in what you can do and still have things come out well. Experiment for yourself and your baking will get better still.

The methods described are ones that we have found to work well. The nature of our bakeries encourages the development of simple and straightforward, yet effective, techniques, and these are what we pass on to you. If your baking experience is limited, some practical advice will come in handy, while even the most seasoned baker may learn something from our approach. This isn't an exhaustive review of techniques; for fancier stuff, consult a more "gourmet" bread book, and for any details you find lacking here, we recommend the ***Tassajara Bread Book*** for its comprehensive instructions.

To eliminate a possible source of extreme frustration, make sure you have all the ingredients and equipment you'll need ***before*** beginning the baking process. Check the recipe, and then your supplies. It will be hard to make challah bread if you're out of eggs, or St. John's Bread without carob powder. In fact, it doesn't hurt to measure out your ingredients ahead of time. They're best at room temperature anyway. Make sure you have some extra flour for kneading, and oil or cornmeal to coat your pans or baking sheet. And check your equipment. Do you have what you need? Probably—you can get by with very little, as we see in the following section.

Useful Tools

You need only a few basic pieces of equipment to follow the recipes in ***Uprisings***. Baking is an ancient method of preparing grains for eating and the tools have been mostly simple and functional. The criteria should be that the tool fit the task and feel comfortable in the hand. So be inventive.

Hands

Fortunately, the most essential tools most of us already possess. Hands get used a lot around our bakeries—to measure, mix, shape, scoop, test and taste. Although the baker's hands need to be, and will grow to be, strong and often calloused by the oven's heat, yet they need to remain gentle and sensitive. They must be able to lightly touch a baked good to test for readiness or caringly form a loaf. Take care of them.

Oven

The heat source for your baking is another important tool. Some baking can be done in the sun or over a fire or griddle, but you'll need an oven for most things. Learn the ways of your oven. Discover its hot and cold spots. While muffins and cupcakes prefer to "jump up" quickly in the hot part of the oven (usually the top shelf), most yeasted goods do well in a more moderate heat (middle perhaps). Borrowing or buying an oven thermometer lets you accurately test the oven. To avoid lopsided cakes, check the levelness of your oven. Unevenness can be remedied either by leveling the entire oven or simply sliding something non-combustible under one side of the baking pan to make it horizontal.

Containers

Next, you'll need a few containers for mixing and baking (though you can mix doughs directly on a surface, by pouring wet ingredients into a well in the flour and mixing with your hands). Mixing containers should be non-porous, washable bowls or pots. A variety of sizes is useful for all-round baking, but you only need one large bowl for bread. As for baking containers, keep in mind that they must be ovenproof and non-toxic. Within those guidelines, be creative. Metal, tempered glass, ceramic and clay molds, pots, and pans are all suitable. A rectangular 4½"x 8½" pan gives you a standard 1½ pound loaf, but round pans and baking sheets will also do fine. Unusual containers for baking bread are empty metal cans and clean clay flower pots. It's best not to wash bread pans—let them get well-seasoned so the bread won't stick.

Utensils

A few simple tools can help you out in your baking. Measuring cups and spoons are useful to get proportions right. A sturdy long-handled wooden spoon (metal is OK) is good for mixing and beating batters and doughs. Also helpful, but even less essential, is a dough knife or scraper of some kind for cleaning encrusted dough from your kneading surface; a more flexible spatula or scraper to thoroughly empty a bowl or pan (you can make a semi-circular one by cutting a firm plastic lid in half); a whisk for beating a bread sponge or muffin batter; a rolling pin (a bottle works fine); a brush for oiling pans or glazing dough; a sieve or sifter to keep lumps out of your dry ingredients; for cookies, a tablespoon, ice cream scoop or small cup for scooping batter, and a cookie press, jar lid or tumbler for pressing them down; and perhaps a rack for cooling your baked goods.

Kneading Surface

One final important tool is the kneading surface for your bread dough. Keep in mind that semi-porous surfaces, such as marble or oiled wood, are the most desirable. But any smooth, clean surface that does not flake or splinter will do. The remaining consideration regarding the work surface is that you arrange it to be at an appropriate height so you can knead comfortably while standing.

Finally, try to bring yourself—your time, thought, and caring—to your baking. We know so well from our bakeries and kitchens that our creations can only be as good as the energy and love that we put into them. OK, we're ready to begin with . . . .

Yeasted Breads

Making the Sponge

The sponge is the batter containing liquid, yeast, sweetener (optional—see below), and some of the flour. When allowed to sit for a period of time, the sponge puffs up. The yeast organisms become very active and produce carbon dioxide, which stretches the gluten in the flour and causes the whole thing to rise. The gluten thus gets a good start in developing its muscle.

The sponge method, fully described in *Tassajara*, is favored by most of our bakeries to produce good texture and rise. It can be omitted, however, as we discuss in the next section.

- **Mix the warm liquid with the sweetener, if used, and stir in the yeast till it dissolves. Beat in a portion of the flour, producing a thick, gloppy batter.**
- **Stir the sponge vigorously with a whisk or wooden spoon for a few minutes (about 100 strokes). You want to remove any lumps and see the batter begin to develop a stretchy texture.**
- **Cover the bowl and let the sponge sit in a warmish place for 30 to 60 minutes, although less is alright.**

Two points about a sponge. First, ***sweetener isn't necessary***. The yeast will feed on the starch in flour, which first must be converted into sugars by the action of enzymes. So an unsweetened sponge will take a little longer to rise.

Second, you may want to ***"proof" or test your yeast*** before making the sponge. This simple step checks that the yeast you are using is good—still alive and ready to activate.

- **Mix a small amount of the warm liquid (¼ - ½ cup) with a little sweetener, and stir in the yeast. If it doesn't bubble and foam within a few minutes, the yeast**

organisms are dead. Perhaps the yeast wasn't fresh enough, or your liquid was too hot. (Dry yeast performs best at 95° to 115°F; fresh or cake yeast at 80° to 105°F.)

If your yeast proofs alive, just add remaining liquid and sweetener and proceed with the sponge.

After being left for a while, the sponge will rise and develop a bulging, frothy top, somewhat reminiscent of geothermal bubbling mud pools. (If it doesn't, start again, proofing your yeast if you haven't already done so.) Keep an eye on a rising sponge — cleaning up an overflow is no joke. You can beat or whisk a sponge that's getting too high, and cut it down to size, but it'll come up again. Don't beat it down too many times, though — this seems to exhaust the gluten.

Omitting the Sponge

As we said, some bakeries don't sponge their bread and it comes out fine. If you want to skip this step, just mix all the ingredients into a dough (starting with liquid, sweetener, and yeast) and begin kneading. But since the gluten hasn't had a workout already, be prepared to knead longer to develop a good elastic texture in the dough. If you're dubious about your yeast, it would be advisable to proof it first before mixing everything or you could waste a lot of food.

Mixing the Dough

The most important point about mixing the dough is to ***leave some of the flour till the end*** so you can adjust the amount. The absorbency of flour can vary a lot, so feel your way, incorporating it gradually.

- **Into the frothing sponge, mix the remaining ingredients, reserving some of the flour. (It may be easier to add chunky ingredients, like nuts or fruits, after you have kneaded for a while.) Stir well with a wooden spoon and/or your hands.**
- **Add flour gradually, until the stirred dough begins to come away from the sides of the bowl and becomes a more compact mass. This tells you that you are ready to start the kneading process.**

Kneading

At this stage, you want to give the dough a thorough massage to achieve a smooth, well-mixed texture and a springy elasticity. This is when you can really develop the gluten and you will feel the dough become more cohesive and bouncy under your hands. (For rolls and yeasted pastries, less kneading will produce a fluffy rather than elastic texture.)

- **Sprinkle your kneading surface with a dusting of flour and tip out a small extra mound of flour to one side. Pat your hands in this, repeating as often as necessary to avoid sticking.**
- **Turn out the dough from the bowl in a compact mass and begin to knead. Putting the base of your palms into the dough, push it down and away from you with a firm, rocking motion. This is not a time to be delicate; push with power, but don't be too rough or you'll tear the dough. Add flour if it seems too sloppy.**

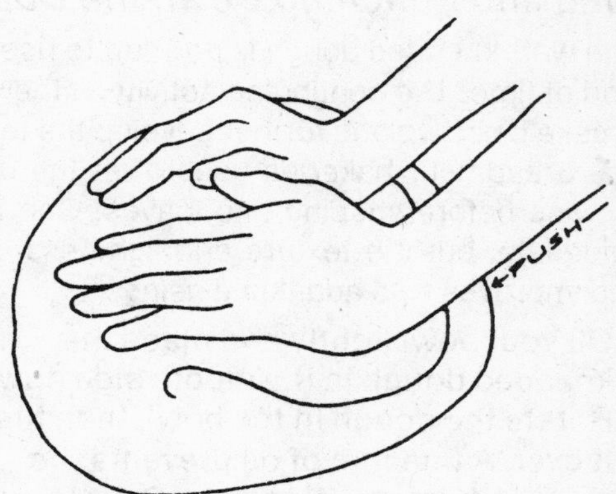

- **After each push, rotate the dough a quarter turn, fold it in half towards you and repeat the process. Try to develop a good rhythm: push — rock — rotate — fold. Keep the flat surface of the dough down on your kneading surface and the folded surface on top.**

You are finished kneading when the dough feels cohesive, smooth, and elastic. This usually takes about 8-10 minutes. Some useful indicators are:

1. The dough no longer feels sticky (see below for exceptions).
2. Little blisters appear just below the surface.
3. When pressed, the dough springs back.
4. When stroked, the dough feels cool and smooth, like your ear lobe. The surface is almost shiny.
5. A cherry-sized piece of dough can be stretched to approximately two inches square before tearing.

The dough may remain sticky while showing other indications of being well-kneaded when it contains any of the following: lots of eggs and butter; some cooked grains; juicy fruits and vegetables; or, most commonly, a fair amount of rye flour. In these cases, avoid adding more and more flour or you'll end up with a dense, unresponsive dough and heavy bread.

If your loaves are to be free-form (baked on a sheet, not in a pan), make the dough firm enough to retain its shape. You'll want it to be on the firm and bouncy side, rather than soft and stretchy.

Rising and Punching Down the Dough

The well-kneaded dough is now left to rise for a period of time. The continuing activity of the yeast will make it puff up and further develop the texture of the bread. Our bakeries usually let the dough rise twice before shaping into loaves. One rising is adequate, but the texture and lightness of the bread improves with additional risings.

- **Oil your bowl lightly and place the kneaded dough in it, smooth side down. Rotate the dough in the bowl, then flip it over. A fine film of oil prevents the surface from crusting over. Cover the bowl with a damp cloth, towel, or apron, or place it in a large plastic bag.**
- **Set the bowl in a warm, draft-free place. You don't want it much hotter than 100° F; the dough will rise in a cooler place, but will take more time.**
- **Leave the dough alone until it has puffed up to approximately double its original bulk. This may take anywhere from 30 minutes to several hours, depending on the temperature and the density of the dough, but usually 45 to 60 minutes is about right. A good test: poke your finger about an inch into the dough. If a hole remains, the dough has risen sufficiently. If the hole slowly springs back, leave the dough to rise some more.**
- **When fully risen, punch down the dough by thrusting your fist into it repeatedly (this is great fun with 100 lbs. of bread dough!). You want to flatten most of the air out.**
- **If you are having a second rising in the bowl, cover again and let sit until nearly doubled. This will probably take 30-45 minutes. Punch down.**

Now, with your once- or twice-risen dough, you are ready to shape the loaves and leave them for the final rising.

Shaping the Loaves

There are as many different ways to shape loaves as there are bakers! The two principal concerns are getting the air out of the dough and having a nice smooth top to your loaves as they fit snugly in the pans or sit handsomely on the baking sheet. Feel your way with these aims in mind. We describe some common methods below, in case you need help.

Regular-shaped Loaves

- **Perform a kind of one-handed kneading, pushing with one hand while rotating and folding in the far edge of the dough with the other. Just do this briefly until you have a compact round-oval blob with the smooth surface on the bottom.**
- **Flatten this lightly to an oblong or round-cornered rectangle, about the length of your pan. (Or adjust your kneading to achieve this shape right away.)**

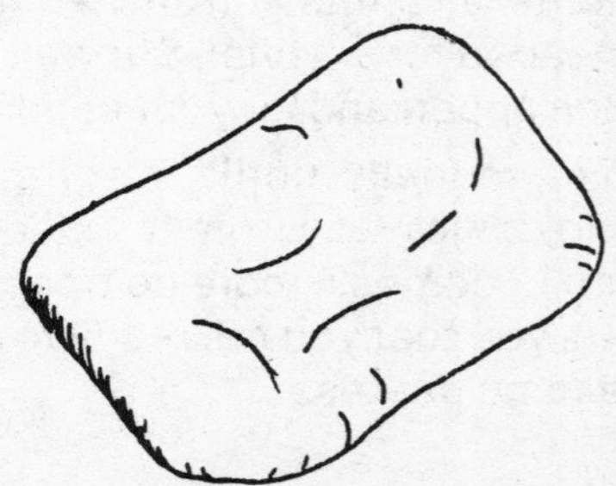

- Pick up the edge of the dough nearest you and roll it up in a fairly tight roll.

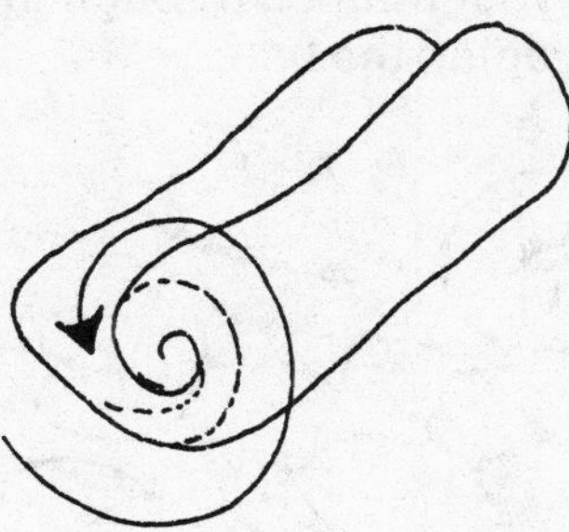

- Pinch the dough together along the seam, then tuck in and tidy up the ends of the loaf. Gently roll the loaf on the seam a few times to perfect the shaping.

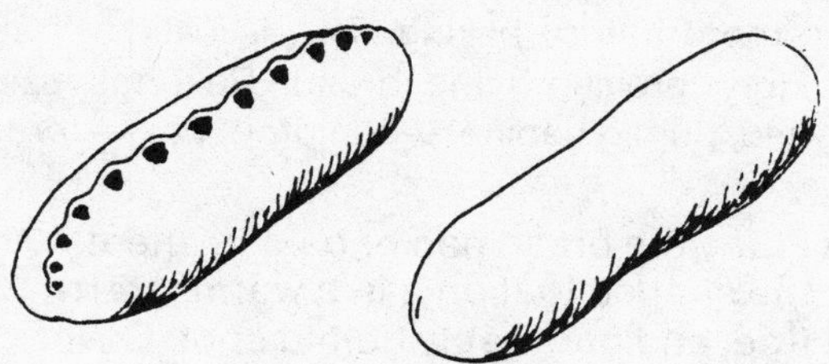

- Place smooth side up in an oiled bread pan.

Round Loaves

If this is to be a free-standing loaf, remember to have the dough firm enough to hold its shape without support.

- Briefly knead the dough, pulling in the farthest edge and rotating the dough until you have a compact round blob with the smooth surface on the bottom. Squeeze and pinch the folded-in edges together.

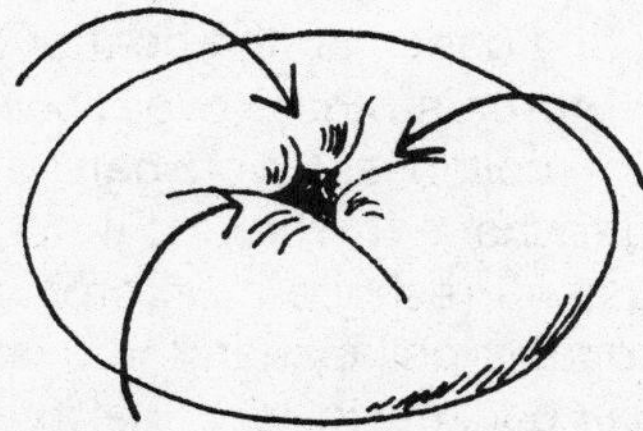

- Flip the dough over. Cup the left side of the dough with your left hand, and the right side with your right. Shuffle the dough around with your hands in a circular direction, shaping and perfecting a symmetrical round loaf.

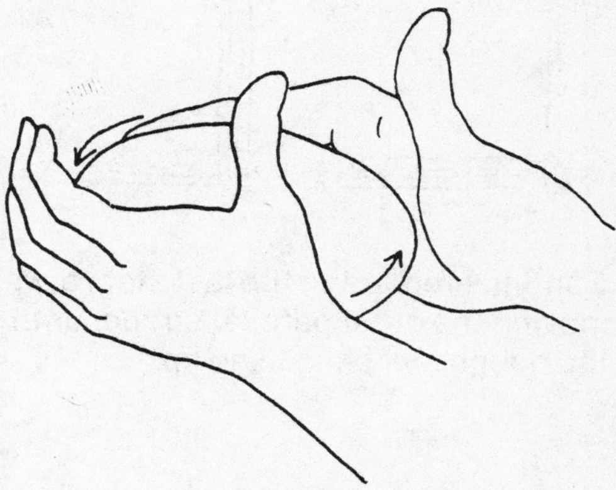

- Place on an oiled or cornmeal-dusted baking sheet.

French-style Long Loaves (Baguettes)

Unless you have a long, thin pan, remember again to make a firm-textured dough so it doesn't flatten too much on the baking sheet. Then merely adapt the regular loaf shaping to produce a long loaf with somewhat tapering ends (or see method under Whole Wheat-Rye French Bread).

Braided Breads

These are very easy and look great. You can place a smaller braid on top of a larger one for a really pretty loaf.

- Divide dough into three equal parts, and roll out each ball until it's a rope about twice the length of your intended loaf.
- Attach the three strands at one end, and line two of the strands parallel to each other and at right angles to the third.

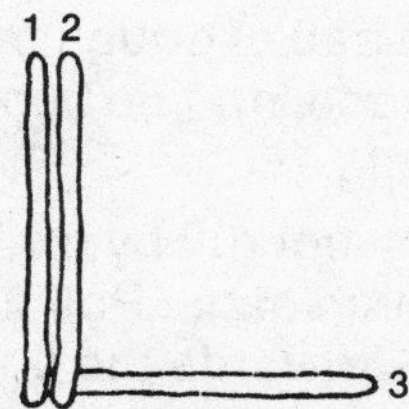

- Take the outer parallel strand, bring it over the other parallel strand, and place it parallel to the original single strand. (Don't cross the original single strand!) Repeat.

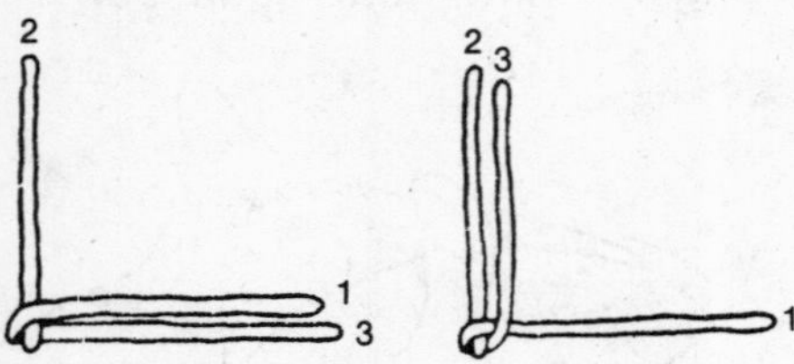

- Continue repeating the last step, always moving the outer parallel strand, until the dough has been used up.

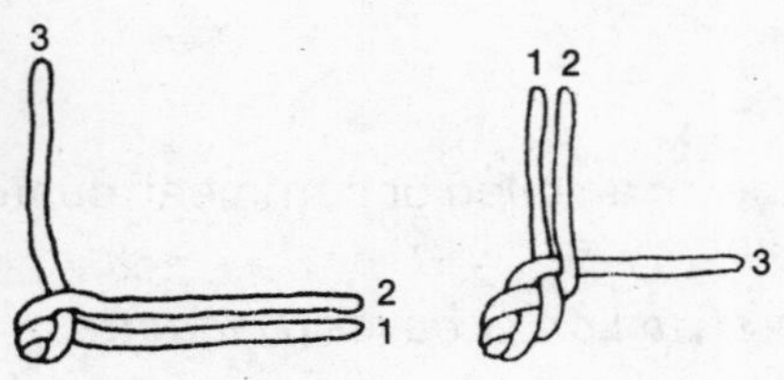

- Pinch the three ends together to complete the loaf.
- Place in an oiled bread pan or on a dusted baking sheet.

Rolls

The shapes of rolls are limited only by your imagination! Play with small blobs of dough and see what you can come up with. Rolls can be set on a baking sheet or in a muffin pan. A few suggestions:

- Shape a regular round roll like a mini round loaf.
- Divide roll into three round balls and tuck into a muffin pan, for cloverleaf rolls.
- Roll out the ball of dough into a long sausage shape, and tie knots, make spirals, twists, etc.
- Make a crescent roll by rolling out into a flat triangular shape. Roll up tight from a wide edge towards the point. Curve into a semi-circle.
- For bagels, either join the ends of a sausage shape, or make a round ball and push your thumbs through the center, shaping the hole.

Final Rising

After your loaf has been shaped, it must rise once more before baking. This is called "proofing" (or "proving") the bread. Bakeries use a warmed, humid cabinet—the proof box—for this step.

- Place the bread pan or baking sheet with the shaped loaf on it in a warm, draft-free, and preferably humid spot. Cover with a damp cloth, or place in a plastic bag.
- Let the loaf rise till it's about doubled in size – usually about 20-30 minutes. (Allow less time for rolls.)

At the end of this final rising, the loaf is ready to bake if it looks quite puffed up, with a kind of inflated tension to its surface. In a bread pan, the sides of the loaf will come up to the top of the pan while the center of the loaf's top will be an inch or two above the pan. A common test is to gently press the loaf with the tip of a finger. A soft impression that doesn't bounce back indicates that the bread won't rise much more and it's time to bake. A little resistance to your touch is alright, though—the bread needs a last bit of rising power when it first goes into the heat of the oven. If you loaf "overproofs" (gets overblown-looking and wrinkles or collapses), you can take it out of the pan and reshape it. Then let it rise again in the pan. If you don't reshape an overproofed loaf, the top will probably collapse in the oven, or you may get large air pockets in your final loaf.

Just prior to baking, some bakers like to make one or more shallow slashes on the top of the loaf with a sharp knife. This relieves surface tension and allows the loaf to rise in the oven without splitting (it also looks nice). This is most often done on free-form loaves. To glaze breads, brush lightly with milk or egg for a shiny crust, or spray or brush with water (and again in the oven) for a chewy crust. (Brushing with oil ***after*** baking produces a soft crust.)

Baking

The oven should be up to full heat when you put the bread in. Bread is usually baked at 350° F for 45 minutes, but some bakeries bake for 30-35 minutes at 400° F. The recipe will specify.

- **Gently put the loaf into the preheated oven (the middle shelf is often a good spot for moderate heat).**
- **Check the loaf after the recommended baking time. It should be golden brown. Take it out of the pan; the bottom corners should be firm, not soft, and the loaf should sound hollow when solidly thunked with a finger or knuckle. If it doesn't feel and sound right, return the bread to the pan and the oven, and give it more time.**
- **When you are satisfied that the bread is done, take it out of or off the pan right away and place it on a rack to cool.**

Oven temperature gauges being notoriously unreliable, it's a good idea to keep an eye on your breads as they bake until you learn the characteristics of the oven. If a loaf darkens prematurely, place another pan over it, tent it with foil or parchment, or turn down the oven a little.

Storing the Bread

Bread keeps best in an airtight bag in a cool, well-ventilated spot. Make sure it is completely cooled before bagging it, or the moisture that builds up will give you wet bread that molds rapidly.

Keep bread in the refrigerator if you're keeping it for more than two or three days, especially in summer. Refrigeration retards molding, but the bread will become drier and less flavorful. A tablespoon of vinegar in a loaf acts as a preservative to some extent. Bread can be frozen, but loses texture and some taste. Use immediately after thawing and don't refreeze. Slicing the loaf before freezing allows you to thaw just the amount you want at any one time.

Slightly stale bread can be reheated satisfactorily in a 350° F oven for 10-15 minutes. You can heat even small amounts if wrapped in foil. Sprinkling the oven floor with drops of water or quickly brushing a loaf all over with water or milk, and then placing unwrapped in a hot oven for 10-15 minutes, really rejuvenates a loaf and gives it a nice crusty surface.

Old bread can be used in a number of ways: for breadcrumbs, soft or toasted; croutons; rusks or zwieback; French toast and garlic bread; or recycled in recipes such as Pudin de Pan and Peasant Bread (see Index).

Slice bread with a serrated knife if possible. If you use a regular kitchen knife, make certain it is very sharp or it will tear the bread. If you're slicing a warm loaf, wash and dry the blade after every one or two slices; this prevents the blade from sticking to the bread and tearing it.

Sourdough Breads

The special flavor of sourdough is most commonly associated with San Francisco. Legend has it that sourdough originated with the bakers in the California mining camps during the gold rush days. What sets sourdough apart from other types of bread is the inclusion of a sourdough "starter", or culture, for leavening and taste-enhancing purposes. This starter is nothing more than a blend of water and flour which has been left to ferment, producing the distinctive sour taste.

- **To make sourdough starter, combine ⅓ to ½ cup of any flour with 1 cup of water. Keep it in a warm place and stir daily for one week. Your starter is then ready for use.**
- **Keep the starter in the refrigerator when not in use. It will keep there indefinitely as long as it is occasionally "fed". Feed it by stirring in a tablespoon of flour every week. It's easy to save some starter every time you use it to make a batch of bread.**

Great tasting sourdough breads require nothing more than flour, water, and starter (see recipes by Nature's Bakery and Manna Bakery). Sourdough starter can be included in other doughs as well to add unique flavor (see Sunrise Bakery).

Unyeasted Breads

Unyeasted breads are not hard to make and have their own unique appeal. They require basically the same methods as yeasted breads. However, since they have to develop their own yeasts, they need to rise for a long time. The dough is usually made the day before and left to sit overnight. Avoid using bowls made of aluminum or plastic, since the dough tends to absorb molecules of these materials.

After placing the loaves in the pans, cut deeply down the center of the loaf lengthwise, or make deep diagonal cuts across the top, to allow carbon dioxide to escape. Brushing the tops with oil or water helps avoid drying out during the last rising.

Unyeasted breads need to bake longer than yeasted ones—often up to 1½ hours at 350° F. The recipe will specify. The bread is done when the sides and bottom are darkish brown and hard, and the bread sounds hollow.

Essene Bread

Standing somewhat apart from the mainstream of Western baking tradition are the essene breads. Just the name seems to suggest something mysterious, even exotic, and certainly complicated to create. True, essene bread *is* different from the ordinary yeasted loaves with which we are familiar, but it is also simple to prepare, exceptionally nutritious, and best of all, a real taste treat.

What Is It?

With no pun intended, essene bread is the very essence of simplicity. Its only required ingredient is sprouted grain, and you can easily sprout your own. The sprouts are ground to a doughy consistency, shaped into loaves, and baked at very low heat until crusty on the outside but still moist and chewy inside. Nothing else is needed: no yeast, sweeteners, flour, oil, salt, and of course, no chemical conditioners or preservatives! You can add other items to the dough—nuts, seeds, dried fruits, chopped apple, or spices—and they can give exciting new tastes and variety to your breads. But these ingredients are just nice, not necessary. Plain essene bread has a surprisingly sweet and nutty-rich flavor all its own.

Hard whole wheat berries are used most frequently, and work extremely well. When sprouted, they become very sweet (since, through sprouting, the starches in the grains are converted into sugars), and once ground, produce a workable dough which holds together well when shaped into loaves. But other grains can be used too, and each will have its own characteristics of taste and texture. Rye berries, for example, also become sweet when sprouted, yet they have a taste which is distinctly different from wheat. Other possibilities are soft whole wheat (more crumbly and milder-flavored than hard), triticale, barley, millet, and oats. Combining different grains produces interesting new flavors.

Historically, essene bread is one of the earliest varieties of bread. It derives its name from a recipe of the ancient Essenes as recorded in ***The Essene Gospel of Peace***, a 1st Century Aramaic manuscript. The speaker is Jesus Christ.

> "'How should we cook our daily bread without fire, Master?' asked some with great astonishment.
>
> 'Let the angels of God prepare your bread. Moisten your wheat, that the angel of water may enter it. Then set it in the air, that the angel of air also may embrace it. And leave it from morning to evening beneath the sun, that the angel of sunshine may descend upon it. And the blessing of the three angels will soon make the germ of life to sprout in your wheat. Then crush your grain, and make thin wafers, as did your forefathers when they departed out of Egypt, the house of bondage. Put them back again beneath the sun from its appearing, and when it is risen to its highest in the heavens, turn them over on the other side that they be embraced there also by the angel of sunshine, and leave them there until the sun be set.'" (p. 37)

Nutritionally, essene bread is a rich resource. Made of 100% sprouted grain, it contains much of the goodness of the sprouts themselves—low in fat, abundant in protein, natural sugars, fiber, vitamins, and minerals, all made very digestible by the presence of numerous enzymes in the sprouts. Heat is an enemy of many vital elements in food. Cooking, especially at high temperatures, can destroy high proportions of vitamins and enzymes. Because essene bread is baked at low temperatures (200° F - 275° F), the chance of nutrient loss is correspondingly less.

How to Make It

You will need a few items of basic equipment to make your essene bread. Nothing special is required; most of the essentials will already be in your kitchen.

1. ***Containers for sprouting.*** Large-mouthed glass jars are ideal, but any container that holds water will work fine (large plastic tub, soup pot, etc.)
2. ***Breathable tops for the sprouting containers.*** A piece of fine screening or cheesecloth is best, placed over the container's mouth and secured with a strong rubber band (or you can punch holes in a screw-on lid that fits your container). Anything which will allow air and water, but not sprouts, to pass through easily is fine.
3. ***Grinder.*** A hand-operated food or meat grinder is the least expensive and psychologically most satisfying, but a Champion Juicer or food processor works well.
4. ***Miscellaneous items.*** You will also need a large bowl to hold your dough, a cookie sheet, and, of course, an oven (except in the case of sun-baked, or dried, wafers and patties).

The ingredients are unbelievably simple. Just buy a quantity of the grain you've decided to use. But remember, the grain must be suitable for sprouting; therefore, you need uncooked, unsprayed, ***whole*** berries. Neither cracked wheat nor pearled barley, for example, will sprout. Hard red winter wheat works extremely well, and it is very inexpensive when bought in bulk from your local food coop or natural foods store.

To sprout the berries, follow these simple steps:

1. Measure the desired amount of berries. 1 cup of berries gives you about 2 cups of dough.
2. Soak berries overnight in the sprouting container, using twice the berries' volume in water.
3. In the morning, drain off the soaking water through the breathable top. (Save this mineral-rich liquid for drinks, soups, or to water your plants.)
4. Place the jar in a dark place, and rinse with cool water twice each day. Drain thoroughly. This helps make the sprouts less prone to spoilage. Occasionally shake the jar vigorously to keep the roots from matting together in a solid, unmanageable clump.
5. Sprouts are ready when the sprout hairs are about 2 times as long as the berry—usually 2½ to 3 days after soaking—and have a sweet, mild taste.
6. Skip the last rinse before grinding so that the berries won't be too moist.

To make your dough, take the sprouts when they have reached the right length, and put them through the grinder. (Oiling the grinding parts before use helps prevent sticking.) The result should be a juicy, sticky dough that is mottled light and dark brown in color; the consistency is somewhat similar to raw hamburger.

The dough is ready to use as soon as it emerges from the grinder. If you can't continue at that point, cover the dough tightly with food wrap and place in the refrigerator. Also, if you are going to add nuts or fruit to the dough, now's the time. Soaking dried fruit first (20-30 minutes in hot water) will give the fruit a pleasing, juicy texture.

To shape the loaves, wet your hands well and take a quantity of dough; one large handful will make a nice roll while a big two-handed scoop will give you a larger loaf. Work the dough with your hands briefly to produce a smooth surface and to insure that there are no air pockets inside. No kneading is required. Shape into round loaves, with slightly flattened tops. Rewet your hands (and working surface if necessary) before handling each new loaf. Place on a cookie sheet that is lightly oiled or dusted with cornmeal to prevent sticking. These are now ready to bake.

To bake essene bread, place in a 200°-275° F oven for about 2-3 hours (less for rolls) till the outside is firm and the bottom, though not hard, is firm enough to spring back slightly after a gentle prod with the thumb. The inside will be quite soft—a firmer texture develops upon cooling. Essene can actually be baked at a wide variety of temperatures, from as low as 120° (for 8-10 hours) up to 300°. Bear in mind that if you bake the loaves too long, they will tend to dry out on the inside. Also, baking at too high a temperature will tend to overcook the outside of the loaves. And both of these probably cause excessive loss of nutrients. To help prevent drying out, some bakeries spray the loaves with water both before and during baking.

For storage, let the loaves cool on a wire rack after removing from the oven (try not to eat *all* of them while still warm). When completely cold, store in sealed plastic bags. If you're going to eat your essene bread within 3-4 days, keep it out of the refrigerator as it will stay moister this way. Otherwise refrigerate; it'll keep up to 4 weeks. Essene bread can be frozen.

Quick Breads and Muffins

These are quite simple and fast. They use baking powder or soda to achieve a light texture, and require no kneading or rising times. The same batter can be poured into a loaf pan or baked as muffins or cupcakes. You can produce a batch of hot muffins from scratch in not much more than half an hour, so they're ideal if you're short of time.

The most important thing to remember when making muffins and quick breads is to ***mix gently and quickly*** and, once mixed, to pour the batter into the pans and ***bake right away***. The leavening agents will begin to act when combined with liquid or when stirred about—not so fast that you need to rush, but have your pans oiled and oven fully heated before the final mixing of ingredients. (You can preheat the oiled pans too, if you like.)

- **Combine all the dry ingredients in one bowl, sifting the baking powder or soda. Combine all the wet ingredients in another container, first creaming the oil or butter well with the sweetener to ensure lightness.**
- **Combine the wet with the dry ingredients, stirring lightly and just enough to moisten the dry ingredients (some lumps are OK).** ***Don't beat!***
- **Fill oiled pans or muffin cups about ¾ full with batter (remember it'll rise in the oven).**
- **Place in fully preheated oven. The temperature is usually 350°-400° for these baked goods. Muffins bake for 20-30 minutes, loaves for an hour or more. Test for doneness by inserting a knife, fork, or toothpick into the center – it should come out cleanly, and not be gooey. When done, the top will feel springy and the sides will brown a little and begin to pull away from the pan. If the top darkens prematurely, place a pan or foil over it or turn down the oven until the inside is cooked.**
- **Once out of the oven, let sit a few minutes before removing from the pan. Then cool on a rack. Refrigerate quick breads if you're keeping them longer than two or three days – they mold fairly fast. They will dry out somewhat, though, if refrigerated or frozen. Reheating in foil works well.**

One final point about quick breads and muffins. Since they don't require gluten, whole wheat flour isn't necessary. You therefore have a lot of leeway, for you can substitute just about any flour (grain or legume) for the flour in the recipe. Have fun experimenting.

Cakes and Brownies

These are usually made in the same way as quick breads: combine wet—combine dry—mix them together lightly—pour batter into oiled or floured pans and bake right away. Test for doneness in the same way too. Cakes may call for mixing ingredients in a somewhat more elaborate manner—the recipe will give directions. Cake batters can usually be baked in muffin pans for light cupcakes.

Pies

Many people avoid pie-making because they think it's a special art. It's just not true. Pies are very satisfying to make, and not hard. They also look—and taste—great! In particular, crusts are not difficult and can be put together quickly from a wide range of ingredients. We suggest below several different ways to give a pie a crust; these just indicate the potential. Experiment with your own ideas.

1. A crumb crust or granola crust; for example, cookie crumbs, toasted bread crumbs, or granola, bound together with oil, butter or juice, plus honey and spices if you like.
2. Raw bread dough, rolled out thin and baked without rising.
3. Slices of already-baked bread, laid overlapping and rolled out thin, to cover the pie plate.
4. A tasty blend of grains and nuts which can be served raw. For example, for an 8-9'' pie, let 1½ cups rolled oats and ½ cup chopped almonds sit for half an hour in about ½ cup cider or fruit juice. Press with wetted hands onto an oiled pie plate.
   This crust can be chilled (it'll stay crumbly), or baked (which holds it together well).
5. Just sprinkle the pie plate with wheat germ or crumbs, or forget the crust entirely and make pudding instead of pie!
6. Make a pie crust from flour and oil or butter, with a liquid to hold it together. Here are two—one buttery, the other dairyless—and both easy. In both cases, avoid overhandling and too much flour, for a lighter crust.

Buttery pastry crust—for an 8-9'' pie, single crust

- 5-6 Tbl. cold butter
- 1½ cups whole wheat pastry flour
- 3 Tbl. cold water
- 1 Tbl. vinegar

Work the butter into the flour, breaking it down into small lumps with a fork or your fingers. Rub it in until it's like fine breadcrumbs in texture. Mix in water and vinegar, adding a little flour, if needed, to make a soft, rollable dough.

Roll out on a lightly floured surface to fit pie plate.

Rub butter paper around plate to grease it.

Lift pastry carefully and press onto plate, trimming the edges and patterning with a floured fork, or fluting the edges with fingers or a spoon.

Prick the crust several times with a fork.

Bake at about 375° for 10-15 minutes for full baking or 5-10 minutes for partial baking. It's OK to bake it longer at 350° or shorter at 400°.

Dairyless pie crust—for an 8-9'' pie, single crust

- ¼ cup mild oil
- 1½ cups w.w. pastry flour
- ½ cup water

Mix all ingredients together, adding a little extra liquid, if needed, to make a rolling consistency. Roll out and proceed as for buttery crust. Bake for slightly less time.

Cookies

The recipe instructions are usually adequate for these simple treats. Here are a few tips:

- **Mix wet ingredients separately from dry ingredients, and combine them. Cream butter or oil well with the sweetener for a light, smooth texture.**
- **The batter needn't be scooped out right away unless it contains a lot of baking powder or soda.**
- **Scoop blobs of between 1 tablespoon and ¼ cup (depending on cookie size) onto oiled baking sheet. You can use a spoon, cup or ice cream scoop, dipping in water every now and then. Space cookies to allow for spreading if the recipe mentions this.**
- **To flatten cookies, use your fingers, a cookie press, the bottom of a tumbler,**

or a fork, dipping often in water to prevent sticking.

- Bake as directed in the recipe, usually at 350° for 10-20 minutes. Cookies will often still be soft when done, firming up as they cool. Look for light browning and firming around the edges. Gently lift one cookie with a spatula and see if the bottom looks nicely browned. In general, remove immediately from sheet and cool cookies on a rack.

One last point about baking powder or soda in cookies. This is usually given as an optional ingredient. We tested recipes both with and without it. Cookies made with these leavening agents come out slightly lighter and with a more porous texture, while omitting it produces a somewhat firmer cookie that needs a little longer baking time. Taste-wise, there isn't a great deal of difference, except for that hint of soda which some people don't like. For what it's worth, the majority of the tasters preferred the cookies made without baking powder or soda.

Substituting Ingredients

One of the most exciting aspects of whole grain baking is the opportunity it offers for exploring new combinations and tastes. A major feature of this in our bakeries is the active search for ingredients and methods that make our whole grain goods even healthier, but no less delicious. As we saw in "Foods for Whole Grain Baking," a growing number of people are becoming aware of undesirable effects associated with eating various foods: for example, dairy products, eggs, leaveners, fats, sweeteners, wheat, and salt. To accommodate these preferences, many bakers have experimented with ways to bake deliciously without using these ingredients. *Uprisings* contains a number of dairyless, eggless, and wheatless recipes, as well as the "Index by Special Dietary Characteristic" to help you find recipes which don't contain the food you wish to avoid.

Below we suggest some substitutions that should make it easier to alter any recipe in *Uprisings* to suit your dietary viewpoint, as well as convert an old favorite of your own to a more nutritious version. Or simply use these suggestions to increase the versatility of your baking, to replace an ingredient you're out of, or to save on costs. Don't expect the results to come out exactly the same as the original, and be prepared to experiment to see what works best in each case. The following substitutions are meant only as guidelines which some bakers have found helpful. Please let us know of any others you've had success with.

Suggested Substitutions

Brackets [] denote a more healthful variant of the undesired ingredient, but not a real alternative.

Asterisk (*) indicates when substituting a liquid for a solid or dry ingredient, to reduce other liquids and bake slightly longer at a lower temperature (by about 25°).

Eggs

For one egg, substitute:

- 1 Tbl tahini plus 3 Tbl liquid
- 1 Tbl garbanzo flour plus 1 Tbl oil
- 1 Tbl lecithin granules plus 3 Tbl liquid
- 1 Tbl arrowroot powder plus 3 Tbl liquid
- 4 Tbl of: 1 part flaxseed plus 3 parts water, blended smooth
- 3 Tbl liquid plus 1 Tbl of blend of: 2 parts arrowroot, 1 part tapioca flour, 1 part slippery elm
- [2 egg whites]

Dairy products (1 cup, unless noted)

Whole milk

- Soy milk
- Seed or nut milk: grind sunflower or sesame seeds, almonds or cashews, then blend with water into milk; or soak, and blend with fresh water.
- [Skim milk]

Milk powder

- Soy powder
- [Whey powder]

Yogurt, sour milk, buttermilk

- Soy milk curdled with 2 tsp lemon juice
- Soy yogurt

Butter

- Soy or vegetable oil margarine
- 2/3 - 1 cup oil*

Cream cheese

- Tofu
- Cashew cheese: grind or blend cashews to fine powder, then blend into thick cream with water or juice

Sour cream

- Soy yogurt
- [Yogurt]

Salt

Quantities of salt substitutes should be determined according to taste. See our section on "Salt".

- Herbs, onion powder, caraway seeds
- Seasonings like vegetable powder or nutritional yeast
- Powdered kelp, other seaweeds
- Lemon juice (in goodies)
- [Tamari or miso] (contain salt from the fermenting process)
- [Sea salt or solar salt, instead of commercial table salt]

Leaveners

Yeasted breads

- Sourdough or unyeasted breads
- Essene bread
- Baking powder-or soda-leavened loaves

Baking powder or soda

- Add some cornmeal or coarse-ground rice flour; they tend to absorb water as they bake, expanding and creating some lightness.
- Replace some of the flour with rolled oats or granola; these contribute texture and may add some lightness.
- Try making a paste with a little yeast, water, and flour: let sit 30-60 minutes, then use.*

Commercial baking powder (equal quantities)

- [Commercial low-sodium baking powder]
- [Homemade baking powder: blend 2 parts arrowroot, 1 part baking soda, 1 part cream of tartar]

Sweeteners (1 cup, unless noted)

White sugar

- 1/2 cup honey or maple syrup*
- 2/3 cup malt syrup*
- 2/3 cup date sugar

Honey

- Maple syrup
- 1 1/3 cups malt syrup

Honey, malt syrup, maple syrup

- Date butter: soak dates or date pieces in a little hot water till soft. Blend to a smooth paste. (Other dried fruits can be used, but date butter is sweetest and smoothest.)
- Fruit purees

Solid Fats (1 cup)

- 2/3 - 1 cup vegetable oil*

Wheat (1 cup, unless noted)

White flour

- 7/8 - 1 cup whole wheat flour (absorbency varies)

Whole wheat pastry flour

- Hard whole wheat flour (except in cakes)
- Other flours: rye, barley, rice, corn, oat, millet

Whole wheat bread

- 100% rye bread
- 100% triticale bread
- Essene bread (Most essene bread is made with sprouted wheat; however, many people who suffer reactions to wheat do not have the same problems when it has been sprouted.)

Protein

This refers to the combining of different protein sources to make "complete" protein, a concept popularized by Lappe's first edition of *Diet for a Small Planet.* However, the 1982 edition emphasized that this is not necessary for good health. Add a little:

- Milk powder, other dairy products
- Whole or ground sesame or sunflower seeds
- Legumes, such as soy or garbanzo flour, tofu, or peanuts

Problems and Solutions

Time

There are a number of breadmaking shortcuts which are simple, save time, assist planning, and help cope with interruptions:

1. ***A bread sponge or dough can be refrigerated*** (or put in any cool spot) to slow down yeast activity and hence rising. If you're interrupted while making bread, refrigerate covered until you return. Then allow to warm up and continue where you left off. This also enables you to prepare dough for later baking (for example, if you want fresh bread for dinner but have to go to work). Refrigerate the covered dough just before or just after shaping. When ready to prepare the dough for baking, place it in a warm place to rise (allow for warming-up time) and proceed as usual. (Refrigerating pre-shaped cinnamon rolls or bagels overnight gives you the best kind of "fast food" breakfast!)
2. ***Dough can also be frozen.*** Divide the dough into loaf-sized pieces, flatten (for even thawing), and wrap loosely. Trays of shaped rolls or bagels work very well when frozen for later use. Remove from the freezer, then allow to warm up and rise.
3. ***Don't forget that dough can rise and be punched down several times***, if you're able to check back briefly at intervals (or have someone else do so). The cooler the spot it's left in, the less frequently it need be checked.
4. ***One or more of the following shortcuts can help speed up the baking process.*** ***Yeasted doughs:*** (1) omit the sponge step, but knead vigorously; (2) let dough rise only once before shaping; (3) provide a warm, moist place for rising; (4) bake at higher temperatures for shorter times (400° F for 30-35 minutes); (5) make rolls or bagels instead of loaves — they can require less kneading, and quicker proofing and baking. ***Other baked goods:*** Unyeasted breads aren't usually a good idea for an emergency loaf. However, a few of the unyeasted breads in ***Uprisings*** are fairly fast (but not sweet); rice bread, Irish soda bread, and buckwheat bread are examples (see Index). The sweeter quick breads and muffins can be made at short notice as a substantial and appealing accompaniment to a hastily planned meal. You can rustle up a batch of hot muffins, for instance, in perhaps forty minutes. For a sweet treat, cookies are the fastest to produce. A time-saving practice used in our bakeries is gathering in advance the measured dry ingredients for a batch of goodies and storing them in a container in the fridge for use at a moment's notice. Fully mixed cookie batter (not containing baking powder or soda) can also be refrigerated for later scooping and baking.

Cost

A major anxiety for almost everyone these days is the cost of food. Baking at home is, of course, an excellent way to save on your expenses. Here are some further tips.

1. ***Locate the nearest food coop store or buying club***, to obtain cheap, bulk ingredients. Look in the phone book under "Health Food Stores" or "Grocery Stores", or ask at a health food shop or restaurant. Get involved with a buying club where groups of people buy supplies at wholesale prices — these aren't hard to start, by the way, and save a lot of money. Most health food stores and supermarkets are more expensive because they're making a profit.
2. ***Choose cheaper ingredients whenever possible.*** Compare the prices of oils, for instance, and buy the lower-priced safflower rather than sesame oil. For sweetening, honey and malt cost less than maple syrup, and some honeys can be much cheaper than others. (For both oils and honeys, however, be on the alert for the cheaper, highly processed versions which are best avoided.) When choosing dried fruits, raisins will probably be less expensive than currants or dates, and preformed date pieces may be a good buy. For texture and crunch, sesame and sunflower seeds make a low cost addition to your baking; in particular, sunnies

are a good replacement for the more expensive nuts. The prices of dried fruits and nuts may fluctuate over the year, perhaps being lowest after harvesting in the fall. Bulk amounts bought when prices are down can be stored for use over a period of time. Obviously, these are only rough guidelines—just shop with care and awareness. One final thought: "Substituting Ingredients" (see above) may give you some ideas for alternative ingredients that will save you money.

3. ***Keep your baking simple.*** Whole wheat berries and flour aren't expensive and you can make a good basic loaf without oil, salt, or sweeteners. So home-baked whole wheat bread is very economical. An inexpensive way to flavor your basic bread is with herbs, chopped onion, or other chopped vegetables. Try a few apple chunks with cinnamon, or raisins or sunflower seeds. For variety, basic bread dough can be shaped into rolls, bagels, or cinnamon buns, or braided, glazed, and sprinkled with poppy seeds.

Quantity

If you want to feed a lot of people or have extra bread to store, here are some suggestions.

1. ***Breads:*** you can easily knead a four-loaf batch of dough (double any recipe in *Uprisings*). Stagger baking, if necessary, by letting half the dough rise an extra time, or put some in the fridge for later proofing and baking. You can also freeze unbaked dough (see above, under "Time").
2. ***Other baked goods:*** you can make up to four dozen muffins at once, if you have the oven space to bake them all at one time (if the batter sits too long between mixing and baking, it won't rise nicely in the oven). Virtually any cookie recipe can be multiplied as many times as you like. Don't use baking soda or powder if the dough will have to sit while the first batch bakes. Cookies or sweets such as unbaked halvah, fudge, or fruit and nut balls are the easiest things to produce in quantity. In addition, premixed doughs can be refrigerated for later scooping or shaping.

One Final Suggestion for finding solutions to your baking problems, whatever they may be. Get help! Involving other people can give you support and other opinions in a crisis, an extra pair of hands to halve the labor and save time, or merely a good time for everyone concerned. Buying supplies with others can reduce your food costs considerably. This is probably the most important thing we've learned in our bakeries—work together with other people and virtually any problem can be solved. Share your troubles and successes, don't be afraid to experiment, and most importantly, enjoy yourself.

Equivalents of Weights and Measures

Liquid Measure

		3 teaspoons (tsp or t)	=	1 Tablespoon (Tbl or T)		
		2 Tbl	=	1 ounce (oz)		
		4 Tbl	=	¼ cup (cup or c)		
16 Tbl	=	8 oz	=	1 cup	=	½ pint (pt)
		2 cups	=	1 pt		
		2 pt	=	1 quart (qt)		
128 oz	=	16 cups	=	4 qt	=	1 gallon (gal)

Dry Measure

16 ounces (oz) = 1 pound (lb)

Volume/Weight Equivalents

Water:

1 pint = 1 pound = 2 cups

Honey:

1⅓ cups = 1 pound (1 cup = ¾ lb)

Whole Wheat Flour:

1 pound = 3½ cups (approximately)

American/Metric Conversions

Liquid:

1 tsp	=	5 milliliters (ml)
1 Tbl	=	15 ml
1 oz	=	30 ml
1 cup	=	235 ml (about ¼ liter)
1 qt	=	.95 liter (l)
1 gal	=	3.8 liters

Dry:

1 oz	=	28 grams (gm)
1 lb	=	454 gm
2.2 lb	=	1 kilogram (kg)

Temperature Conversions

° Fahrenheit		° Celsius
250	=	130
300	=	150
350	=	180
400	=	200
450	=	230

To convert °F to °C,
subtract 32, multiply by 5, and divide by 9.
[(°F − 32) × 5 ÷ 9 = °C]

American/English Equivalents

1 U.S. tsp (5 ml)	=	1 English tsp (5 ml)
1 U.S. Tbl (14.2 ml)	=	4/5 English Tbl
1¼ U.S. Tbl	=	1 English Tbl (17.7 ml)
1 U.S. cup (8 oz)	=	4/5 English cup
1¼ U.S. cups	=	1 English cup (10 Imperial oz)
1 U.S. pint	=	5/6 Imperial pint
2½ U.S. cups	=	1 Imperial pint (20 oz)
U.S. weights	=	English weights

For practical purposes, a two-loaf batch of bread in English measures would use:

just under 1 Tbl yeast
2-4 Tbl sweetener
1 pint or 2 cups water
4-5 cups flour

The Bakeries

Bakery Locations

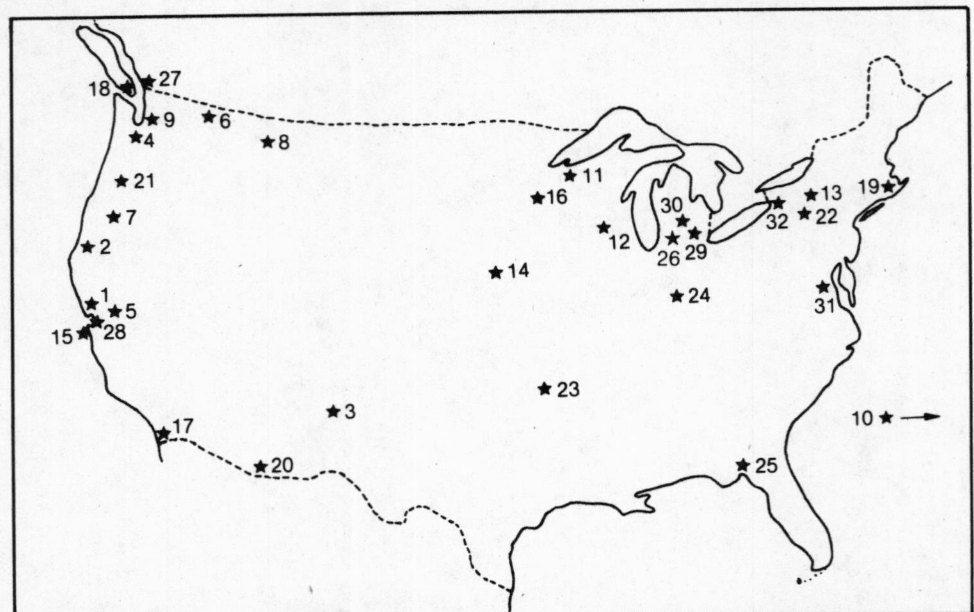

1. **Alvarado St. Bakery**
   5625 State Farm Drive,
   Rohnert Park, CA 94928.
   (707)-585-3293

2. **Arcata Coop Bakery**
   811 "I" Street,
   Arcata, CA 95521.
   (707)-822-9221

3. **The Bakery Cafe**
   118 Yale St.,
   Albuquerque, NM 87106.
   (505)-255-0749.

4. **Blue Heron Bakery**
   4935 Mud Bay Rd.,
   Olympia, WA 98502.
   (206)-866-2253.

5. **Blue Mango Restaurant**
   330 "G" St.,
   Davis, CA 95616.
   (916)-756-2616.

*6. **Dharma Crumbs Bakery**
   282 W. Astor,
   Colville, WA 99114.

7. **Good Bread Bakery**
   Jacksonville, OR 97530.

*8. **Honey Bear Bakery**
   20 First St. W.,
   Kalispell, MT 59901.

9. **Little Bread Company**
   8050 15th Ave. N.E.,
   Seattle, WA 98125.
   (206)-525-5400.

10. **Manna Bakery**
    Niasstraat 54,
    1095 XR Amsterdam,
    Netherlands. 020-350548.

11. **Millstone Bakery**
    631 W. Bayfield St., Box 113,
    Washburn, WI 54891.
    (715)-373-2322.

12. **Nature's Bakery**
1019 Williamson St.,
Madison, WI 53703.
(608)-257-3649.

13. **On The Rise Bakery**
200 Walton St.,
Syracuse, NY 13202.
(315)-475-7190.

14. **Open Harvest Bakery**
2637 Randolph,
Lincoln, NB 68510.
(402)-475-9069.

15. **People's Bakery**
3489 16th St.,
San Francisco, CA 94114.
(415)-863-9660.

16. **People's Company Bakery**
1534 E. Lake St.,
Minneapolis, MN 55407.
(612)-721-7205.

17. **Rebel Bakers**
1863 Bacon St.,
San Diego, CA 92107.
(619)-223-8826.

18. **Rising Star Bakery**
424 Craigflower Rd.,
Victoria, B.C. V9A 2V7, Canada.
(604)-386-3880.

19. **Slice of Life Bakery**
146 Charles St.,
Cambridge, MA 02141.
(617)-547-9157.

20. **Small Planet Bakery**
411 N. 7th Ave.,
Tucson, AZ 85705.
(602)-884-9313.

21. **Solstice Bakery**
350 E. 3rd,
Eugene, OR 97401.
(503)-342-7404.

22. **Somadhara Bakery**
215 N. Cayuga St.,
Ithaca, NY 14850.
(607)-273-8213.

23. **Summercorn Bakery**
401 Watson St.,
Fayetteville, AR 72701.
(501)-521-9338.

24. **Sunflour Bakery**
419 E. Kirkwood Ave.,
Bloomington, IN 47401.
(812)-336-7160.

*25. **Sunrise Bakery**
Tallahassee, FL.

26. **Grain Dance Bakery**
Paw Paw, MI.

27. **Uprising Breads**
1697 Venables,
Vancouver, B.C. V5L 2M1, Canada.
(604)-254-5635.

28. **Uprisings Baking Collective**
2424 Ridge Rd.,
Berkeley, CA 94709.
(415)-649-1165.

29. **Wildflour Community Bakery Coop**
208 N. Fourth Ave.,
Ann Arbor, MI 48104.
(313)-994-0601.

*30. **Wolfmoon Coop Bakery**
East Lansing, MI.

31. **Women's Community Bakery**
736 7th St. S.E.,
Washington, D.C. 20003.
(202)-546-7944.

32. **Yeast West Bakery**
241½ Lexington Ave.,
Buffalo, NY 14222.
(716)-833-5537.

* denotes bakeries closed at time of publication.

SANTA ROSA
CALIFORNIA

we are dedicated to providing non-alienating work with decent wages and benefits for the workers. we supply our wholesale customers with daily delivery service locally. we recently moved and now do some retail sales from the bakery, though we'd like to expand this. we are legally incorporated as a co-operative under the california co-operative corporation code.

PEASANT BREAD

2 x 1½ LB. LOAVES

A HANDY USE FOR OLD BREAD

2¼ CUPS WARM WATER
2 TSP MOLASSES + 1 TSP MALT
1 TBL YEAST
2 CUPS HARD WW FLOUR

1½ CUPS CRUSHED TOASTED BREAD
2½ CUPS HARD WW FLOUR
1 TBL VINEGAR
1 TSP KELP
2 TBL OIL
½ TSP SALT (OPT.)

MIX TOGETHER FIRST FOUR INGREDIENTS, AND BEAT WELL. LET SIT UNTIL PUFFED UP. ADD REST OF INGREDIENTS, ADDING FLOUR AS NEEDED TO GET A SOFT TEXTURE. KNEAD DOUGH UNTIL IT'S ELASTIC. LET RISE TILL DOUBLED IN SIZE, PUNCH DOWN AND LET RISE AGAIN. PUNCH DOWN AND SHAPE INTO TWO LOAVES. PLACE IN OILED BREAD PANS AND LET RISE AGAIN. (THE SECOND RISING BEFORE SHAPING MAKES BREAD A LITTLE LIGHTER.) BAKE AT 350° FOR 45 MINUTES.

Carrot Celery Bread

2 x 1½ lb loaves

A simple bread with a robust flavor.

2 cups warm water
¼ cup honey
1 Tbl yeast
5½-6 cups hard w.w. flour
½ lb grated carrot
½ Tbl celery seed
2 Tbl oil
1 tsp salt

Mix water, yeast and honey. When the yeast has dissolved, beat in about 2 cups of the flour. Let this sponge sit until doubled and puffy. Now add remaining ingredients, reserving flour and adding it to make a soft kneading texture. Knead dough well, until it's elastic. Let dough rise in a warm place until doubled in size. Punch down. Let rise again, shape into loaves and let rise in oiled pans. Bake at 350° for 45 minutes.

POTATO DILL BREAD

2 - 1½ lb loaves

Delicious with a fresh salad or cool cucumber soup.

- 2 cups warm water
- ¼ cup molasses
- 2 Tbl malt syrup
- 1 Tbl yeast
- ½ cup bran
- 1 tsp salt
- 3 Tbl vinegar
- 2 Tbl dill weed (dried)
- 1 medium potato, grated
- 5 cups hard w.w. flour

MIX TOGETHER WATER, MOLASSES AND MALT. STIR IN YEAST AND LET IT DISSOLVE BEAT IN 2 CUPS OF THE FLOUR. LET THIS SPONGE SIT TILL PUFFED UP. ADD ALL REMAINING INGREDIENTS, ADDING FLOUR AS NEEDED TO MAKE A SOFT TEXTURE. KNEAD DOUGH WELL TILL IT'S STRETCHY. LET RISE IN A WARM PLACE TILL DOUBLED IN SIZE. PUNCH DOWN. LET RISE AGAIN AND SHAPE INTO TWO LOAVES. LET THESE RISE IN OILED PANS. BAKE AT 350° FOR 45 MINUTES.

WITH THE OCEAN AND THE REDWOODS AROUND US, AND THE MORNING FOG THAT ROLLS AWAY FOR RELAXED SUNNY DAYS, YOU KNOW THAT YOU ARE IN NORTHERN CALIFORNIA! OUR BAKERY IS PART OF PERHAPS THE LARGEST CO-OP IN NORTH AMERICA — AN EX-SUPERMARKET STORE, NOW PACKED WITH ALL KINDS OF GOOD FOOD AND SUPPLIES, AND EMPLOYING ABOUT 80 WORKERS. THE BAKERY REMAINS A SMALL, LARGELY AUTONOMOUS COLLECTIVE OF SEVEN PEOPLE, WHICH STRIVES TO SUPPLY CHEAP EVERYDAY BREADS TO A BROAD CROSS-SECTION OF THE COMMUNITY, AS WELL AS A RANGE OF FANCIER BREADS, GRANOLAS AND GOODIES, MADE WITH AN EYE TO BOTH NUTRITIONAL CONTENT AND INNOVATIVE TEXTURES AND FLAVORS.

9-GRAIN BREAD

THIS BREAD WILL NOT ONLY NOURISH YOU, IT WILL SURPRISE YOU WITH ITS UNIQUE AND DELIGHTFUL FLAVOR AND TEXTURE. DEFINITELY WORTH THE EXTRA EFFORT OF FINDING THE 9-GRAIN MIX INGREDIENTS. THE MIX WILL KEEP WELL IN THE REFRIGERATOR – WE'RE SURE YOU'LL WANT TO MAKE THIS BREAD AGAIN (TRY A HANDFUL IN PANCAKES!).

<u>9-GRAIN MIX:</u>

	MAKES 2 1/4 CUPS	MAKES 10 CUPS
TRITICALE FLOUR	1/2 CUP	2 CUPS
BUCKWHEAT GROATS OR FLOUR	1 Tbl	1/4 CUP
FLAX MEAL (GRIND FLAXSEEDS)	1 Tbl	1/4 CUP
MILLET (WHOLE)	1/4 CUP	1 CUP
CORNMEAL	1/3 CUP	1 1/3 CUPS
SUNFLOWER SEEDS	1/2 CUP	2 CUPS
OATS	1/4 CUP	1 CUP
SOY FLOUR	1/4 CUP	1 CUP
SOY GRITS	1 1/2 Tbl	3/8 CUP

MIX THESE UP AND YOU'RE READY TO MAKE BREAD!

- 2 1/3 CUPS WARM WATER
- 2/3 Tbl BLACKSTRAP MOLASSES
- 1 3/4 Tbl MALT SYRUP
- 1 Tbl YEAST
- 1 1/8 CUPS 9-GRAIN MIX
- 5 1/2 CUPS HARD WHOLE WHEAT FLOUR
- 1 tsp SALT
- 3 1/2 Tbl OIL

MIX THE WATER, MOLASSES, MALT AND YEAST.
ADD THE 9-GRAIN MIX, FLOUR, SALT AND OIL (YOU CAN ALSO MAKE A SPONGE AND WAIT, BUT IT'S NOT NECESSARY).
MIX, AND KNEAD DOUGH WELL.
LET RISE, SHAPE INTO LOAVES AND LET RISE AGAIN IN OILED BREAD PANS. BAKE AT 350° FOR 45 MINUTES.
MAKES 2 × 1 1/2 LB LOAVES.

WHEAT SPROUTS BREAD

NICE CHEWY-CRUNCHY BREAD, SWEET AND NUTRITIOUS.

2 CUPS WARM WATER
2 tsp MALT
2 Tbl MOLASSES
1 Tbl YEAST
5 CUPS HARD WHOLE WHEAT FLOUR
½ LB (ABOUT 2 CUPS) WHEAT SPROUTS*
1 tsp SALT
2 Tbl WHEY POWDER (OPTIONAL)
3 Tbl OIL
1½ Tbl SOY FLOUR

MIX TOGETHER WATER, YEAST, SWEETENERS AND TWO CUPS FLOUR. LET SIT TILL BUBBLY. THEN ADD REMAINING INGREDIENTS, AND KNEAD WELL, RESERVING OR ADDING A LITTLE FLOUR TO OBTAIN A GOOD ELASTIC TEXTURE. LET RAISE IN OILED COVERED BOWL, SHAPE INTO LOAVES AND LET RAISE AGAIN. BAKE AT 350°, 45 MINUTES. 2-1½# LOAVES.

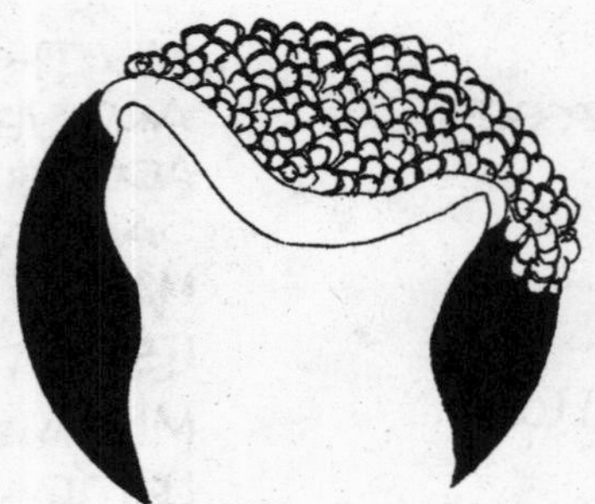

* SOAK WHEAT BERRIES OVERNIGHT AND SPROUT IN CONTAINER, RINSING TWICE DAILY, FOR 2-4 DAYS. THEY GET SWEETER THE LONGER THEY SPROUT.

SWEET OAT BREAD

NOT MANY BAKERIES STILL OFFER A BASIC YEASTED BREAD THAT'S RICH WITH BUTTER AND EGGS. THIS ONE'S DELICIOUS — A GOOD BREAD TO INTRODUCE A FRIEND OR FAMILY MEMBER TO THE DELIGHTS OF WHOLE GRAIN BREAD.

2 1/4 CUPS WARM WATER
1/4 CUP HONEY
1 Tbl YEAST
1 EGG
1/4 CUP MELTED OR VERY SOFT BUTTER
2 CUPS OATS
5-6 CUPS HARD WHOLE WHEAT FLOUR
1/4 CUP SOY FLOUR
1 tsp SALT

MIX THE WATER, HONEY AND YEAST AND LET SIT A FEW MINUTES. ADD REMAINING INGREDIENTS, RESERVING AND ADDING WHOLE WHEAT FLOUR AS NEEDED. KNEAD DOUGH WELL UNTIL IT IS SMOOTH AND ELASTIC. LET RISE, LOAF AND PLACE IN OILED PANS. LET RISE AGAIN, AND BAKE AT 350° FOR 45 MINUTES.
2 x 1 1/2 LB LOAVES

ARCATA ALSO PUT IN POTATO FLOUR AND LECITHIN — INGREDIENTS WE DIDN'T HAVE WHEN TESTING THIS RECIPE. IF YOU'RE INTERESTED, TRY 1-2 Tbl POTATO FLOUR AND 1-2 tsp LECITHIN, AND LET US KNOW HOW IT COMES OUT.

SESAME SOYA BREAD

LOVE THAT CRUNCH!

2⅓ CUPS WATER
3 Tbl BLACKSTRAP MOLASSES
1 Tbl MALT SYRUP
1 Tbl YEAST
5½ - 6 CUPS HARD WHOLE WHEAT FLOUR
2½ Tbl SOY GRITS
¼ CUP SOY FLOUR
⅓ CUP SESAME SEEDS
3⅓ Tbl OIL
1 tsp. SALT

MIX THE WATER, MOLASSES, MALT AND YEAST AND LET SIT A FEW MINUTES. ADD THE REMAINING INGREDIENTS, RESERVING AND ADDING WHOLE WHEAT FLOUR AS NEEDED. KNEAD DOUGH WELL. LET RISE, SHAPE INTO LOAVES AND LET RISE AGAIN IN OILED PANS. BAKE AT 350° FOR 45 MINUTES.
2 x 1½ LB LOAVES.

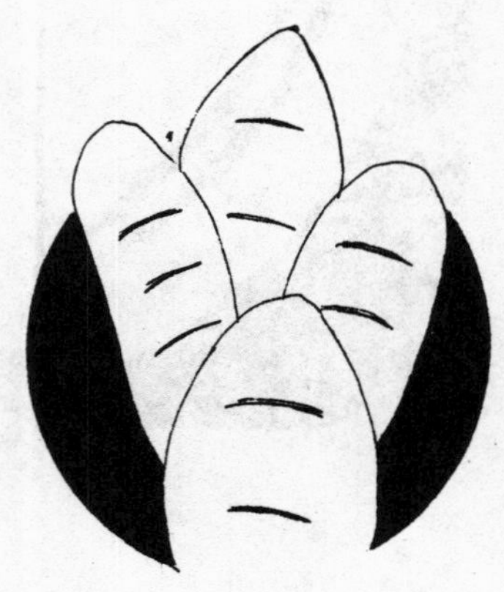

CARROT CAKE OR MUFFINS

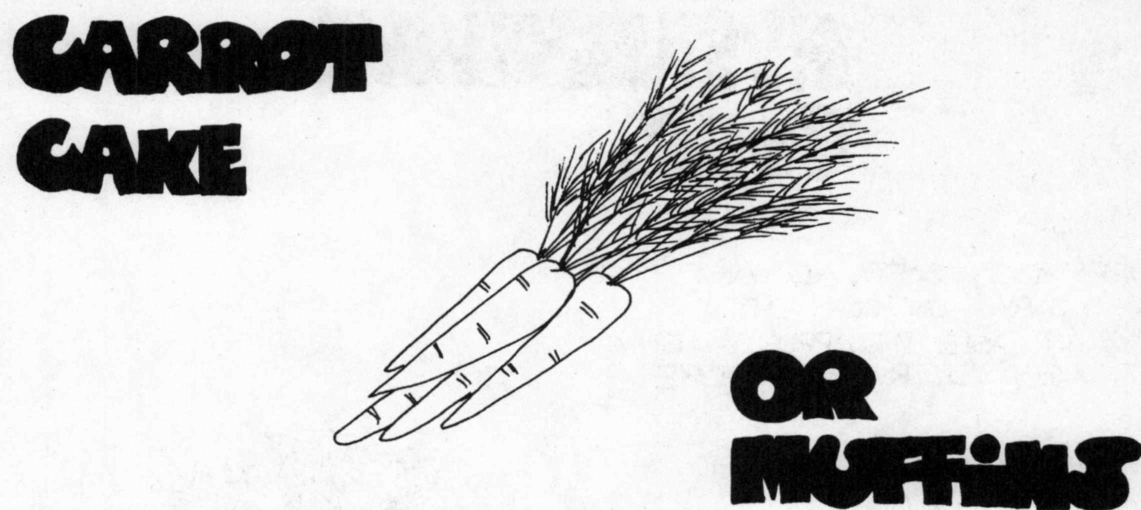

THE PINEAPPLE AND CLOVES ADD A DISTINCTIVE TANG TO THIS LIGHT CAKE.

½ CUP SAFFLOWER OIL
½ CUP BARLEY MALT SYRUP
½ CUP DATE SUGAR
  (OR 2/3 CUP CHOPPED DATES)
½ CUP WATER
2 LARGE EGGS
⅓ CAN CRUSHED PINEAPPLE
½ 1LB GRATED CARROTS
3/8 CUP RAISINS
2½ CUPS WHOLE WHEAT
  PASTRY FLOUR
1 tsp BAKING POWDER
1 tsp BAKING SODA
1¼ tsp CINNAMON
¾ tsp CLOVES
3/8 CUP WHEY POWDER*

CREAM OIL AND SWEETENERS. ADD WATER, EGGS, PINEAPPLE AND CARROTS AND MIX WELL.

IN SEPARATE BOWL, MIX RAISINS, FLOUR, BAKING POWDER, SODA, CLOVES, CINNAMON AND WHEY.

ADD WET INGREDIENTS AND MIX IN JUST UNTIL BLENDED. POUR INTO OILED MUFFIN CUPS (2/3 FULL) OR CAKE PANS. BAKE AT 350° UNTIL TOOTHPICK OR KNIFE COMES OUT CLEAN AND CAKE IS LIGHTLY BROWNED — ABOUT 30 MINUTES FOR MUFFINS, 50-60 MINUTES FOR CAKES.
20 GOOD-SIZED MUFFINS OR 2 - 9" CAKES

*IF YOU FIND WHEY POWDER HARD TO FIND, SUBSTITUTE MILK POWDER OR A LITTLE MORE FLOUR - OR CUT WATER AND OMIT ENTIRELY. YOU CAN ALSO USE LIQUID WHEY, ADJUSTING WATER ACCORDINGLY.

APPLESAUCE CAKE

VERY TASTY, SOFT AND MOIST. RICH AND DARK. ONE COMMENT: "CAN'T TASTE THE APPLESAUCE ENOUGH. I'D TRY IT WITH MORE."

1/4 LB. MARGARINE OR BUTTER
1 CUP BARLEY MALT
1/4 CUP MOLASSES
1 LARGE EGG
1 1/4 CUPS APPLESAUCE
2 CUPS WHOLE WHEAT PASTRY FLOUR
1/4 CUP WHEAT GERM
1 tsp BAKING SODA
1 tsp BAKING POWDER
1 1/2 tsp CINNAMON
1/8 tsp GROUND CLOVES
1/4 tsp NUTMEG
1/2 CUP RAISINS

CREAM THE FIRST THREE INGREDIENTS, MAKING SURE TO CREAM MARGARINE ALONE FIRST UNTIL SOFT AND SMOOTH THEN BEAT EGG AND APPLESAUCE INTO CREAMED MIXTURE.
COMBINE DRY INGREDIENTS. ADD TO WET INGREDIENTS AND MIX TOGETHER LIGHTLY. POUR BATTER INTO GREASED PANS AND BAKE AT 350°:
25 MINUTES FOR MUFFINS
45 MINUTES FOR 9" ROUND CAKE
20 MUFFINS OR 2 x 9" CAKES.

PUMPKIN CUPCAKES

A GREAT TASTING WHOLE WHEAT DESSERT CAKE, THAT'S LIGHT AND AIRY AND SOFT.

3/8 CUP SAFFLOWER OIL
5/8 CUP HONEY
1/2 CUP MOLASSES
1 3/8 CUP PUMPKIN, MASHED
2 LARGE EGGS
1 7/8 CUPS WHOLE WHEAT PASTRY FLOUR
1 tsp BAKING SODA
1 tsp BAKING POWDER
3/8 tsp NUTMEG
3/8 tsp CLOVES
3/4 tsp CINNAMON
3/8 CUP RAISINS

CREAM TOGETHER THE OIL, HONEY AND MOLASSES. BEAT IN THE MASHED PUMPKIN AND THE EGGS. COMBINE THE REST OF THE INGREDIENTS AND ADD THEM TO THE FIRST ONES. POUR THE BATTER INTO GREASED AND FLOURED CAKE PANS, BAKE AT 350° FOR 50-60 MINUTES OR UNTIL IT'S BROWN AROUND THE EDGES AND IT TESTS CLEAN. LET IT SIT FOR FIVE MINUTES BEFORE TAKING IT OUT OF THE PANS. IF YOU MAKE CUPCAKES, FILL THE OILED OR PAPERED MUFFIN CUPS 2/3 FULL AND BAKE THEM FOR 20 MINUTES OR UNTIL DONE.
20 CUPCAKES OR TWO 9"
ROUND PANS.

VERY CAROBY, VERY FUDGY. WATCH OUT!

3/4 CUP BARLEY MALT
1/2 CUP SAFFLOWER OIL
1/4 CUP HONEY
3/4 CUP WATER
3/4 tsp VANILLA
3/4 CUP SHREDDED COCONUT
1 CUP HARD WHOLE WHEAT FLOUR
1/2 CUP WHOLE WHEAT PASTRY FLOUR
3/4 CUP CAROB POWDER
1 1/2 tsp BAKING POWDER

COMBINE THE MALT, HONEY AND OIL AND MIX WELL. STIR IN THE WATER AND VANILLA.

MIX TOGETHER THE DRY INGREDIENTS IN A SEPARATE BOWL. ADD THIS TO THE WET AND MIX TOGETHER LIGHTLY UNTIL INGREDIENTS ARE BLENDED. DON'T MIX LONGER THAN NECESSARY.

POUR INTO OILED PAN AND BAKE AT 350° FOR 20-25 MINUTES UNTIL SLIGHTLY FIRM IN CENTER AND BEGINS TO DARKEN AROUND EDGES. LET COOL BEFORE EATING - EAT WARM IF YOU CAN'T WAIT! (WE RECIPE TESTERS COULDN'T.)

1 10" ROUND PAN.

CAROB COCONUT BROWNIES

EGGLESS, A FINE WAY TO USE SOME OF THE PUMPKIN YOU'VE GROWN IN YOUR GARDEN.

½ LB BUTTER AT ROOM TEMPERATURE
1½ CUPS MALT SYRUP
1½ tsp VANILLA
1½ CUPS MASHED PUMPKIN
3 CUPS WHOLE WHEAT FLOUR
1 Tbl CINNAMON
¾ tsp NUTMEG
½ tsp BOTH CLOVES AND ALLSPICE
1½ CUPS RAISINS

CREAM TOGETHER THE BUTTER AND THE MALT, AND PREHEAT THE OVEN TO 350°. BEAT VANILLA AND PUMPKIN INTO CREAMED MIXTURE. IN ANOTHER CONTAINER, COMBINE FLOUR, SPICES AND RAISINS AND ADD TO THE WET MIXTURE. STIR IT ALL TOGETHER, AND DROP BY TABLESPOONFULS ONTO GREASED COOKIE SHEETS. BAKE THEM FOR 15-18 MINUTES MAKES 4½ DOZEN.

A POPULAR RECIPE, THIS IS NOW MADE BY SEVERAL WHOLE GRAIN BAKERY COLLECTIVES ACROSS THE U.S.

2¼ CUPS SUNFLOWER SEEDS
1¼ CUPS DATE PIECES / CHOPPED DATES
4 TBL PEANUT BUTTER
6 TBL BARLEY MALT
⅛ TSP VANILLA (MORE IF YOU LIKE)
1 TBL WATER

SUNNY DATE CHEWS

MIX PEANUT BUTTER AND MALT TOGETHER, ADDING VANILLA AND WATER. MIX IN SUNNIES AND DATES. PRESS THE STICKY GOO INTO AN OILED PAN - YOU CAN CUT OUT LINES BEFORE BAKING FOR EASY REMOVAL LATER. BAKE AT 350° FOR ABOUT 30 MINUTES. WHEN DONE, IT'LL BE LIGHTLY BROWNED AROUND THE EDGES, BUT STILL SOFT IN THE MIDDLE. LET COOL. IT'LL HARDEN UP TO GIVE YOU A GOOD CHEW.
8" × 8" PAN - 16 × 2" BARS.

WILDFLOUR BAKERY DISCOVERED A DELICIOUS VARIANT: DROP THE MALT AND USE ALL DATES, MASHING EXTRA FOR A GOOD GOO. USE SUNFLOWER OR PECAN BUTTER INSTEAD OF PEANUT BUTTER. BAKE. 20-30 MINUTES. IT MAKES AN INCREDIBLY RICH CANDY.

MUESLi

NO BAKING. MUESLI'S A DELICIOUS UNCOOKED CEREAL OR SNACK MIX ORIGINATING IN SWITZERLAND. MUNCH IT DRY OR EAT WITH MILK, SOYMILK, CIDER OR WHATEVER LIQUID YOU FANCY. SOAKING IT MAKES IT SWEETER. EUROPEANS SOAK MUESLI OVERNIGHT FOR A SUBSTANTIAL BREAKFAST.

3/4 CUP OATS
1/2 CUP WHEAT FLAKES
1/4 CUP RYE FLAKES
1/3 CUP DATES
3/8 CUP RAISINS
1/4 CUP ALMONDS
1/4 CUP CASHEWS OR WALNUTS
3 Tbl SUNNIES

MIX UP! EXPERIMENT WITH THE RATIOS OF DATES AND RAISINS FOR DIFFERENT DEGREES OF SWEETNESS. USE YOUR IMAGINATION WITH THE OTHER INGREDIENTS TO CONCOCT YOUR OWN FAVORITE VARIATIONS.
15 OZ., ABOUT 3 CUPS.

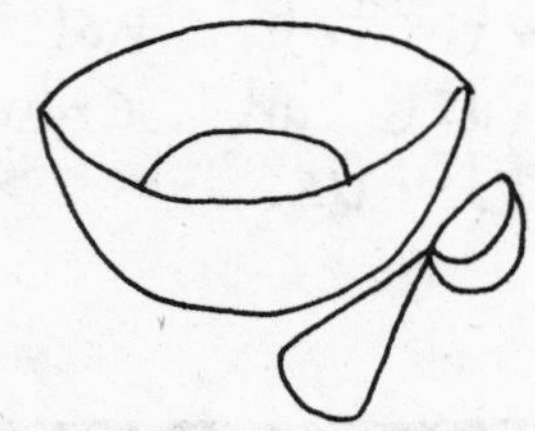

the Bakery Cafe

Albuquerque, N.M.

The Bakery Cafe is not a place — it is people. The Bakery has as its impetus, frame of reference, and goal the desire to provide handsomely offered, delicious vegetarian meals and baked goods at reasonable prices. Everything from bread to yogurt is made on the premises, without preservatives or additives. The Cafe seeks to support both local producers and the established cooperative network.

More importantly, the Bakery Cafe is a radical experiment — a collective whose members actively participate in all decisions. Discussions at weekly meetings thus result in provocations, invocations, multi-faceted repetitions, evaluations, and downright arguments. When the dust settles, everyone shares in the necessary compromises, none of which demand sale of anyone's soul.

Much selfless labor happens here too, as seen in a new baking room that was built in just three days and a garden that almost entirely surrounds the Bakery. It is not an easy place to work. Energy demands run high: workers must do their own jobs well and at the same time be aware of and deal with the moods and frustrations of their co-workers. No, definitely not a punch-in — punch-out job — just an enlightening one.

Come eat with us.

Tahini Coffee Cake

9" round

Blend: ½ c. oil
¾ c. honey
¾ c. tahini
1½ t. baking powder
1 t. nutmeg
½ t. coriander

Add: 2 c. w.w. pastry flour
½ c. sesame seeds
1 c. water

Pour into 9" round cake pan.
Bake 35 - 40 minutes at 350°.

"Delicious"

"Subtly Rich"

"Elegant"

recycle old bread with:

pudin de pan

9"×9" pan

~ soak 5-6 c. bread chunks
in 1½ c. apple juice

~ mix and add:
⅓ c. oil
⅓ c. honey
⅓ c. molasses
½ c. dates

~ add and mix:
1 T. baking powder
1 t. vanilla
1 t. cinnamon

batter should be fairly thick with lumps

~ pour into oiled pan (9"×9" square)

~ bake at 350° check after 30 minutes
should be firm but not dry

comments: very moist, pudding-like

inspirations: substitute maple syrup for molasses
serve with tofu "whipcream" topping

Sesame Halvah,

13" x 9" pan

Toast 6c. sesame seeds in cast iron skillet or oven

Blend seeds in blender 1 cup at a time

Add and mix:
- 1½ c. honey
- 1 T. ginger
- 1 t. cinnamon
- 1 t. allspice

Pat into 9" x 13" pan.

... Carob - Coated

In pan over boiling water melt
- 2 c. carob chips
- ¼ c. water

When smooth, spread over sesame mix. Let cool. Cut.

"Ambrosia!"

Striding among misty dawn premonitions of the new day, or streaking by pheasant, deer and Kingfisher by bicycle, we come to roost for another unpredictable workday at the Blue Heron Bakery. Set among miles of glistening MUD when the tide is out helps nurture appreciation of essential beauty. A glance out The back at rich pond life blooming, or a side view toward forested hills above Mud Bay even through the front windows often reveals our inspirational mascot, soaring and squawking.

Working in all combinations of 3-5 shifts/day we're now 5 fellows and 3 women. Anyone can try any part of our tasks, trading around to learn and avoid needless boredom. Lots of people contact keeps us spunkier, baking in full view of customers, scurrying around on delivery, or staffing the bustling Farmers' Market booth seasonally. Night bakes allow space for rambunctious adrenalin, deliberation, whim, and just living through the process. All Kinds of energy go in and each person's bread shows its own faces. The cooperative energy that spawned us now feeds into a web, both directions, from growers-millers-truckers-bakers-co-op foodstores, restaurants and ever faithful smiling customers at our door.

Beginning with huge spoons, bowls, willing notions, arms and zeal, this place keeps changing: a display case, a proof-box, more ovens, a cooler, a new mixer... it's no longer asking any one of us to continue it. Bakery life beguiles and transforms and becomes lots of wonderfully curious people — FRIENDS —

Potato Buttermilk Bread

-no sweetener- 2 x 1½# loaves

A pretty bread with a rich cheesy aroma.

5 TBL warm water
1 TBL yeast
½ lb. raw unpeeled potatoes
1⅗ cups buttermilk
1 tsp salt
5½-6 cups hard WW flour

Dissolve yeast in water. Grate potatoes or put through food-grinder and add to buttermilk. Add this to yeast. Stir in salt and flour, adding flour as needed for a soft, kneadable texture. Knead dough until it's springy and elastic. Place in oiled bowl — cover & let rise till doubled in bulk. Punch down, shape into 2 loaves, & let rise again in oiled pans. Bake at 350° for 45 min.

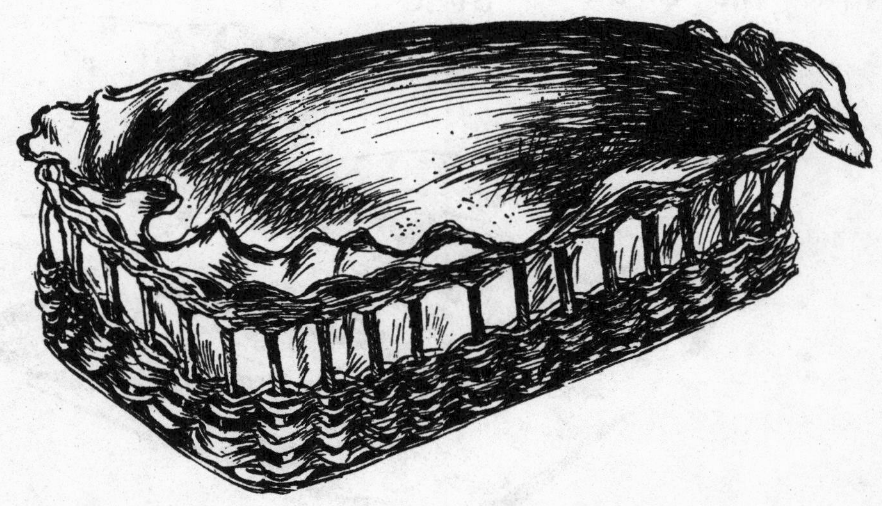

Hearty Whole Grain Black Bread 2 round loaves

Good Flavor → easy to make → 2 very pretty loaves!

2½ cups warm water
¼ cup medium dark molasses
1½ Tbl. yeast
3 cups hard WW flour
⅓ cup sifted carob powder
¾ cup cornmeal
½ cup rye flour
¾ cup rolled oats or rye flakes
¾ cup wheat germ
3 Tbl. oil
1 tsp. salt

Make a sponge by mixing water, molasses and yeast, and 2½ cups WW flour. Allow to bubble (about 30 min.). Add carob powder, corn meal, rye flour, rolled oats or rye flakes, wheat germ, oil and salt to sponge. Mix together. Turn out onto flour dusted surface and knead, adding more WW flour until the moist, sticky dough has body. Let dough rise 30 minutes, approximately, in a warm place, covered with a damp cloth, sitting in an oiled bowl. Punch down. Let rise another 15 min. Punch down again. Shape into loaves. Place on oiled or cornmeal-sprinkled tray. Bake 15 min. at 350° then reduce heat to 325° to avoid scorching the crust. Bake for another 35 minutes, until the bread is done.

CHEESECAKE

one $9\frac{1}{2}$" cheese cake

Excellent.

Cut a piece of baking wax paper to fit bottom of spring form pan, and $1\frac{1}{2}$" strips around sides. Assemble in pan...

CRUST:

1 cup wheat germ
½ cup ww flour
½ cup chopped walnuts
½ cup finely shredded coconut
¼ cup butter
¼ cup honey

Thoroughly mix dry ingredients. Melt the butter, stir in honey. Then briskly stir honey/butter into dry ingredients. Use fingers to mold thin layer of crust mix around edges first, about 1"- 1¼" tall. Then tamp the rest over the bottom of the pan (keep hands less sticky by dipping them in water.)

FILLING:

1½ lbs cream cheese (the best you can afford)
½ cup honey (warm)
2 eggs
1 tsp vanilla
(squeeze of lemon)

Whip filling ingredients together to get a smooth consistency. Fill raw shell with cheese mixture evenly, and bake at 325° for 20-25 min.

TOPPING:

1 cup yogurt
2 Tbl honey

Remove and top with honey/yogurt. Spread evenly. Return to oven and bake 5-10 min. longer.

Cinnamon Rolls

one dozen

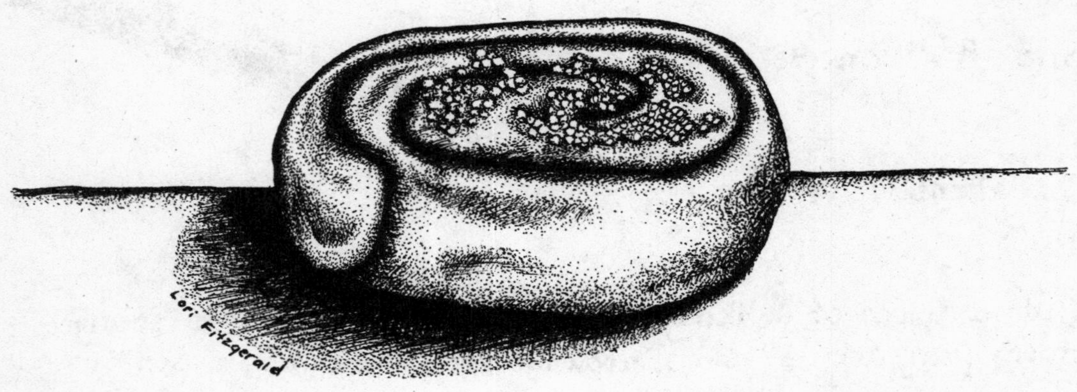

"There is nothing like a warm cinnamon roll...."

1⅓ cups warm water
2 Tbl yeast
¼ cup honey

4½ cups WW pastry flour
⅓ cup dry milk
1 tsp. salt
2 eggs
¼ cup oil

¼ cup butter
½ cup honey
cinnamon
½ cup raisins

Sprinkle yeast on water and stir in ¼ cup honey. Allow to bubble up. While waiting, measure out and stir together dry ingredients. Crack the eggs and beat them well in a separate bowl. Stir the flour, dry milk and salt into the sponge, until it begins to look evenly balled-up. Add eggs. Mix or knead until it looks even then add oil in a steady trickle. Keep mixing to get oil evenly distributed - dough will be tacky. (Keep total mixing time around 5 min. to prevent dough from getting tough.)

Turn dough into oiled bowl. Shape quickly into compact ball. Cover; allow to rise 30-45 min.

Meanwhile melt butter and whip with honey.

When dough is puffy, don't punch it down.
Roll out on a table, shaping it into an even log with your hands (use a good "forearm bounce"!) until close to desired length, then roll out 20-22" wide with your best rolling pin. Dough should be about $\frac{1}{3}$" thick.

Pour a small am't. of whipped honey butter over length of dough and spread it with a plastic spatula or scraper to make a very thin film.
Scrape excess back into bowl and save for topping. (Keep it warm- set it near the oven.)
Sprinkle film with cinnamon and raisins. (Be liberal!)

Roll the dough up into a log again, trying to wind it up firmly. (Even it out.)

Cut log into $\frac{3}{4}$" wide slices + place in oiled flat pans. Leave space for dough to rise.

Let rise in warm, moist place - 40 min. - 'til they begin to fill the pan.

Bake at 350° in the middle of the oven for 15-20 minutes til golden.

Invert onto rack, place cool pan over exposed bottom. Return upright. (Rolls should pop out.)
Brush on honey butter for a mellow golden finish.

WE ALL KNOW WHAT TO DO NEXT!

CAROB CHIP BARS

17" x 12" pan or equivalent

very rich and delicious.

1¼ cups butter
3/4 cup honey
1/3 cup malt
1/3 cup molasses
3 eggs
1 TBL vanilla

Cream butter till smooth, then cream in honey, malt and molasses. Beat in eggs and vanilla.

2½ cups WW flour
3/4 TBL b. soda
2 cups unsweetened carob chips
1¼ cups sunflower seeds

Combine flour & soda & blend into creamed mixture. Finally stir in carob chips & sunflower seeds. Bake in oiled pan at 325°-350° for 20-25 min., till lightly browned.

COCONUT DREAM BARS

17" x 12" pan

A luxurious treat for special occasions!

crust:
1 cup butter
1/2 cup honey
2 tsp vanilla
2 cups WW pastry flour
2/3 cup rice flour

Cream butter, then cream in honey & vanilla. Add flours and blend. Spread crust in oiled pans & bake at 325° for 10-15 minutes.

topping:
2 eggs
1/2 cup yogurt or buttermilk
1 cup honey
3/8 cup molasses
2 tsp vanilla

Beat eggs, and mix in yogurt, honey, molasses & vanilla.

3/8 cup WW pastry flour
1/2 tsp b. soda
1/2 cup finely shredded coconut
1/2 cup wheat germ
1 cup chopped almonds

Combine dry ingredients and stir them into egg mixture. Spread this over partly-baked crust. Sprinkle a little extra shredded coconut on top. Bake at 325° for 20-30 min till firm and lightly browned.

(Walnut-Raisin / Date-Cashew) Ultimate Oatmeal Cookies
- 2 dozen -

These are big, thick, chewy, delicious cookies! YIKES!

- 4½ cups rolled oats
- 1¼ cups wheat germ
- ¾ cup powdered milk
- ¾ cup coconut flakes
- ⅔ cup walnuts or cashews
- ⅔ cup raisins or dates
- ½ Tbl. cinnamon
- ¾ cup honey
- ¾ cup oil
- 3 eggs

Warm the honey, beat the eggs into the oil, then whip all three together until the mixture is smooth. Mix the rest of the ingredients together in a large bowl, making a "well" in the center. Pour the honey-oil-egg mixture into the well, and then quickly toss, stir and turn the mixture, using your hands to get to the bottom of the bowl.

When it is evenly mixed together, let the dough sit 20-30 min., covered. (this helps the dough bind, and the cookies won't crumble as easily) Portion the batter out as well-packed ¼ cup blobs on greased cookie sheets. Squash the cookies so they are just about ½" thick and rounded, and bake at 325°-350° for about 15 minutes until they are a nice light brown.

Blue Mango

Davis, Ca.

The Blue Mango Restaurant has been serving nutritious vegetarian meals, whole grain breads and delicious desserts since 1979. Our stated purpose is to promote "nourishment, consciousness and creativity." We are located in the small university/agricultural community of Davis, in the California Central Valley.

The Blue Mango is a workers' cooperative. All aspects of the business are decided by a consensus of the workers. All tips are shared and everyone receives the same hourly wage. We support local small farmers by purchasing their seasonal organic produce. The Restaurant provides a meeting place for local groups with community concerns, and a showcase for local artists and musicians.

Within the collective, our breads and desserts are prepared by a five member bake team. We use organic ingredients whenever possible. We prefer to allow the customer a wider choice by offering both whole grain and honey desserts, as well as cakes and brownies incorporating refined sugar. In addition, we are evolving baked desserts and breads for those who have allergies or are diabetic.

Our daily fresh baked goods are sold at the restaurant, at local food co-ops and at a farmers' market. We also enjoy baking special orders and free birthday cakes for our workers.

Fruit Bars

Filling #1 Dried Peaches, Apricots or Figs

4 cups dried fruit
4 cups water
1 T lemon juice or to taste

> Slice fruit into small pieces, cook in water over medium heat until all water is absorbed. Stir often to prevent burning. Remove from heat. Stir in lemon juice.

Filling #2 Fresh Dates

4 cups dates, sliced
2 cups hot water
dash soda

> Let above ingredients rest in bowl for 15 minutes.

> Mash mixture and stir in: ½ t. cinnamon
2 T lemon juice
1 cup walnuts

Crust:

<u>mix</u>: 4 cups whole wheat flour
4¼ cups oats
1 T cinnamon
¼-½ T lemon rind

<u>cut in with fingers</u>:
1¼ cups soy margarine or butter

<u>add</u>:
1¼ cups honey

> Oil a 9" x 13" pan. Spread ½ crust mixture and pat down.

> Spread filling. Crumble second half of mixture on top but do not pat down.

> Bake @ 325° for 40 minutes or until top is light brown.

Banana Creme Cake

A honey version of a Boston creme pie

Cake

- whip 1 minute: 7 egg yolks, room temperature
  - ½ cup oil
  - 6 T honey
  - 2 t. vanilla
- combine: 2 cups whole wheat pastry flour
  - 1 T baking powder

  mix into above mixture on low speed.

- in separate bowl, whip until stiff but not dry:
  - 7 egg whites, room temperature
  - ½ t. cream of tartar

  fold egg whites into first bowl.

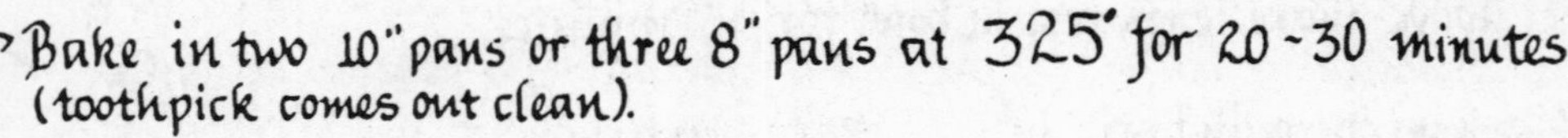

- Bake in two 10" pans or three 8" pans at 325° for 20-30 minutes (toothpick comes out clean).

Filling

- Heat in double boiler until very hot:
  - 2 cups milk
  - 6 T honey
  - ¼ t. salt
- combine: 5 T whole wheat pastry flour
  - 2 T cornstarch
  - ½ cup milk
- Add to hot milk, stirring until thick and continue to cook for 3 minutes. Cool, covered, without stirring.

Assemblage

- Spread a thin layer of pudding over first layer. Arrange sliced banana (¼" thick) all over and cover with pudding (if using three 8" pans repeat for second layer). Place last layer on top and cover with pudding.

  Frost sides of cake with:
  - 1 cup heavy cream, whipped, with
  - 2 t. honey folded in.

We are a small collective in a rural area of Northeastern Washington. Our bakery is in our local food co-op and we sell our goods there as well as sending them to other areas of Washington and Idaho. We supply the community with whole grain breads, goodies and granola.

Herb Bread

2 x $1\frac{1}{2}$ lb. loaves

The herb flavors blend nicely in this attractive bread.

Make a sponge of:

- $2\frac{2}{3}$ cups lukewarm water (85-100°F)
- 1 Tbl. yeast
- 2-4 Tbl. honey, molasses or barley malt
- 2 cups hard whole wheat flour

Blend thoroughly and let the sponge rise until doubled in bulk - about one hour.

Mix into the sponge:

- 2 tsp. each of basil, oregano and marjoram
- 2 tsp. each of onion and garlic powder
- 1 tsp. salt (optional)
- 3 Tbl. oil, soft butter or margarine
- $3\frac{1}{2}$ - 4 cups hard whole wheat flour

adding flour as needed. Knead the dough until its elastic. Let dough rise again in oiled, covered bowl until doubled in bulk - about one hour.

Punch dough down and shape into loaves. Let rise in greased loaf pans 15-25 minutes.

Bake at 350° for about 45 minutes.

Be gentle when you touch bread
Let it not be uncared for, unwanted
Too often bread is taken for granted
There is such beauty in bread:
Beauty of sun and soil;
Beauty of patient toil;
Wind and rain have caressed it,
Christ often blessed it -
Be gentle when you touch bread.

Raisin Date Bars

9" x 13" pan

Really luscious! These are great with the raisin date topping but you can also bake the crust and serve it plain or covered with fresh fruit.

Crust:
- ½ lb butter
- ¾ cup honey
- 1 Tbl. vanilla
- 1½ cups coconut
- 3 cups whole wheat flour
- 1½ tsp. baking powder
- ¾ cup slivered almonds

Topping:
- 2 cups raisins
- 2 cups dates (chopped)
- 2 tsp. arrowroot
- 2 tsp. cinnamon, allspice or ginger

Crust: Mix all ingredients together. Pat into a 9" x 13" baking pan. Bake at 350° until the edges start to brown, about 30 minutes. Take out of the oven and spread with the topping of your choice.

Topping: Simmer the dried fruit in water until soft. Mix in the arrowroot and spices. Spread on the crust, sprinkle with coconut or crumbs and bake at 350° until light brown on top, about 15-20 minutes.

Carob Tofu Bars

9" x 13" pan

These have a mild carob taste.

Bottom: 1 cup butter
½ cup honey
1½ cups sunflower seeds
3 cups whole wheat flour

Mix the crust ingredients together and press into a 9" x 13" baking pan (save a little to sprinkle).

Topping: ¾ cup carob powder
3½ lbs. tofu
1 tsp. vanilla
1 cup honey
¼ cup peanut butter

Mix topping ingredients together in a blender or with a mixer or by hand if you work hard to get them very smooth and well blended. Spread the mixture on the crust.
Sprinkle with the crust you saved or with coconut. Bake at 350° until light brown on top, about 20-30 minutes.

Raisin Sunnies

5-6 dozen

Sweet, and simple to make. Salt free and eggless.

1 Tbl. vanilla
1 cup oil
1 cup honey
4 cups sunflower seeds
3½ - 4 cups whole wheat flour
1 cup raisins

Preheat the oven to 350°. Mix the ingredients together in any order that you like, but be sure to add the flour last. The dough shouldn't be too sticky, but it shouldn't be like bread dough either. Put the little cookies on greased cookie sheets and bake until the edges are brown, about 15 minutes.

Carob Chip Chews

Yields 4 dozen great, sweet tasting cookies that rival the chocolate version.

1 cup honey
1 cup butter
½ tsp. vanilla
1 cup coconut
1 cup carob chips
1½ cups rolled oats
1½ cups whole wheat flour

Mix everything together and scoop onto greased cookie sheets. Bake at 350° about 10 minutes or until light brown.

the good bread bakery

Ashland, Oregon

We are a collective of two and we work at home making twenty or so kinds of bread from organically grown grains which we stone grind. Our bakery makes only bread and an occasional batch of sweet rolls. We figure, since there are so many sweets around, we'll concentrate on bread.

Some of our bread is soft, moist and slightly sweetened and some is good old bread – just flour, water and salt.

We don't believe in making a lot of money or working too hard and it feels good to make a living providing something that's good for people and doing it with minimum adverse effects on the Earth. We use organically grown grains both for health and to support farmers who take good care of their land.

Grandpa's Farm Bread

— an unleavend bread — 2 Loaves

Unique and terrific! We testers loved this bread; the salt-free version was a favorite.

$\frac{1}{3}$ cup rice 3 cups water	Simmer for 3-4 hours, with a lid; replace water if needed. The rice will expand and make a thick creamy goo. After simmering, add enough water to make 3 cups. Let cool to lukewarm.
1 tsp salt 2 Tbl oil $1\frac{1}{2}$ cups rye flour $\frac{1}{2}$ cup corn meal $5\frac{1}{2}$ cups hard ww. flour	Add everything but the ww flour to the rice mixture and stir well. Add the ww flour a cup or so at a time, stirring it in well each time, until you've added just about all of it and you can turn the dough out of the bowl and knead it.

Knead well, adding flour if needed to make a nice smooth dough. Shape into two regular loaves. Place on a flat oiled pan, cover with a wet towel so it won't dry out. Let it sit eight hours minimum – up to fifteen hours is okay. Then, uncover, make 3 or 4 slits in the tops, $\frac{1}{2}$ inch deep, squirt or brush with water and bake:

30 minutes at 425°F

then 60 minutes at 375°F

Place the racks higher in the oven than usual— about 2/3 of the way up. Bread bottoms will still be dark. This bread keeps well, slices thin and is a good chew.

Hearth Rye Bread   2 loaves

...firm with a crunchy crust, easy to slice and delicious chewy inside. Not hard to make.

2¾ cups lukewarm water
1 Tbl yeast
¼ cup Chia seeds (if available)
½ cup cornmeal
2 cups hard ww flour

1 tsp salt
2 Tbl oil
1 Tbl Caraway seeds*
1½ cups rye flour
2⅓ cups hard ww flour

*A nice touch, if you can grind your own flour, is to grind the caraway seed with the rye flour. Mix them together so the caraway seeds won't gum up your stones, say the bakers!

Put water in a bowl and sprinkle on yeast. Let sit until yeast dissolves. Add chia seeds and cornmeal so they can absorb water now instead of drying out the dough later. Then beat in the 2 cups ww flour. Beat well. Cover and let rise 30 minutes or so. Don't let it rise so long that it falls.

Then add salt, oil, caraway and rye flour. Mix well. Stir in the ww flour, adding more if needed until you can turn the dough out and knead it. Knead until dough is smooth and feels good. Put it back in the bowl, cover, let rise 30-60 min. Again, don't let it rise so long that it falls. That will cause a sour taste to develop.

After it's risen, punch it down and let it rest a few minutes to relax the gluten and make it easier to knead. Then divide in half, shape each half into a nice round loaf, place on an oiled flat pan, cover, let rise until just about doubled. Then brush or squirt with water.

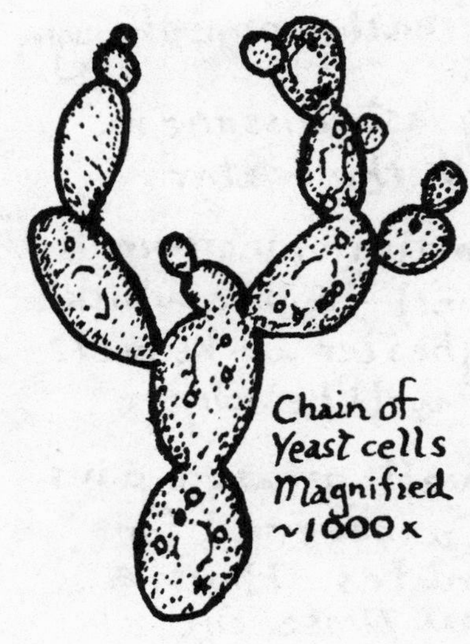

Chain of Yeast cells Magnified ~1000x

Bake for 50 minutes at 400 - 425 °F. A small pan of water placed on your lowest oven rack will help develop this bread's fine dark crust.

Karen from Good Bread adds this helpful hint: With stone ground flours, the less flour you add the better, because the flour tends to absorb the water slower than a finer grind of flour. You think the dough is just right, but after it rises, it has dried out. If your loaf rises slow and not at all in the oven and is crumbly when cut, you probably put in too much flour. If it spreads flat on the pan, rises quickly and then falls in the oven, you probably had the dough toowet. It should be <u>just</u> dry enough to knead.

Rice Bread

2 LOAVES

A wheatless, dairyless, eggless and unsweetened bread that is high in protein and low in calories. Slices make an excellent substitute for biscuits in peach or strawberry shortcake. Many of our recipe testers preferred this bread without salt—the flavors of the different grains really come through.

2½ cups warm water
1 Tbl yeast

Let the yeast dissolve in a bowl with the water.

1 Tbl oil
½ tsp salt
½ cup sunflower seeds
¼ cup rolled oats
¼ cup soy flour
2 cups rice flour
½ cup millet flour

Add all remaining ingredients, and beat well – a wire whisk or hand eggbeater works best. The batter will be soupy.

Pour into well-greased pans and let rise uncovered for 20-30 minutes. HANDLE GENTLY AT ALL TIMES OR BATTER MAY COLLAPSE.

Bake at 375°F for 1 hour. Let cool 3-5 minutes in the pans, then turn out onto a rack for further cooling.

Note: Try grinding your own rice and millet flours using a hand mill or electric blender. You can better control the texture and the resulting fresh flavors will be a pleasant surprize.

Kalispell, Montana

About the Honey Bear:

Co-operatively owned and collectively managed, the Honey Bear provides the Flathead Valley with a variety of organic whole wheat bread products and sweets, especially ginger bears, our mascot. The bakery serves quick light lunches, along with fresh ground imported coffee and herb teas to complement our pastries.

Pita or Pocket Bread

Makes 7 4oz. pita

A nice light, soft pocket bread. Stuff it with any filling you fancy for a sandwich or a meal.

1 Tbl. honey
2 tsp. yeast
1 cup warm water
3½ cups hard WW flour
½ tsp salt
1½ Tbl oil

You can mix in a little garlic powder, or other spices/herbs, for interesting flavors.

Mix together honey, yeast, water and 1 cup flour to make a sponge. Let sit until bubbly.

Mix in remaining flour, salt and oil. Dough should be moist, but not sticky. Knead well. Let dough rise in oiled bowl until double. Divide into 7-8 pieces, roll into balls, and roll out into flat rounds about 6" across. Place on a baking sheet that's been lightly oiled or dusted with corn-meal, flour or sesame seeds. Let rise until slightly puffy. Bake in a <u>hot</u> oven - 500° - 550° - on the bottom shelf of the oven, or slip pita onto preheated sheets before putting them in. Only a sudden blast of heat will make the "pockets." It's a good idea to start with just 2 pita on the sheet to make sure the oven is hot enough. Bake at 500° for 10 minutes or at 550° for 4½-5 min.

BAGELS - sesame garlic or plain

8 sizeable bagels

Eggless. A handsome bagel. Double the recipe if you expect company - they'll disappear fast. Omit the sesame and garlic for plain bagels.

2 tsp. yeast
2 Tbl. honey
1½ cups warm water
1 cup hard WW flour

} mix together and let sit until bubbly

2¼ cups hard WW flour
½ tsp salt
1½ Tbl oil
2½ Tbl sesame seeds
½ - 1 Tbl garlic powder (to taste)

} Add remaining ingredients to sponge and knead dough well.

Let dough rise in an oiled bowl that's covered until double in size. Punch down and divide into 8 pieces.Δ Shape into round rolls, then push thumbs through center and shape the hole.

Δ Pan of boiling water - start to heat before you poke the holes
½ Tbl honey (optional: some say honey helps the glaze)

Drop the bagels into boiling water right away after shaping them. Leave for about a minute - they'll puff up fast. Remove and put on oiled pan. Bake at 350° for 20-25 minutes or at 400° for 10-15, until lightly browned.

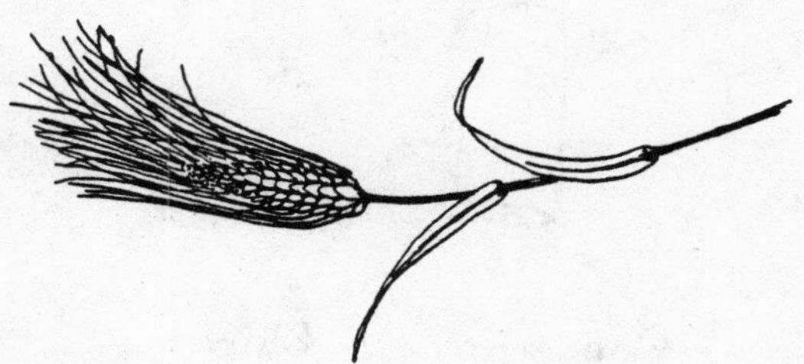

Roll-Ups

1½ lbs dough makes 8-10 luscious slices

A brilliant idea from the Honey Bear bakers! Rollups are quick, can be any size, use any bread dough, and contain any two layers of filling. You might start with pizza rollups, apple-cheddar cheese, or cinnamon-date-pecan. Rollups have the virtue of being adaptable to any season, in any region – sort of a baked form of appropriate technology! → Basically, you roll-out bread dough into a rectangle and lay the first layer of filling – chopped vegies or sliced fruit (raw) –

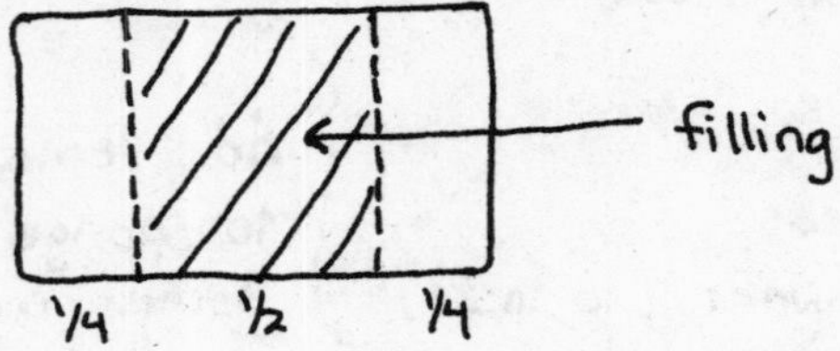

on the center panel, not too thick. Then fold in the two side panels so they just meet in the middle and cover the filling:

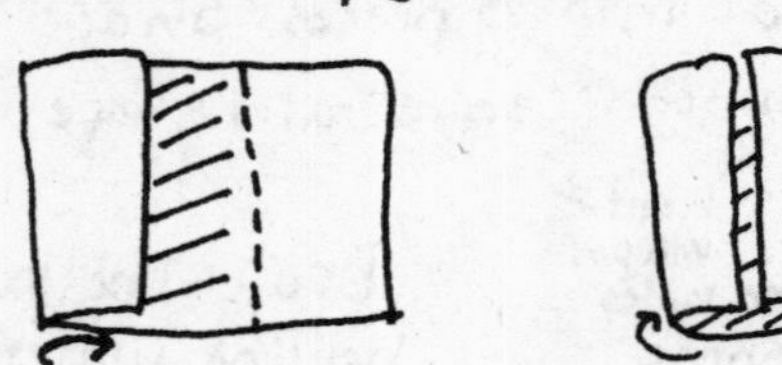

Now lay, sprinkle or smear more filling on one of these side panels, and fold over again so the filling is covered.

If you like, try and pinch the flap seam so filling is enclosed, although if you've been lavish with the filling this may be impossible. Place your creation on an oiled or floured baking sheet. Brush the top with water and sprinkle with sesame, poppy or caraway seeds or nuts if you like. Don't proof it; bake right away at 350° for 30-35 minutes. While it's still hot, slice into hunks. The layers of filling may ooze out temptingly and the smell will be wonderful! With a bottom layer of vegetables, tomato slices or sauce and herbs, and a top layer of grated cheese, you get a pizza rollup. A bottom layer of apple slices crowned with melty-type cheese makes a luscious snack. A blend of fruits or fruit sauces with nuts and spices makes a scrumptious sweet pastry. Rollups may be just the incentive you need to make your weekly supply of bread-double a recipe and use one loaf for dinner or dessert! With two people working in the kitchen you could divide the labor and reap double benefits!

Ginger Bears ⟨no eggs, no dairy⟩ About 1½ dozen

Honey Bear's mascot - wonderful!

½ cup soy margarine
½ cup honey
½ cup black strap molasses
} cream together well

¼ tsp. ground cloves
¼ tsp nutmeg
¼ tsp cinnamon
¼ tsp fresh grated ginger root, or if you have to compromise, ⅜ tsp ground ginger
} Add and mix well with creamed mixture.

½ tsp baking soda dissolved in
¼ cup hot water
} Add, and mix in well.

2¾ cups WW flour (plus a little more for rolling out the dough) } Stir in, blending until smooth.

Chill the dough. Roll out on lightly floured surface till ¼" thick. (You can work in a little extra flour if need be, for good rolling texture.) Cut into bears, or some other shapes. Place on greased cookie sheets. Bake at 325° for 15-20 minutes. (Be careful not to burn these or make them too crispy. They get firmer as they cool.) Cool and remove from sheets. If you leave these out in an accessible place while you go for a walk, be sure to take one with you for they will surely disappear.

Sesame Dream Bars

1 9" x 13" pan

Honey Bear's latest hit. A toasty-tasting custard topping on a rich cakey bottom. The measures become a bit odd when this recipe is made home size - Consider it proof that you're getting the real thing.

Custard topping

Start this first.

1½ eggs (1 large / 2 small)
1 cup warm water
} Beat together

1 cup honey
½ Tbl. vanilla
¼ Tbl. almond extract
¼ tsp. baking powder (rounded)
⅜ cup (6 Tbl.) WW flour
} Beat into first mixture & let custard sit one hour. Meanwhile, make the crust.

⅝ cup (½ cup + 2 Tbl.) toasted coconut
⅝ cup toasted sesame seeds
¼ tsp. cream of tartar
} Add to topping *just* before pouring into crust.

Crust

(Do while custard is sitting.)

1¼ sticks (½ cup plus 2 Tbl.) margarine
⅝ cup honey
} Cream together

¼ tsp. baking soda
¼ tsp. baking powder
1⅞ cups WW flour

Mix in soda, powder and flour. Spread in greased pan + bake for 10 min. at 325°. Cool for 5 min., then pour in topping...

Before you pour the topping in, add coconut, sesame seeds and cream of tartar. Beat, then pour over crust. Bake at 325°-350° for 20-30 min. until firm + browned. Cool. Cut into squares.

Peanut Granola Chews

1 9" x 13" pan

These are excellent for quick energy, they're filling and nutritious. If you're short on time, peanut granola chews are the way to go. No baking.

1 cup honey
2 cups peanut butter
1 tsp. vanilla
½ cup coconut flakes
½ cup sunflower seeds
½ cup bran (wheat or other)
¼ cup sesame seeds
¼ cup raisins or date pieces
4 cups oats
½ cup water

Cream honey and peanut butter together with a wooden spoon if you've got one. Add the vanilla. Mix the coconut flakes, sunnies, bran, sesame seeds and raisins or date pieces together. Add to creamed mixture. Stir in oats and water. Mixture should be moist and it should mold together.

Press into a greased 9" x 13" pan. For nice variations, try adding wheat germ, peanuts, rolled corn or rye, poppy seeds or cinnamon- not all at once, we hope! More water may be necessary. Refridgerate one hour. Cut into small pieces and enjoy.

You could wrap a few pieces up and give them to your neighbors.

little bread company

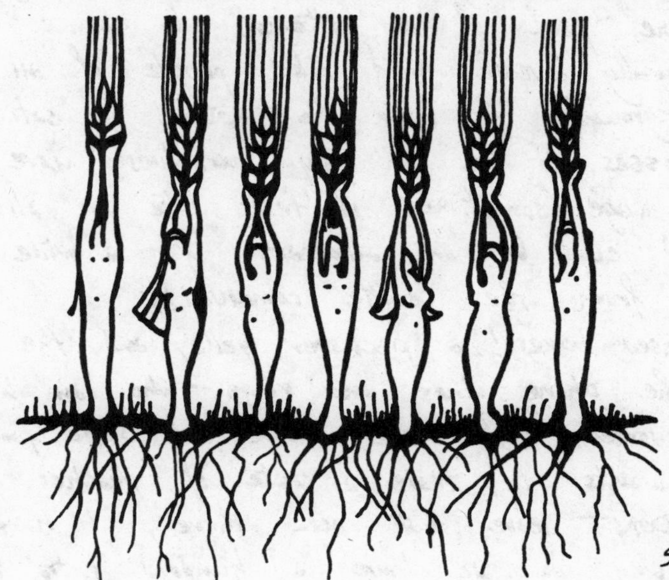

seattle, washington

Monday morning, 6 a.m. pitch black and cold and probably raining -- hands like bagels warming before the oven, sourdoughs baking, round and round, rump ends of loaves swirled like the curlique tails of pigs -- big and rosy, crisp crust, soybean margarine melts into the silky inside.

Little Bread Company, begun in 1969 in the kitchen of a natural foods restaurant in Seattle's Public Market. Grew to inclusion in the Seattle Worker's Brigade, a co-operative of worker-managed businesses, including a warehouse, a grocery, a mill run by women, a restaurant and Little Bread Company. When we became too big for the confines of someone else's oven we moved north to a building of our own. The Brigade disbanded in 1977, and LBC was incorporated as an autonomous business.

Like many collective businesses, we have paid more attention to the collective than to the business. Recently though we've decided to take ourselves more seriously as a business--not only to survive in the eighties but also as one part of an attempt to make Little Bread more culturally diverse. We'd like people of all colors/classes/backgrounds to have the option of satisfying work and no bosses. If we can pay ourselves more than a subsistence wage (sometimes it feels like an allowance) Little Bread can be an alternative for a wide variety of people from the Seattle community.

I need boxes! a packager yells, and the slicer wails on and the phone rings and rings--who can help the warehouse women unload the truck and some farmer from Wenatchee wants to trade a crate of peaches for a bag of oats--DON'T leave that rack there, I haven't mopped yet and why do we have a hundred extra bagels and we're all wearing skirts, men and women alike, thin material swishing around our legs this summer morning, sweaty and hot as we rock the Beatles at the top of our lungs--yah yah yah...

Although women and men work at LBC, we're committed to employing more women than men. We define ourselves as feminists--that is, we assert and affirm the dignity and strength of women, and work to understand and break down cultural stereotypes and barriers. We affirm the tradition of women and food. For centuries women of all colors grinding grain, wheat, rice and corn between stone and stone. Strong hands working the grain with water, deft hands patting out tortillas or chapatis or thick crusted loaves. Women hefting sacks and scooping flour, women repairing machines and unloading hundreds of loaves from an 8-racked rotary oven--and always, the dough alive beneath our skilled fingers. Ironically, in many Hispanic countries, the most derogatory word for lesbian is 'tortillera', which means tortilla maker.

Sesame Chews

1 small shallow pan - 4"x4" or 6"x6"
or 8" round pan

½ cup honey
¾ cup crunchy peanut butter
1 cup sesame seeds
1 cup buttermilk powder *
3 Tbl. water
2 Tbl. chopped nuts or coconut

Preheat oven to 350°.
Mix and heat honey and peanut butter in oven for 15 minutes. Stir to heat evenly through.
Toast sesame seeds for 15 minutes, then mix with buttermilk powder and water.
Stir both mixtures together thoroughly to form a thick fudge-like consistency (add a little extra water, if needed).
Lightly oil pan or tray. Roll out the gooey mixture on the pan; it may help to oil the rolling pin too.
Top with chopped nuts or coconut. Refrigerate.
Cut into 12-16 sweet, crunchy pieces.

* Try ½ milk powder, ½ whey powder or all milk powder if buttermilk powder is not available.

Carob Chews

1 small shallow pan - 4"x4" or 6"x6" or 8" round pan

½ cup honey
¾ cup crunchy peanut butter

Preheat oven to 350°. Mix and heat in oven 15 minutes, stirring to heat evenly through.

½ cup carob powder
1 cup buttermilk powder *
2 Tbl. water

Mix together, mashing out any carob lumps.

2 Tbl. chopped nuts or coconut

Stir both mixtures together to form thick fudge-like consistency. Proceed as for sesame chews, p.103.

* see note for sesame chews.

GRANOLAS

Here are the recipes for four kinds of granola.
The 4-grain mix is made up of oats plus smaller amounts of barley, wheat and rye flakes.
You can come up with your own preferred blend of course

Each recipe makes 4-5 lbs.

Jane Cooner (after Courbet)

The method's the same for each:

Mix wet ingredients
Mix dry ingredients
Combine them, stir together well.
Spread on a large sheet (17" x 25")
or 2 smaller sheets.
Bake at 325°
for 20-30 minutes
Add raisins or dates *after* baking.

Maple Granola

Delicious maple flavor.

Dry:

- 10 cups oats
- 3 cups 4-grain mix
- 1 3/4 cups sunflower seeds
- 1 cup sesame seeds
- 2 cups coconut

Wet:

- 1 1/2 cups maple syrup
- 1 cup safflower oil
- 2-3 tsp. water, as needed

over..

Peanut Cashew Crunch

Speaks for itself!

Dry: 10 cups oats
$3\frac{1}{2}$ cups 4-grain mix
$\frac{3}{5}$ cup raw peanuts
1 cup chopped cashews
$\frac{1}{2}$ cup sesame seeds

Wet: $\frac{9}{10}$ cup safflower oil
$\frac{3}{5}$ cup honey
5 Tbl. molasses

Add: $\frac{1}{2}$ cup raisins

Jane Grover (after Millet)

Aunt Louise's Coco·Date Granola

Sweet and simple.

Dry: 10 cups oats
$3\frac{1}{2}$ cups 4-grain mix
$1\frac{1}{2}$ cups shredded coconut

Wet: 1 cup safflower oil
1 cup honey
4-5 Tbl. water, as needed

Add: $\frac{1}{2}$ cup chopped dates
or date pieces

Holy Granola

Nice touch of almond.

Dry: 10 cups oats
$3\frac{1}{2}$ cups 4-grain mix
$\frac{3}{5}$ cup chopped almonds
1 cup sesame seeds
$\frac{3}{5}$ cup sunflower seeds

Wet: $\frac{9}{10}$ cup safflower oil
$\frac{3}{5}$ cup honey
5 Tbl. molasses
few drops almond extract

Add: $\frac{1}{2}$ cup raisins

MANNA

Amsterdam, Holland

Our bakeries (one for sourdough bread and one for pastries and cakes) are a division of The Manna Working Community. This Community started exactly eleven years ago and consists now of the following departments: 1) A central depot, which buys, packs, and distributes only organically grown products 2) A workshop which is making tofu, seitan, and the products that are made from them 3) A workshop where we make peanut butter, hazelnut butter and other kinds of butters 4) A workshop where we make muesli and granola 5) The bread and pastry bakeries 6) And last but not least six shops in Amsterdam and four shops outside of Amsterdam. Besides them we sell our products to another two hundred shops all over Holland.

The philosophy of Manna is based on Macrobiotic Principals. To guarantee the quality of our products Manna strives for a system whereby we buy the products directly from the farmer or the producer, and whereby natural agriculture and pure manufacturing techniques prevail.

Our sourdough bread bakery started in 1974 and was the first real (this means yeast-free) sourdough bakery in Holland. At this moment we are making about 20 kinds of bread, consisting only of organically grown wheat flour, sea salt, sourdough and water. Our grains are milled on a windmill since a few months ago also on a watermill. Most of the wheat is imported from France, since there is not enough production of Dutch grains, and the quality of the french grains for baking bread is much better. Other ingredients we use for making our breads are: hazel nuts, sesame seeds, currants, raisins and brown rice. One of our most successful breads is **Rice bread**. Here is the recipe:

We make a dough of whole grain flour and for every 100 parts of dough we put 50 parts of cooked brown rice. Let it bake for 80-90 minutes at 390°F. This is a delicious bread.

The pastry bakery makes pastry, cakes, etc. without sugar, yeast, baking powder, butter, honey, milk, etc. Some of the products are sweetened with fresh or dried fruits or with malt syrup (yinnies). All the flours and grains are organic, and when using oils we use cold-pressed unrefined vegetable oil.

At this moment there are working twenty people in our bakery and distribution system. As a whole Manna is a non-profit organization and all the people earn the governmental prescribed minimum wage. In the whole Manna working community there are at this moment a hundred persons working.

MANNA
NON-PROFIT WERKGEMEENSCHAPPEN VOOR NATUURVOEDING EN -GENESWIJZE
Stichting Natuurvoeding Amsterdam

Sourdough Bread

2 loaves

"You will find that this bread needs more craftmanship, time and patience. But once you succeed in creating a sweet, nice looking, character-full bread you will see it's going to serve peoples health and happiness."

A. Preparation of the **mother dough** (starter)

The motherdough is the medium to raise the dough. Mix 1/3 cup organic hard whole wheat flour with 1/2 cup water in a porcelain cup. Cover this porridge with a cotton cloth and let it stand draft-free at 70°F. Stir it up a little in the morning and in the evening. As soon as the porridge starts to bubble and slightly starts smelling sour (after 2 to 4 days), mix about 1/2 cup flour into the porridge and knead it. Let this dough stand for approximatly 5 hours to rise until the volume has doubled. The motherdough is ready now.

B. Preparation of the **breaddough**.

Mix 3 cups lukewarm water with maximum 2 tsp. sea salt and the motherdough in a bowl. Mix this with about 6 1/2 cups hard whole wheat flour. Knead for 10 minutes, until you get a flexible dough. The dough will be more sticky than a regular dough. You can keep a cup of water close by, moisten your hands and the kneading surface to keep from sticking. Now, take off a piece of this dough (3/4 cup) and put it in a glass jar into the refrigerator, to use the next baking day. Let the dough rest, covered with a cotton cloth for 90 minutes at 75°F.

C. the modelling

Make a flat piece of dough of the doughball and double it twice firmly and roll it. Put this dough with the seam side down in an oiled baking pan. Spray the top with water and put it in a closed box for 3 hours or so. this should be a rather warmish temperature (79°). You can boil some water, and put the steaming pot inside the oven with your raising dough. Don't turn the oven on. Reheat the water on top of the stove as needed.

D. the baking

Put an ovenproof dish full of water in the oven and turn it on to 357°F. When the oven is hot spray the top of the dough once again and put it in the oven. After 10 minutes lower the temperature to 310°F. the total baking time is 70 minutes, approximately.

for Currant-Raisin bread

Wash 1/6 LB. currants and 1/3 LB raisins with cold water and let them soak for about 30 minutes in hot water. Make a dough as described above, using pastry flour if you like, and make the following additions: 3 TBL. CORN OIL, 1 TBL. Barley malt, cinnamon or vanilla to taste. add the raisins and currants just at the end of your kneading. follow for the rise, the modelling, and baking the same procedure as for the sourdough bread.

one last bit from the Manna Bread Bakers ... "Important for keeping a good sourdough is to keep it away from yeast, alchohol, beer etc. Use as much as possible well-water and when the air is pure your bread will be heavenly sweet, especially with stone-ground fresh flour!"

We plan to stone-grind our own flour within two years .... the mill had to be left out of the budget for the time being .... hence our name!

Heading north into Washburn, WIS. along the big waters of Chequamegon Bay, it's hard to miss a golden plump slice of bread dangling in the breeze above a cuffed hand whose pointing finger directs visitors up the steps, across the porch, and through the doorway of the little white store front. It's the Millstone Bakery, where customers and visitors are welcome to watch co-owners Josh and Jane as they mix, loaf, proof and bake their hearty whole grain breads and goodies. Located in a small but busy rural community, Millstone receives support from a large elderly population, a friendly mainstream community, as well as from the enthusiastic northern cooperative community. Millstone is small, but will be distributing its breads, including whole wheat hamburger buns and Mideastern pocket bread, to area food coops, restaurants, and small grocery stores. We need everyone's business: "real" good bread and cooperative ideals just may rub off and become habit-forming!

Swedish Tea Ring

1 large tea ring – a dozen good servings

A beauty! Ideal for dessert or snack.

Dough:
1 cup warm water
1 Tbl yeast
1/4 cup honey
1/4 cup dry milk
1 egg
1 cup WW pastry flour

Mix all together, and let this sponge sit until bubbly and risen.

3 Tbl oil
1 tsp salt
2 1/4 – 2 1/2 cups WW pastry flour

Add these ingredients to sponge. Mix and knead until dough is soft and springy. Let rise in oiled bowl until dough is doubled in size.

Filling:
1 cup raisins
1/2 tsp cinnamon
1/4 tsp nutmeg
1 Tbl orange (or apple) juice
2 Tbl honey
1 tsp vanilla

Mix and simmer till thickened. Stir occasionally to prevent burning.

Roll out dough on lightly floured board to 12" by 14" rectangle. Spread with filling. Roll up tightly as jelly roll. Place on oiled baking sheet; join ends so filling won't come out while baking. Snip 1" slits around the edge of the ring with scissors at about 1½"–2" intervals. Let rise until doubled in size. Brush with milk or eggwash. Bake at 350° until golden brown – about 30 minutes. (Ring is sweet enough and attractive without glaze, but you might choose to use a glaze or roll-icing.)

Hot Cross Buns

16-20 buns

"Delicious, plump and tender," write the Millstone bakers. "A Knockout," say the recipe tasters. The richness and the sweet orange fragrance make these <u>too</u> good to save for Good Friday!

2 cups milk
8 tsp butter
1/2 cup honey
2 Tbl yeast
5 1/4 cups ww pastry flour

Combine milk and butter. Bring to a boil, then cool to lukewarm. Add honey and yeast. Mix. Stir half the flour into yeast-milk mixture. Cover and let rise 30 minutes.

2 eggs
1 tsp salt
4 tsp cinnamon
rind of one orange, finely grated
1 1/2 cups raisins

Add remaining ingredients. Knead dough until it is nice and springy. Roll out; divide into 16-20 pieces. Round pieces into buns; place on oiled baking sheets and let rise for 30 minutes. Slit each roll lightly on top in the shape of a cross. Brush with beaten egg.

1 egg
a little honey

Bake at 350° for about 30 minutes till browned (Millstone's instructions were: 150° for 30 minutes, then 350° for 30 minutes. We didn't try this - but <u>you</u> can - ours still came out beautifully). Cool and glaze with beaten egg white mixed with a little honey - our testers found these hot cross buns were great even without the glaze!

MADISON, WISCONSIN

In Madison, Nature's was but one of many organizations that grew out of the social movements of the late sixties. Since then Madison has also seen the formation of several storefront cooperatives, a cooperative regional food distributing warehouse, a co-op pharmacy, a co-op bookstore, a co-op auto repair shop, a co-op fabric store, a collectively managed legal firm, and more. Some of these businesses went under; most of them are going strong.

Nature's has always attracted people that want to put their vision of people working cooperatively into practice. For several years it struggled along while its workers continually left the business after burning out from very low pay, an unorganized and shaky business set-up, and a lack of means to solve the problems that would come up between people. A few years ago some of the bakers began to set the bakery on a new course. Since then, working conditions have improved greatly and staffers now stay with the bakery for years. Here are some of the ways we run things that help:

* We have a spoken understanding of what each of us is at the bakery for, and we've reached agreements of what we will expect of each other.

* We have a high regard for an efficient business. We put this into practice by continually working to better organize the business.

* We compensate ourselves well. For us this involves paying ourselves (at a rate we decided on and eventually met) for virtually all the time we put into any aspect of the business. We have a food allowance and assistance with health insurance. We've organized things so that those who want them can take very long vacations. And we try to recognize each other's good work.

* We've learned how to have very efficient business meetings.

* We're very careful who we hire.

* We have regular, and gentle, staff evaluations. We have "feelings" meetings. We've gotten good outside help to learn ways to better get along. We're all committed to trying hard to deal with the interpersonal problems that are bound to come up. This involves some time, a lot of vulnerability, and, ultimately, a lot of growth. This ends up being one of our biggest compensations.

It means a lot to us that this bakery of ours is part of a greater network of organic farmers, warehouse workers, researchers, activists and store-keepers that are all working for a positive change in how food is grown and distributed.

Whole Wheat Bread

Makes 2 1½ lb. loaves

♡ good, basic whole wheat ♡

Sponge

2 tsp. malt
2⅓ cups warm water
1 Tbl. yeast
4 cups hard w.w. flour

Mix the malt, water and yeast and let sit until yeast rises to the top. Mix in the flour (100 strokes or more). Let the sponge sit in a warm, damp place (or under a damp towel) for 20-30 minutes— until roughly doubled.

4 tsp. oil (safflower is good)
2-2½ cups hard w.w. flour
1-2 tsp. salt
3 Tbl. sunflower seeds (optional)

Add the remaining ingredients to the sponge, mix and knead well until thoroughly mixed, smooth and elastic. Let dough rise, as the sponge did, 20-30 minutes.

Loaf the dough and place in oiled pans. Let rise, and bake at 375° for 40-50 minutes or until the bread comes easily out of the pans. The bottom edges and sides of the loaf should be hard - especially at the corners.

Swedish Rye Bread

makes 2 loaves
a lovely rye loaf with a distinctive anise flavor

Sponge

1 Tbl. yeast
5 Tbl. molasses
2½ Tbl. oil
2 cups water (warm)
2 cups hard w.w. flour

Mix the water, molasses, oil and yeast well, and allow the yeast to rise. Then add the flour and let this sponge rise 20-30 minutes in a warm, damp place until double in size.

1⅔ cups hard w.w. flour
2⅓ cups rye flour
½ whole orange - juice & peel (chopped medium fine)
2 Tbl. anise
2 tsp. salt and 4 tsp. water

Mix the rest of the ingredients together, and then add to the sponge. Knead until very well mixed. Let this rise until it is approximately double its original size.

Loaf on lightly oiled surface and place in well oiled pans. Allow to rise again. Bake at 325° for approximately 75-80 minutes, or until bottom edges and corners are hard and dark golden brown.

- Unleavened -

BUCKWHEAT BREAD

Makes 2 loaves

A very versatile dough that can be used for pizza crusts, rolled thin for crackers, etc. And it has that same delicious buckwheat flavor of old fashioned breakfasts.

½ cup buckwheat groats
1½ cups water

Roast groats gently, then add water, cover, bring to a boil, and simmer 'till water is absorbed (about 15 min.).

2 cups hard w.w. flour
2 cups buckwheat flour
1¼ cups water
Optional: 2 Tbl. sunflower seeds

Mix together all remaining ingredients with the groat mixture. If you decide to add the sunflower seeds, a nice touch is to roast them gently before adding. Knead 'till dough is still moist, but no longer sticky.

Shape into round, flat loaves that are about 1½ inches in height. Decorate loaves with original designs and bake at 400° for 40-45 min.

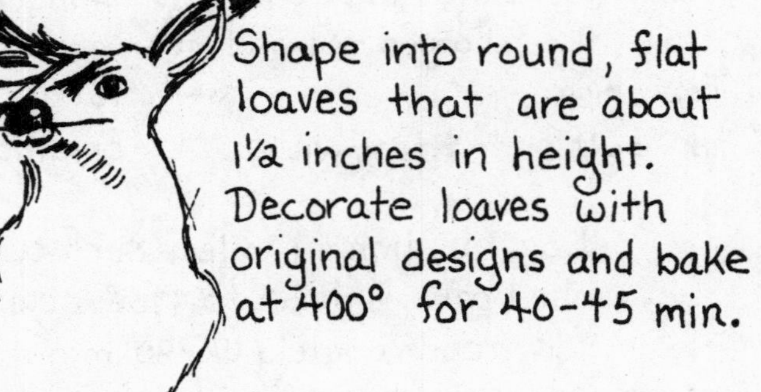

Sourdough is slow magic . . .

2 loaves

Simplicity is the essence of these breads. No oil, salt or sweetener is used in the dough, only flour, water and microbes.

Basic Recipe

1 cup liquid sourdough starter
2 cups water
5 cups (and a bit more) hard w.w. flour

Combine starter and water in an earthenware or enamel pot or bowl and let stand overnight in a warm place.

Add flour until a stiff dough is formed. Knead for twenty minutes, adding flour until the dough is not sticky. Lay the dough in a clean, oiled bowl, cover the bowl with a damp cloth and stand it in a warm place until it has doubled in volume. This could take all day or only a morning depending on how fast your culture is growing. Be patient.

When the dough has risen, punch it down so it can breathe. Let it rise again. If you like it very sour let it rise several times before baking. Simply punch it down every time it doubles until you are ready to bake. Be patient. Each rise may take as much as 4-5 hrs.

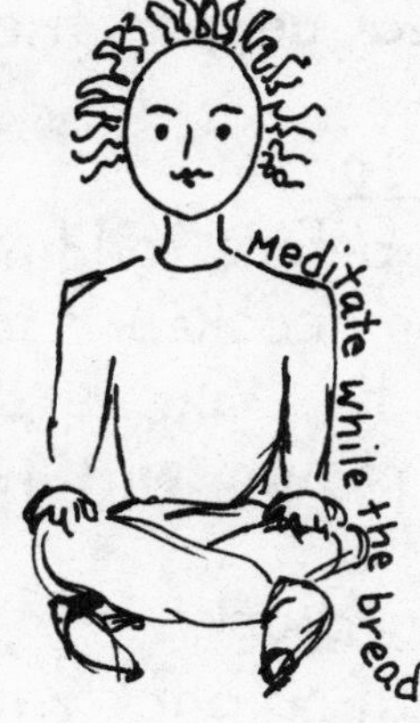

(continued on next page)

Sourdough Continued

Before the last rise knead the dough and shape it into two loaves. Use either loaf pans, or shape into long loaves and bake on an oiled cookie sheet. Slit the tops with a sharp blade. Be especially patient during the last rise. Four hours in the bread pans is not a long time for sourdough. Bake at 375°-400°F until the loaves are well browned and baked through. With experience you will learn to gauge rising times, baking temperature and baking time to suit your tastes and the culture's needs. (First baking trial: 20 minutes at 400°, then 60 minutes at 325°)

Sourdough Variations

Herb Sourdough:

Just before adding the flour, stir the following into the starter liquid:

3/4 tsp. each oregano, marjoram, basil or thyme, dill or celery seed
1 tsp. garlic powder

Proceed as for the basic recipe.

Rice Bread:

Just before adding the flour, stir into the starter liquid 4 cups cooked rice or other whole grain. Then add enough flour to make a stiff dough and proceed as usual. This recipe will make 4 loaves instead of 2.

Rye Sourdough:

Use all or part rye flour instead of whole wheat.

WHEAT SPROUT CRACKERS

makes 15 1" X 3" crackers

½ pound wheat sprouts (see about wheat sprouts pg. 39.)
1 Tbl. unrefined oil
w.w. [pastry] flour (pastry flour makes a less tough cracker)

Grind the sprouts in an old meat grinder or a food chopper (like the kind Universal makes).* Use the finest blades. The sprouts should be finely ground enough so that they resemble tuna fish salad.

Add the oil and mush it all together until the consistency is uniform. Then knead in enough flour to make a dough that can be rolled out (the amount of flour depends on how long the sprouts are — somewhere around one cup, but it varies alot). The dough should be soft enough to roll out well, but stiff enough to not be sticky or fall apart.

Roll out on a floured surface to about ⅛ inch thickness. Cut into shapes. Place on slightly oiled cookie sheets (if they're well seasoned sheets, you may not need oil). Bake at 300° for around 20 minutes until slightly browned and stiffer. They will still be soft, but become crisp as they cool.

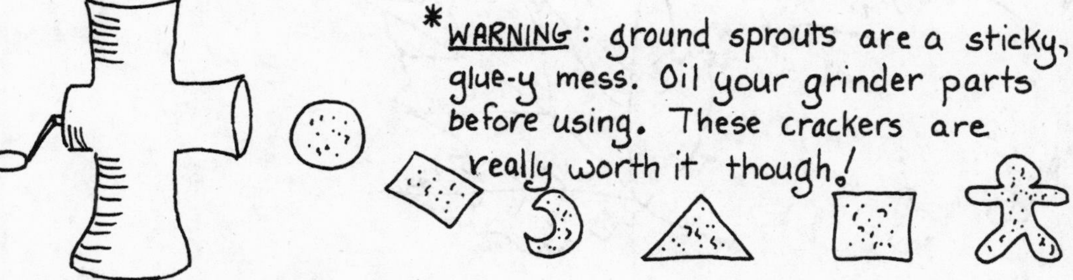

*<u>WARNING</u>: ground sprouts are a sticky, glue-y mess. Oil your grinder parts before using. These crackers are really worth it though!

CAROB NUT BARS

makes 20 1½" X 2" bars

A very tasty snack or dessert, and much more nutritious than the familiar sugar and chocolate variety. The Kids will love them – and that includes Kids of all ages!

¼ cup oil
¼ cup tahini
¾ cup maple syrup

Combine the wet ingredients in a bowl, and beat well.

¾ cup chopped walnuts or pecans
½ cup carob powder
2 cups w.w. flour

Combine and thoroughly mix the dry ingredients in a separate bowl. Then combine the wet mixture with the dry, pack into an oiled 6"x 10" pan, and cover with wax paper.

Chill in refridgerator for several hours (or overnight). Then bake at 375° for 10-12 minutes.

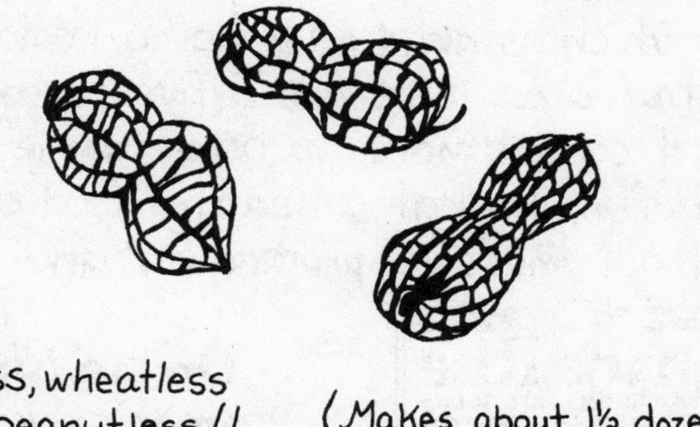

Peanut Minus Cookies

- eggless, dairyless, wheatless but not peanutless!!

(Makes about 1½ dozen)

¼ cup millet
½ cup water
1½ cups natural peanut butter*
1 cup barley malt syrup
¾ tsp. vanilla
¾ cup chopped roasted peanuts
¼ cup corn meal
¼ cup rye flour

Place millet and water in a small saucepan and bring to a boil. Lower heat and simmer until millet is tender and water absorbed. Meanwhile, stir together the malt syrup, the peanut butter, and vanilla extract. In a separate bowl combine remaining ingredients. Add dry ingredients and millet to the wet ingredients and mix well. The dough will be quite sticky. Spoon dough onto greased cooky sheets and flatten with your fingers (wet your hands first). Bake at 350°F for 12-15 min. or until dry and nicely browned. They will firm up as they cool.

*We use the kind with no salt or added oil.

On the Rise started in 1980 in an abandoned warehouse district which is gradually being reclaimed as a retail and residential area. We are a five-person collective. We have a special commitment to using whole, regional, seasonal foods defining what a healthy food economy would look like without massive processing and transportation.

On the Rise grew out of the progressive political community in Syracuse. Bonds of mutual support between our collective and other collectives and individuals in our community have made it possible for on the Rise to grow and prosper over the past 5 years, and to make our contribution to a healthier, more peaceful world.

We also try to bake low on the food chain. We have developed substitutes for milk and eggs we want to share.

Eggless Baking:

Combine one part flax seeds with 3 parts water and blend until flax seeds are completely decimated. This should have the consistency of eggs. Use 1/4 cup in place of egg in cake, muffin and cookies recipes.

Raw Soymilk for Baking

Soak 3/4 pound of dried soybeans overnight. Drain and grind in mill or pulverize in blender with a small amount of water. Pour 8 cups boiling water over beans and let stand for 5-10 minutes. Strain. Use this rich milky liquid as a substitute for milk in baking.

Potato Water

Pour 9 cups boiling water over 1# finely grated potato. Let sit 5-10 minutes. Strain and use.

3 seed bread

One of the best breads we tested.
Rich–moist–scrumptious! for 2 loaves

Soften 1T. yeast in
2¼c. warm potato water
¼c. honey
Stir in 3c. hard whole wheat flour
Let rest 15-20 minutes.
Add 3/8 c. Safflower oil
¼c. honey
3/8 c. poppy seeds
3/8 c. Sesame seeds
3/8 c. Sunflower seeds
1 t. salt
1½c. rolled oats (prepared ahead of time with ¾c. boiling water poured over the oats—use warm)

Slowly add enough flour to the dough to make it workable and knead for 10–15 minutes. (about 1½-2c.)
Let rise till doubled in a covered, oiled bowl and then shape into 2 loaves. Let rise again in the pans. Bake at 350° for 45-50 minutes.

Substitute 1½c. raisins, 1½T. cinnamon, ¼c. oil for seeds & oil to make a hearty oatmeal cinnamon raisin bread.

DAILY BREAD

for 2 1½ lb. loaves

a dark, hearty, and very tasty version of the basic whole wheat loaf

Soften 1 T. yeast
in 2 c. warm soymilk
1 c. warm water
3 T. honey

Next stir in 4 c. hard whole wheat flour.
Let rest for 15-20 minutes.
Add 3/8 c. oil
3 T. molasses
1½ t. salt

Add enough flour to the dough to be able to work it with your hands. Knead for 10-15 minutes. Let rise in a warm place in an oiled bowl until doubled. Divide into 2 loaves and let rise again in the pans.

Bake at 350° for 45 minutes.

corn muffins

makes 16 muffins

mix 1½ c. whole wheat pastry flour
3 c. corn meal
2 T. baking powder

blend and add
6 T. honey
½ c. safflower oil
2 c. soymilk
¾ c. ground flaxseed mixture

divide batter into 16 oiled muffin pans and bake at 375° until bright golden color comes out (about 30 minutes).

Blueberry Muffins

16 muffins

moist & rich

mix 4 c. whole wheat pastry flour
1 T. baking powder
1 t. ground cardamon
1 1/3 c. blueberries

Blend and then add
1/2 c. safflower oil
1/2 c. honey
1 1/2 c. soymilk
1/2 c. ground flaxseed mixture

Fill 16 oiled muffin tins level.
Bake at 350° until tops are light brown (30-40 minutes)

This recipe works well with peaches or pears

Oatmeal raisin cookies

2 dozen ENORMOUS cookies

lightly toast 4 c. oats
1 c. sunflowerseeds

Add 2 c. whole wheat pastry flour
4 t. baking powder
4 t. cinnamon
2 c. raisins

blend and add 1 c. safflower oil
1½ c. honey
½ c. water
1 c. ground flaxseed mixture
1 t. vanilla

Using an #8 ice cream scoop (½ cup) drop cookies on to oiled sheet. Bake at 350° for 20-25 minutes

Open Harvest Bakery in Lincoln, Nebraska, is a part of Open Harvest Inc., a Not-for-Profit whole foods cooperative. Open Harvest was formed to provide a nonprofit alternative food market place whereby minimally processed quality food is distributed through the cooperative energy of the membership. By offering nutritious food and information about such food on a not-for-profit basis, Open Harvest will strive to serve as an educational organization for the welfare of the community.

The bakery began in 1977 in the basement of a local church and has grown since then to provide baked goods to the local community on a regular basis. All our baking is done using whole grains, minimally processed foods such as honey and molasses, nuts, seeds, and fresh and dried fruits, all of the highest quality available. We obtain most of our ingredients through Blooming Prairie Warehouse in Iowa City, Iowa. This is a collective warehouse which supplies goods to food buying clubs and coop store fronts in Iowa, Nebraska, Missouri, South Dakota, and Arkansas. We try to use organically grown, locally grown foods whenever possible. We use worker members to provide labor in store and bakery activities. Members provide as much as fifty percent of the labor in the bakery, which allows us to produce a wide variety of baked goods, including bagels, pita bread, cinnamon rolls, pizza, croissants, fig bars, and wedding cakes, as well as basics such as breads, granola, cookies, and crackers. It is truly a joy to be able to provide the community with good quality, nutritious, fresh baked goods.

CHALLAH

(Jewish Egg Bread)

yields two very large or four regular loaves

A very rich and beautiful bread for special occasions.

make a sponge of:

2 1/2 cups warm water
1 1/2 - 2 TBL. yeast
2 - 4 TBL. honey
4 eggs, lightly beaten
4 cups hard w.w. flour

When sponge is puffy, add and knead till elastic:

1/4 cup oil or soft butter
2 tsp. or less salt
4 - 5 1/2 cups hard w.w. flour

In oiled covered bowl, let rise until doubled in bulk, about one hour. Punch dough down gently and let rise again about one hour.

After the second rising, divide the dough into two to four sections, depending on how many loaves you want. Knead each into a ball, and braid. (see "Shaping", p. 35). You can make single braids or double ones – a smaller braid on top of a larger one. Tuck the ends under and place on an oiled baking sheet. Let rise for 20-25 minutes. Do not let the dough overrise; it should be firm, to keep the shape of the braid. Brush loaves with beaten egg yolk, and sprinkle with poppy or sesame seeds. Bake for 40-60 minutes at 375°.

Pita

-no sweetener- yield - 10-12 pitas

This bread is also called pocket bread. It is baked at a high temperature which causes it to puff up, leaving a hollow center. You can cut it in half or split it open to stuff it with any sandwich filling.

Mix, and stir 100 strokes:

1½ cups warm water
1 TBL yeast
1 tsp salt (optional)
1-2 cups hard w.w. flour

Add:

1½-2 cups hard w.w. flour

Oven 475 degrees.
Knead into a stiff dough. Cover and let rise about 45 minutes. Cut into about 3 ounce pieces. Shape into balls and roll them into circles about 5-7 inches in diameter. Let the pitas rise 30-45 minutes in a warm place. Bake on preheated baking sheets on the lowest shelf of the oven for about 6 minutes.

Lemon Wedding Cake

2 - 8" cakes

A light and springy cake with a wonderful lemon flavor.

1 cup honey
½ cup oil
1 cup milk
2 egg yolks
2 ¼ tsp. vanilla
juice and rind of 3 lemons (approximately 3 TBL. rind)
2 ⅓ cups w.w. pastry flour
1 ½ tsp. soda
2 egg whites

Preheat oven to 350°. Lightly grease and flour two 8" cake pans.

Separate egg yolks from whites and beat whites to stiff peaks. Set aside. Combine honey and oil and mix well. Combine milk, egg yolks, vanilla and juice and rind of lemons. Add this mixture to the honey mixture. In a separate bowl, combine flour and soda. Add to this the wet mixture and stir well. Genlty fold in whipped egg whites with a metal spoon and pour into prepared pans. Bake 25 minutes.

yield - 12 muffins

Banana Muffins

A light, moist muffin. A dab of frosting makes instant cupcakes.

2 - 2 ½ ripe bananas - mashed with a fork

1 egg, slightly beaten	1 ½ TBL. water
⅓ cup oil	1 ⅓ cups w. w. pastry flour
2 TBL honey	2 tsp. baking powder
½ tsp. vanilla	¼ tsp. nutmeg.

Mix mashed bananas with beaten egg, oil, honey, vanilla and water.

In another bowl combine dry ingredients. Make a well in the center and pour in wet mixture all at once. Stir just until moistened - batter should be lumpy. Fill greased tins ⅔ full and bake 30 - 35 minutes, at 350°.

Corn Muffins

yield: 12 muffins

Preheat oven to 325 degrees.
Beat egg. Mix well with oil, honey, and milk.
In separate bowl, mix flour, cornmeal, baking powder, and mace. Add wet mixture to dry mixture, stirring briefly, just until mixed.
Fill greased muffin tins to two-thirds full, and bake for 20-25 minutes.

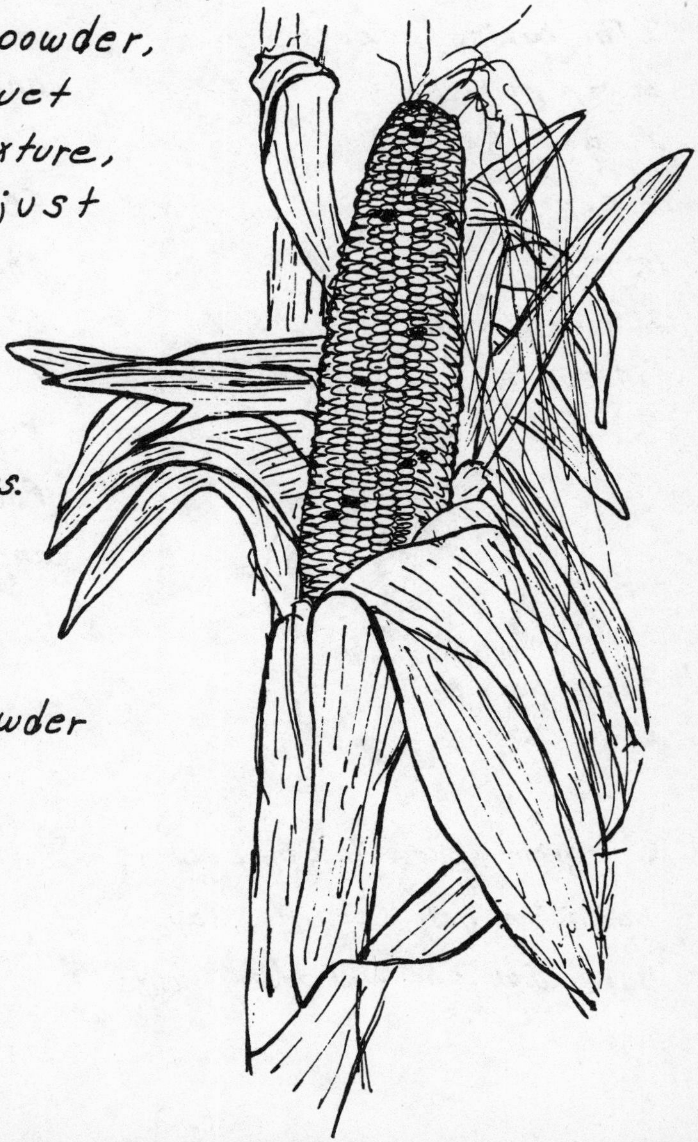

1 cup w.w. flour
3/4 cup cornmeal
2-3 tsp. baking powder
1/2 tsp. mace
1 egg
2 TBL. oil
2-4 TBL. honey
1 cup milk

Seven Grain Currant muffins

21 Large muffins

This recipe will reward your efforts with light colored muffins that have a lovely taste and texture.

3½ cups 7-grain flour *
2 TBL baking powder
½ tsp nutmeg
2 eggs, beaten
¼ cup oil
½ cup honey
2 cups milk
3/8 cup (¼ cup + 2 TBL) currants

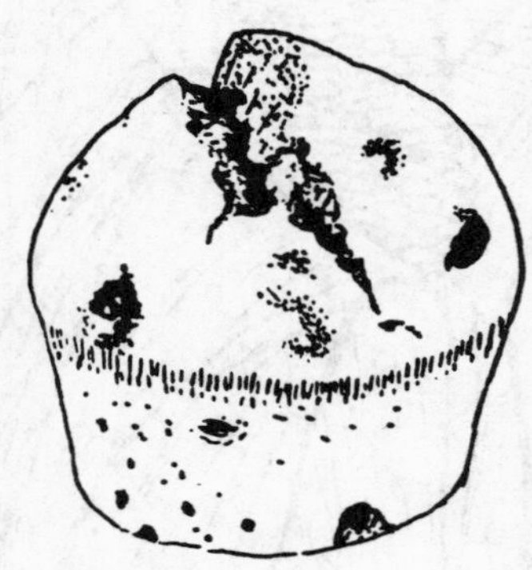

Set the oven at 350°. Mix together flour, baking powder, and nutmeg.
In another bowl, beat the eggs, add honey and oil, then the milk.
Stir the liquid ingredients into the flour mixture, then fold in the currants.
Pour into oiled muffin tins and bake for 20-25 minutes.

* 7-grain flour: ½ cup each - barley, millet, rice, rye, soy, hard w.w. and w.w. pastry flours

Sunny Seed Cookies

4 dozen

These very sweet treats can be made "in a flash" with a few ingradients on hand.

Mix together in a bowl the oil, honey, vanilla and water. Add and mix flour and sunflower seeds. Drop by spoonfuls on an oiled cookie sheet. Bake at 350° for 12-15 minutes until lightly browned.

Peanut Butter Crunchies

24 2 inch cookies

1 cup peanut butter
1/2 cup honey
1 tsp. vanilla
3/8 cup oil
1 cup w.w. pastry flour
1/2 cup wheat germ
1/2 cup coconut
1/2 cup sunflower seeds

Mix peanut butter, oil, honey and vanilla. Mix, in a separate bowl, flour, wheat germ, coconut and sunflower seeds. Add dry ingredients to wet and stir. Place by rounded spoonfuls on oiled baking sheet. Press down slightly. (They don't spread much) Bake at 350° 10-15 minutes, until golden. Let them cool on baking sheets before you try to move them - they'll be soft when still hot.

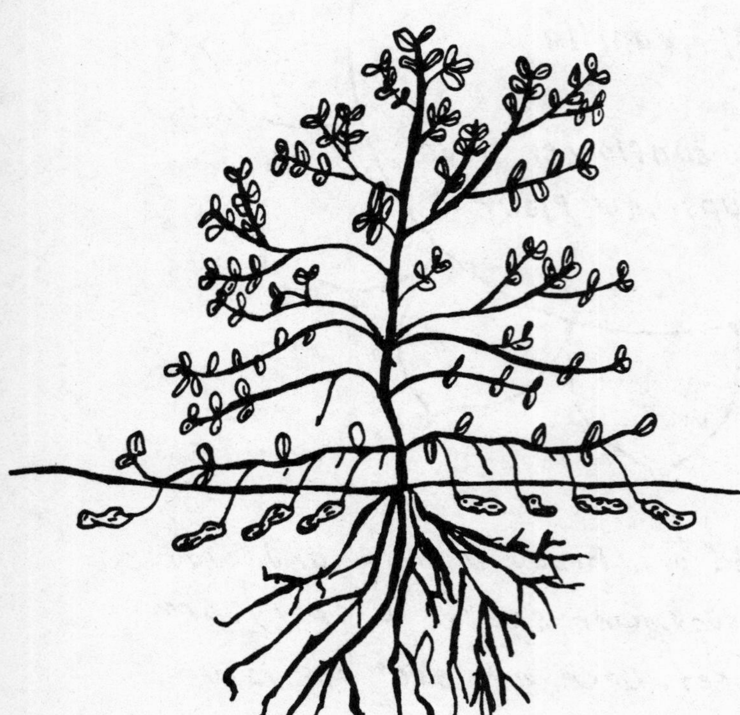

San Francisco, Cal.

Being almost 10 yrs. old, People's Bakery is one of the older collective bakeries. We now consist of 14 people who somewhat reflect the diversity of San Francisco in that some of us are people of color and many of us are gay. We are also, by the way, mostly women. We opened a cafe 2 yrs. ago. Over the 10 yrs. our clientele, especially wholesale, has changed from a very intense, comfortable network of collectives to the competitiveness of all of San Francisco. We don't have any volunteer labor... It's been a struggle !!!

Triticale Sunflower Bread

2×1½ lb. loaves

Good flavor in this simple bread.

2 ¼	cups	warm water	Mix together and let sit until sponge bubbles.
¼	cup	malt syrup	
1	Tbl.	yeast	
2	cups	hard w.w. flour	
¼	cup	soy flour	Add to sponge. Mix and knead well until texture is elastic.
½	cup	sunflower seeds	
3/5	cup	rolled triticale flakes	
1½	tsp.	salt	
2	Tbl.	oil	
3½	cups	hard w.w. flour	

Let dough rise in oiled covered bowl until doubled. Shape into 2 loaves and let rise again in oiled pans. Bake 350° for 45 minutes.

Bran Wheat Germ

2 × $1\frac{1}{2}$# loaves

A good-tasting high-fibre bread.

2½ cups warm water 2⅓ Tbl. molasses 1 Tbl. yeast 2 cups hard w.w. flour	Mix together, let sit until bubbly.
scant ½ cup bran scant ½ cup wheat germ 1 tsp. salt 1½ Tbl. oil 3½-4 cups hard w.w. flour	Add these to sponge and mix. Knead until texture is elastic.

Let dough rise in oiled covered bowl, until doubled in size. Shape into 2 loaves, let rise again in oiled pans.

Bake 350° for 45 minutes.

Hazel's Prune Nut Bread

A unique blend of nuts and fruit!

Delight yourself and your family and friends. You can add more prunes and hazelnuts for sheer extravagance!

2 × 1 ½ lb. loaves

2 ½ cups warm water
¼ cup molasses
1 Tbl. yeast
2 cups hard w.w. flour

Mix together and let this sponge sit until bubbly.

½ cup oats
¼ cup filberts/hazelnuts
2 ounces pitted chopped prunes
¾ cup coconut
¾ tsp. cinnamon
⅛ tsp. nutmeg
1 tsp. salt
1 Tbl. oil
4 cups hard w.w. flour

Add these ingredients to the sponge. Mix well. Knead the dough until nice and springy.

Let rise in oiled covered bowl until double in bulk.
Punch down and shape into 2 loaves.
Let rise again in oiled pans.
Bake 350° for 45 minutes.

People's Bakery label people, by Melissa Bay Mathis

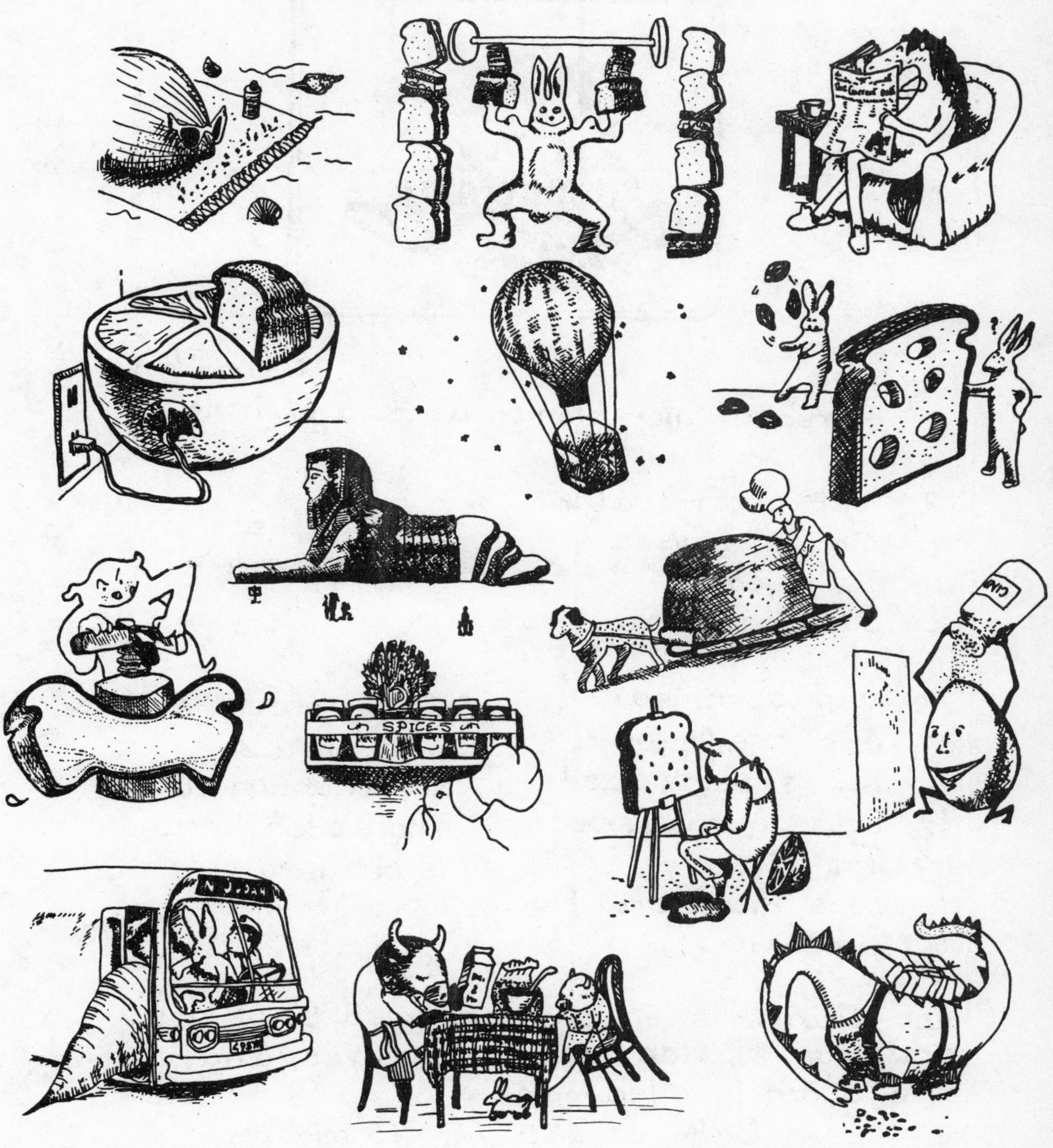

~Tamari Almonds, Hi-Protein White Bread, Carrot Currant Oat Cookies, Orange Wheat Bread, Light Rye, Raisin Bread, Apple Cider Bread, Onion Rye Poppyseed Bread, Rye Caraway Bread, Herb Bread, Lemon Sesame Date Bread, Egg Cinnamon Bread, Carrot Scallion Bread, Raisin Granola, Harvest Trail Mix ~

Corn Rye Bread

2 × 1½# loaves

A really nice blend ~ dark and inviting

2¼	cups	warm water	Mix together. Let sit until bubbly.
1½	Tbl.	molasses	
1	Tbl.	yeast	
2	cups	hard w.w. flour	
¾	cup	cornmeal	Add these ingredients and mix well. Knead dough until good elastic texture is obtained.
¾	cup	rye flour	
6	Tbl.	sesame seeds	
1¾	Tbl.	caraway seeds	
1½	Tbl.	oil	
4	cups	hard w.w. flour	
1	tsp.	salt	

Let dough rise in oiled, covered bowl, until doubled. Divide into two loaves, and let rise again in oiled pans.

Bake at 350° for 45 minutes.

We can't rave enough about this great bread. It looks darkly wonderful, smells enticing and the unique flavor will delight you.

People's Bakery originated the recipe, now a top favorite made by several bakeries in the area and across the country~ including Wildflour in the Midwest.

2 × 1½ lb round loaves

2 2/3	cups	water	5	Tbl. soy flour
1/4	cup	malt	3/5	cup sesame seeds
5 1/2	cups	hard w.w. flour	1	cup rolled oats
2 2/3	Tbl.	carob powder	3/5	cup chopped dates
1	Tbl.	oil	1	tsp. salt (optional)

Mix all ingredients together. Knead well for a soft pliable dough. Place in oiled bowl (not iron or aluminum) and cover well with towel. Let sit overnight. Next morning, shape into 2 round loaves, let sit for an hour or so in a warm spot. The bread may or may not rise at this point ~ don't wait forever! The lighter and softer the dough, the more chance of a rise. Before baking, cut a cross lightly on top to prevent cracking. Bake 350° for 50-60 minudes until browned and hollow sounding when tapped.

Irish Soda Bread

2 ~ 2 lb. round loaves

Absolutely delicious. A huge hit with everyone. Very easy ~ no yeast or rising involved. Make it soon!

7 cups hard w.w. flour
1 1/3 tsp. baking soda
1 tsp. salt
4 tsp. caraway seeds
1 3/4 cups currants

Mix these together.

2 tsp. grated lemon peel
1 cup cold water
1 1/3 cups buttermilk
2 2/3 Tbl. honey
2/3 cup oil

Mix these together. Add to dry mixture and blend well.

Knead briefly and shape into 2 round loaves. Place on oiled sheet, cut across top if desired to prevent cracking during baking. Bake right away at 350° for about an hour or 375° for about 45 minutes, until nicely browned on top.

people's company bakery
1534 e. lake st.
minneapolis minnesota 55407
612-721-7205
worker controlled

PEOPLE'S COMPANY IS ENTERING A NEW GROWTH PERIOD, AS WE ENJOY OUR ELEVENTH YEAR AS A WORKER OWNED AND MANAGED COLLECTIVE BAKERY. IN 1971, IT WAS INITIATED BY SOME OF THE FERVENT ALTERNATIVE COMMUNITY, CONCURRENT WITH PEOPLE'S PANTRY, LATER TO BECOME NORTH COUNTRY CO-OP. IN 1976, WE BEGAN CONSOLIDATING A VERY LARGE COLLECTIVE TO THE PRESENT 14. SEVERAL MEMBERS HAVE BEEN WITH US NEARLY ELEVEN YEARS, AND THE NEWEST AT LEAST TWO. WE SUPPLY MANY OF THE FOOD CO-OPS OF THE UPPER MIDWEST IN ADDITION TO OTHER INSTITUTIONS. WE ALSO WELCOME RETAIL CUSTOMERS TO OUR SPACIOUS STOREFRONT IN THE HEART OF MINNEAPOLIS. ON AVERAGE, WE MAKE 850 LOAVES OF BREAD SIX NIGHTS A WEEK, AS WELL AS PRODUCING A WIDE SELECTION OF GOODIES AND GRANOLA. WE ATTRIBUTE MUCH OF OUR SUCCESS IN ACHIEVING A CONSISTENTLY HIGH QUALITY BREAD TO THE EXCELLENT HIGH PROTEIN ORGANIC NORTH DAKOTA WINTER WHEAT AND OTHER STONE GROUND FLOURS MILLED FOR US WEEKLY BY MARK AND JENNIFER SCHWARTZ OF LITTLE BEAR TRADING CO., COCHRANE, WISCONSIN.

vegie bread

YIELD: TWO 1½ LB. LOAVES

NO EGGS OR DAIRY

A MEAL IN A SLICE! THIS BREAD IS DELICIOUS - IT SMELLS LIKE PIZZA. EXCELLENT WITH SOUP OR SALAD, OR WITH GRILLED CHEESE ON IT.

1⅔ CUPS WARM WATER
1 Tbl YEAST
1½ Tbl HONEY
CHOPPED VEGIES:
- 2 MEDIUM TOMATOES
- 2 MEDIUM CARROTS
- 1-2 STICKS CELERY
- 1 MEDIUM ONION
- ½ GREEN PEPPER

1½ Tbl OIL
5-6 CUPS HARD WW FLOUR
1 tsp SALT (OPTIONAL)
DRIED HERBS:
- 2 tsp OREGANO
- 2 tsp GARLIC POWDER
- 2 tsp BASIL
- 1 tsp MARJORAM

MIX WATER, YEAST AND HONEY. LET SIT A FEW MINUTES TIL FROTHY. ADD ALL REMAINING INGREDIENTS, RESERVING SOME FLOUR. MIX IN WELL.... BEGIN TO KNEAD THE DOUGH WHEN SOFT BUT NOT TOO STICKY. ADD FLOUR AS NEEDED- THE VEGIES WILL RELEASE SOME LIQUID AS YOU KNEAD, BUT WATCH YOU DON'T ADD TOO MUCH FLOUR AND MAKE THE DOUGH STIFF. WHEN SPRINGY AND PLIABLE, LEAVE DOUGH COVERED IN AN OILED BOWL TO RISE. WHEN DOUBLED IN SIZE, PUNCH DOWN AND SHAPE INTO 2 LOAVES. LET RISE AGAIN IN OILED BREAD PANS. BAKE AT 350° FOR 45 MINUTES.

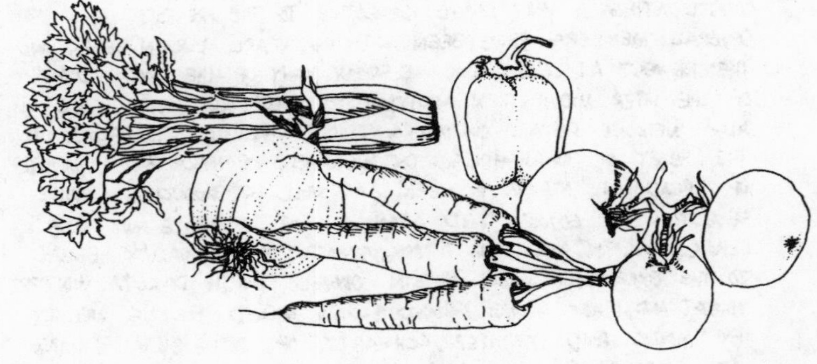

cheddar cheese bread

YIELD: TWO 1½ LB. LOAVES

WITH ALL THAT CHEESE, YOU WON'T BELIEVE IT'LL WORK, BUT IS IT GOOD! WE TRIED IT WITH SWISS CHEESE TOO - EXPERIMENT!

2½ CUPS WARM WATER
1 Tbl YEAST
2 Tbl MALT SYRUP
5½ - 6 CUPS HARD WW FLOUR
½ LB. GRATED CHEDDAR CHEESE*
  AT ROOM TEMPERATURE
2 tsp GARLIC POWDER
1 tsp CARAWAY SEED
1 tsp SALT (OPTIONAL)

* WILDFLOUR DOUBLES THE CHEESE AND OMITS THE MALT AND SEASONINGS.

YOU CAN START THE YEAST OFF WITH THE WATER, MALT AND SOME FLOUR, AND LET IT SPONGE A WHILE, OR JUST MIX EVERYTHING UP TOGETHER, ADDING FLOUR AS NECESSARY. KNEAD THE SMOOTH, WONDERFUL-FEELING DOUGH UNTIL NICE AND STRETCHY. LET RISE, COVERED, IN THE BOWL UNTIL PUFFED UP. SHAPE INTO 2 LOAVES AND LET RISE AGAIN IN PANS. (ROLLS ARE DELICIOUS, TOO.) BAKE AT 350° FOR 45 MINUTES.

The Holstein

scottish shortbread

YIELD: MAKES THREE ROUNDS 5" ACROSS AND 1" THICK.

THE REAL THING - SINFULLY BUTTERY, MELT-IN-THE-MOUTH SHORTBREADS. VERY SIMPLE, YET SIMPLY DELICIOUS!

1/2 LB. BUTTER
1/4 CUP HONEY
1 3/4 CUPS WW PASTRY FLOUR
7/8 CUP RICE FLOUR

CREAM BUTTER REAL WELL, THEN CREAM WITH HONEY. ADD FLOURS, MIXING IN WELL. DIVIDE INTO BALLS 3" OR 4" IN DIAMETER. PAT THESE INTO ROUNDS 3/4"-1" THICK. PLACE ON GREASED OR FLOURED COOKIE SHEET. IF YOU HAVE A PRESS, FLOUR IT AND PRESS A DESIGN INTO THE ROUNDS. OTHERWISE, PRICK WITH A FORK ALL THE WAY THROUGH TO INSURE EVEN BAKING AND ALLOW AIR TO ESCAPE. EDGES MAY BE FLUTED (NICKED WITH A FORK OR KNIFE) FOR DECORATION. BAKE AT 350° FOR 10-20 MINUTES (VARIES WITH THICKNESS) UNTIL LIGHTLY GOLDEN BROWN AROUND EDGES AND OVER TOP. LET COOL BEFORE REMOVING FROM SHEET. YOU COULD TRY MAKING SMALLER COOKIES, OR A FLATTER, LARGER ROUND THAT COULD BE SCORED INTO PIE SLICES BEFORE BAKING AND BROKEN APART WHEN COOL. VERY DECORATIVE! ADJUST COOKING TIME ACCORDINGLY.

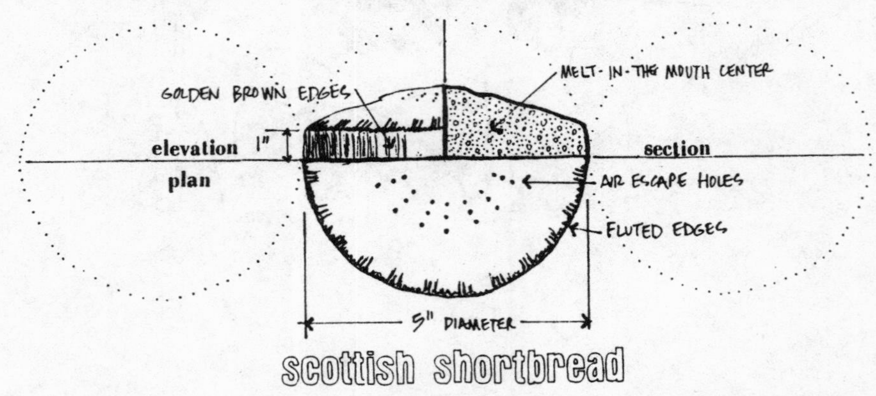

ginger snaps

YIELD: 4-5 DOZEN COOKIES
SIMPLE, BUT VERY GOOD.

NO EGGS OR DAIRY

- 2 1/4 CUPS SAFFLOWER OIL
- 1 CUP MOLASSES
- 1 3/4 CUPS HONEY
- 6 1/2 CUPS WW PASTRY FLOUR
- 3 Tbl GINGER
- SESAME SEEDS

MIX OIL, MOLASSES, AND HONEY TOGETHER. ADD FLOUR AND GINGER. DOUGH SHOULD BE VERY WET. SCOOP OUT ONTO OILED COOKIE SHEETS. SPRINKLE WITH SESAME SEEDS. (THESE COOKIES REALLY SPREAD OUT AS THEY BAKE!) BAKE FOR 10 MINUTES AT 350°.

snap snap snap

granola cookies

YIELD: ABOUT 4 DOZEN 2 1/2"-3" COOKIES
ONE OF OUR TOP FAVORITE COOKIES IN ALL THE RECIPE-TESTING!

NO EGGS OR DAIRY

- 2 1/2 CUPS OATS
- 1 CUP ROLLED WHEAT (OR WHEATFLAKES)
- 1 CUP SHREDDED COCONUT
- 1 CUP SUNFLOWER SEEDS
- 1 CUP WW PASTRY FLOUR
- 1/2 CUP BRAN
- 1/2 CUP SESAME SEEDS
- 1/2 CUP CASHEWS
- 3/4 CUP MILLET FLOUR *
- 1 Tbl. BAKING POWDER
- 1 CUP MAPLE SYRUP
- 3/4 CUP HONEY
- 1 CUP OIL
- 1/2 CUP WATER

PREHEAT OVEN TO 350°. MIX DRY INGREDIENTS TOGETHER. MIX WET MIXTURE. COMBINE WET AND DRY INGREDIENTS. ALLOW TO SIT 20 MINUTES. SCOOP AND FLATTEN ON COOKIE SHEET WITH FINGERS, A PRESS OR THE BOTTOM OF A TUMBLER DIPPED IN WATER. BAKE 18-20 MINUTES OR UNTIL DONE. COOL ON RACK.

* GRIND, POUND OR BLEND RAW MILLET.

cream cheese cookies

YIELD: ABOUT 2½ DOZEN COOKIES
ONE OF THE BEST SELLERS AT PEOPLE'S COMPANY BAKERY.

½ LB. BUTTER
¼ LB. CREAM CHEESE
2 tsp. VANILLA
1 CUP HONEY
2½ CUPS WW PASTRY FLOUR
2 tsp NUTMEG
½ - 1 CUP CRUSHED WALNUTS, PECANS, ALMONDS OR FILBERTS

BEAT BUTTER AND CREAM CHEESE TOGETHER WELL. ADD VANILLA AND HONEY AND MIX WELL. THEN STIR IN THE REMAINING INGREDIENTS. SCOOP WITH MELON BALL SCOOPER OR TEASPOON ONTO COOKIE SHEETS. BAKE AT 350° FOR 15 MINUTES.

poppy seed cookies

YIELD: 3 DOZEN COOKIES
THESE COOKIES ARE DELICIOUS AND BEAUTIFUL.

⅔ CUP BUTTER
⅓ CUP TAHINI
½ CUP HONEY
½ CUP MAPLE SYRUP
2 EGGS (OR 3 Tbl TAHINI)
2½ CUPS WW PASTRY FLOUR
1 CUP RICE FLOUR
1 tsp BAKING POWDER (OPTIONAL)
½ CUP POPPY SEEDS

CREAM BUTTER, TAHINI, HONEY AND MAPLE SYRUP TOGETHER. ADD EGGS (OR TAHINI SUBSTITUTE). ADD PASTRY FLOUR, RICE FLOUR, BAKING POWDER. MIX TOGETHER, THEN ADD THE POPPY SEEDS. (DOUGH IS STICKY.) SCOOP ONTO OILED SHEETS. BAKE AT 350°, ABOUT 10 MINUTES OR UNTIL BROWN.

KRUNCH KRUNCH KRUNCH

krunch bars

YIELD: 16 BARS APPROX 1½" x 2½" NO EGGS, DAIRY OR WHEAT
NOTE: VERY SWEET, SO YOU MAY WANT TO TRY LESS HONEY.

3/8 CUP PEANUT BUTTER
½ CUP HONEY (OR COMBINATION OF MOLASSES, SORGHUM, MAPLE SYRUP OR MALT)
2 CUPS SESAME SEEDS
1 CUP SUNFLOWER SEEDS
1 CUP CASHEWS OR PEANUTS
1 CUP COCONUT

MIX TOGETHER PEANUT BUTTER AND HONEY. ADD ALL OTHER INGREDIENTS AND MIX. DRY MIX MAY OR MAY NOT BE PRE-TOASTED. PRESS MIXTURE INTO 11" x 7" PAN WITH WET HANDS. ROLL TO EVEN OUT TO ½" THICK WITH WET ROLLING PIN. BAKE AT 350° FOR 10-15 MINUTES OR UNTIL EDGES BROWN. CUT WHILE STILL WARM BUT COOL BEFORE REMOVING BARS FROM PAN.

toasted all grain cereal

YIELD: 12 CUPS NO EGGS OR DAIRY
THIS CRUNCHY, NUTTY-TASTING CEREAL IS VERY EASY TO MAKE AND CAN BE COMBINED WITH DRY OR FRESH FRUIT FOR A DELICIOUS BREAKFAST.

7 CUPS ROLLED WHEATFLAKES
3 CUPS OATS
2 CUPS ROLLED RYE FLAKES
½ CUP CORN FLOUR
1 CUP WHEAT GERM
½ CUP CORN OIL
1 CUP BARLEY MALT
¼ CUP BOILING WATER

MIX DRY INGREDIENTS. GRADUALLY TOSS WITH CORN OIL AND BAKE ON COOKIE SHEET AT 350° UNTIL FLAKES ARE LIGHTLY TOASTED, ABOUT 5-10 MINUTES. MIX MALT AND WATER. COVER FLAKES WITH THIS MIXTURE UNTIL COATED. BAKE ON FLAT SHEET UNTIL THE FLAKES ARE CRISPY, ABOUT 15 MINUTES.

"IT'S TOASTED"

REBEL ☆ BAKERS
COLLECTIVE
SAN DIEGO, CA.

THERE WERE MANY THINGS WE WERE TEMPTED TO WRITE ABOUT. WE WANTED TO EXPLAIN EVERYTHING; OBVIOUSLY IMPOSSIBLE IN SEVERAL PARAGRAPHS OR PAGES. WHAT SEEMS MOST IMPORTANT TO EXPRESS HERE IS WHAT WE ARE TRYING TO DO. AND THE ESSENCE OF THAT IS TRYING TO BECOME WHOLE HUMAN BEINGS.

FROM OUR INDIVIDUAL AND COLLECTIVE EXPERIENCE, NOT FROM SOME BOOK, WE REALIZED THAT THE FIRST STEP IN THIS PROCESS WAS THE UNCONSCIOUS OR CONSCIOUS AWARENESS THAT LIFE, NOT MERELY SURVIVAL, IS BASED ON PEOPLE WORKING / PLAYING TOGETHER, STRUGGLING TOGETHER FOR AND AGAINST THINGS, CHOOSING TOGETHER HOW TO WORK / PLAY, HOW TO FIGHT. IT IS IN THIS FIGHT, THIS STRUGGLE AGAINST THE DESTRUCTION AND DEGRADATION OF PERSONALITY, OF PEOPLE AS CREATURES WITH EMOTIONS, OF WHOLE RACES, OF WOMEN, OF THE WORKING CLASS, THAT WE GLIMPSE WHAT IT IS TO BE REALLY HUMAN, TO BE REALLY FREE.

ADMITTEDLY, MOST OF OUR TIME IS NECESSARILY SURVIVAL TIME, CONCRETELY EXPRESSED IN WORKING TO HAVE MONEY OR THINGS TO MAKE IT THROUGH THE DAY, WEEK, OR MONTH. THAT WE TRY TO WORK FROM EACH ACCORDING TO HER/HIS ABILITY, NOT BY A FIXED WEEKLY SCHEDULE OR QUOTA, AND PAID ACCORDING TO HER / HIS NEED, NOT BY TIME CLOCKED OR GOODS PRODUCED, STILL DOES NOT OBSCURE THE TRUTH THAT WE ARE STILL PEDDLERS OF COMMODITIES, OF OURSELVES; THAT WE ARE STILL WORKING TO SURVIVE. WHAT KEEPS US REBEL BAKERS IS NOT ANY WEIRD BUSINESS THRILL, NOR THE HEALTHY WHOLE GRAIN,

DAIRYLESS, EGGLESS SWEETS AND BREADS (ALTHOUGH THIS LATTER ONE IS IMPORTANT TO US), IT IS THE MOMENT BEYOND THE YOKE OF PRODUCE AND SELL, BEYOND CAUSE AND EFFECT, BEYOND DEAD TIME.

WE ALL HAVE HAD THESE MOMENTS — WHEN WE DO SOMETHING FOR THE PURE JOY OF DOING IT. AND THEN WE LOOK AROUND AND SEE ONE ANOTHER DOING IT FOR THE SAME REASON, AND A SMILE AND TEARS WASH OUR FACES. IT IS MOMENTS LIKE THESE, EXULTANT IN THE PROCESS OF CREATION FOR CREATION'S SAKE, AND THEN REALIZING THAT THIS IS MUCH DIFFERENT FROM, IN FACT, ANTITHETICAL TO, AMERIKA'S WAY OF WORKING THAT WE BECOME A POTENTIAL THREAT.

BUT THE LEAP TO BEING AN ACTUAL THREAT, THE LEAP BEYOND THE CRAP OF EVERYDAY LIFE, IS FLEETING IF WE ARE ALONE. THE BARRICADES, THE CREATION OF A SPIRITUAL AND PHYSICAL COMMUNITY OF RESISTANCE AND LIBERATION IS ONLY A DREAM WITHOUT YOU, YOU WHO READ THESE PAGES.

DON'T GO HOME OR INTO THE KITCHEN AND JUST BAKE BY YOURSELF. GET YOUR FRIENDS AND NEIGHBORS AND BAKE WITH THEM, CREATE TOGETHER, DISCUSS WHAT IT MEANS OR WOULD MEAN TO WORK/PLAY COLLECTIVELY.

CERTAINLY DON'T READ A WHOLE BOOK BY AND ABOUT COLLECTIVE AND COOPERATIVE BAKERIES AND BAKING AND JUST USE THE RECIPES. TAKE THE WHOLE SPIRIT THAT WE'VE OFFERED HERE, AND THEN TAKE IT INTO THE STREETS. 'NUF SAID.

OH, YES. WE HOPE YOU WILL EXPERIMENT WITH THESE RECIPES, CHANGING OR ADDING WHATEVER YOU LIKE. BE CREATIVE. WE MADE 15 DIFFERENT EXPERIMENTS FOR THE CARROT CAKE'S TOFU FROSTING. DO THE SAME. NEVER BE SATISFIED. DEMAND THE IMPOSSIBLE.

WHOLE WHEAT-RYE FRENCH BREAD

2 LOAVES

SPONGE:
- 2 CUPS WATER
- 2 1/3 CUPS HARD W.W. FLOUR
- 1/2 TBL YEAST
- 2 TBL MALT

ADD:
- 1 3/4 CUPS HARD W.W. FLOUR
- 1 CUP RYE FLOUR
- 1 TSP SALT
- RICE FLOUR TO COAT

MIX SPONGE AND LET SIT 1/2 HOUR. ADD REMAINING FLOUR AND SALT AND KNEAD WELL. LET DOUGH RISE AND PUNCH DOWN AT LEAST TWICE. DIVIDE DOUGH IN HALF AND ROLL EACH PIECE OUT FLAT. FOLD TWO SIDES IN TOWARD EACH OTHER AND REPEAT.

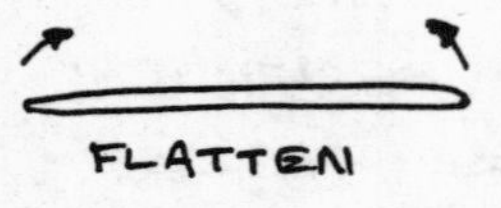
FLATTEN

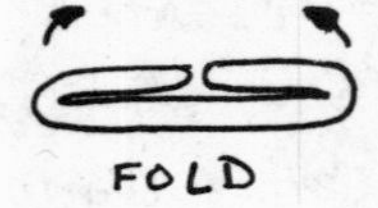
FOLD

FOLD

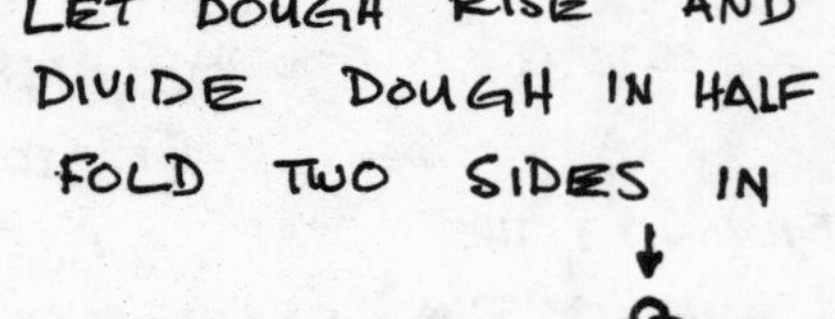
PINCH

PINCH THE SEAMS AND ROLL IT TO FRENCH BREAD LENGTH, TAPERING AT ENDS. ROLL LOAF IN RICE FLOUR UNTIL IT IS NICELY COATED. PREHEAT OVEN TO 475°. PUT PANS DUSTED WITH CORNMEAL OR RICE FLOUR INTO OVEN TO GET HOT. LET LOAVES RISE 15 MINUTES OR LESS SO AS NOT TO SPREAD. PUT LOAVES SEAM SIDE DOWN ON PREHEATED PANS AND MAKE SEVERAL DEEP CUTS INTO THE TOP OF THE LOAF. SPRAY THE LOAVES WITH A PLANT SPRAYER JUST AFTER THEY GO INTO THE OVEN AND EVERY 5-10 MINUTES. BAKE UNTIL SEVERAL COLORS, GOLDEN BROWN TO BLACK, ANYWHERE FROM 40 TO 60 MINUTES.

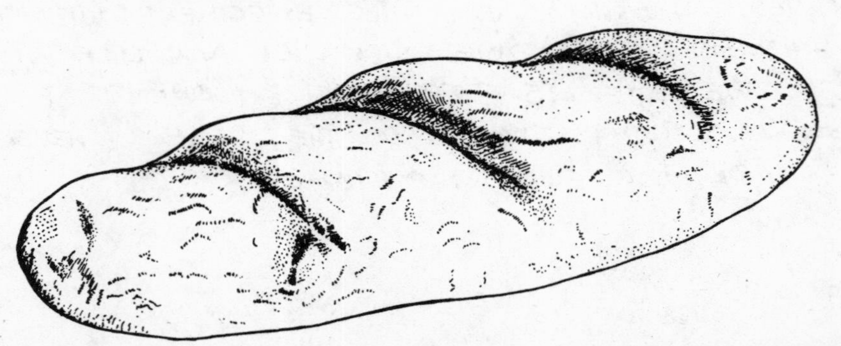

CORN-BENNE MUFFINS

ONE DOZEN

PREHEAT OVEN TO 350°

MIX: 7/8 CUP CORNMEAL
1 CUP W.W. FLOUR
2/3 CUP SESAME SEEDS

MIX SEPARATELY:

1 1/3 CUPS SOY MILK
3/4 CUP MALT SYRUP
2 1/2 TBS OIL

OIL TINS. POUR WET INTO DRY. MIX WELL. SPOON OUT INTO MUFFIN TINS. BAKE AT LEAST 25 MINUTES.

BRAN MUFFINS

ONE DOZEN

MIX: 1 1/4 CUPS WATER
1 CUP MALT SYRUP
1/4 CUP OIL
1/2 TSP VANILLA
(OPTIONAL, AS IS EVERYTHING ELSE.)

MIX SEPARATELY:

2 CUPS BRAN
1 CUP W.W. FLOUR
1/4 CUP CORNMEAL
1/4 CUP MILLET FLOUR
1/8 CUP POPPY SEEDS
1/4 CUP RAISINS
2 TSP BAKING POWDER
1 TSP KELP
1 TSP CINNAMON
1/8 TSP MACE

POUR DRY INTO WET. MIX EVENLY. SCOOP INTO OILED OR PAPERED MUFFIN TINS. BAKE UNTIL WELL-BROWNED, FIRM ON TOP, ABOUT 30 MINUTES.

CARROT CAKE

13" x 9" PAN OR 9" ROUND DOUBLE LAYER

PREHEAT OVEN TO 350°.

MIX:
- 1¾ CUPS W.W. FLOUR
- ⅜ CUP CORN MEAL
- ¼ CUP COCONUT
- ¾ CUPS WALNUTS
- ½ TSP KELP
- ½ TBL BAKING POWDER
- 1 TSP CINNAMON
- ¼ TSP NUTMEG
- ¼ TSP ALLSPICE

MIX SEPARATELY:
- 1½ TBL OIL
- 1¼ CUPS MALT SYRUP
- ½ CUP WATER
- ¼ CUP RAISINS
- 2¼ CUPS SHREDDED CARROTS

OIL PAN(S). POUR DRY INTO WET AND MIX EVENLY. BAKE 35-40 MINUTES. IT SHOULD BE BROWN ON EDGES; A KNIFE POKED INTO IT SHOULD COME OUT CLEANLY

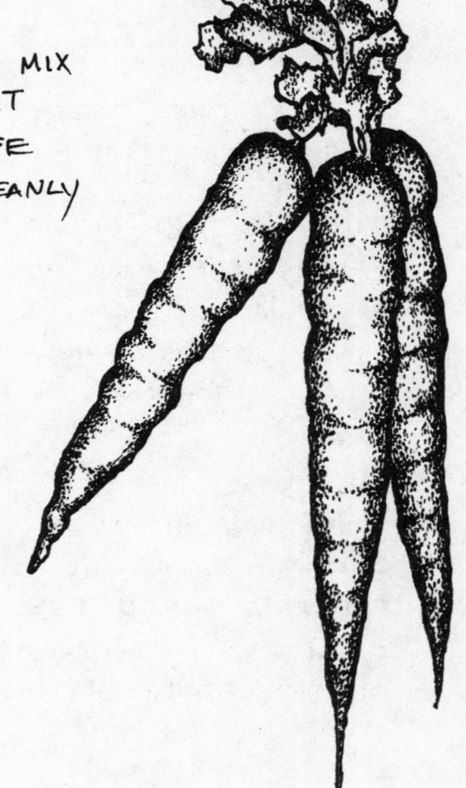

WITH TOFU FROSTING

BLEND:
- 1 LB. TOFU (DRAINED)
- ⅓ CUP MALT
- ¼ CUP COCONUT
- ¼ CUP WALNUT MEAL
- ⅛ TSP SWEET ORANGE OIL

ORANGE-OAT COOKIES

ABOUT 2 DOZEN

PREHEAT OVEN TO 350°

(1) MIX: 1/3 CUP WATER
1 1/4 CUPS OATS
LET SIT...

(2) MIX IN A SEPARATE BOWL:

5/8 CUP CORNMEAL
3/4 CUP SUNFLOWER SEEDS
3/8 CUP WALNUT PIECES
1 TSP CINNAMON
1 TSP KELP
1 TSP BAKING POWDER

(3) ADD, ONE-BY-ONE, TO (1)

1/8 CUP OIL
1 CUP MALT
2 TSP SWEET ORANGE OIL
3/4 CUP W.W. PASTRY FLOUR
3/4 CUP RAISINS
MIX WELL

(4) ADD (2), MIX WELL.
SCOOP ONTO COOKIE SHEET
DO NOT PRESS FLAT.
BAKE 20-25 MINUTES
'TIL BROWNED ON BOTTOM.

CAROB BROWNIES

FILLS 25" x 8" TRAY

PREHEAT OVEN TO 350°

MIX: 3 1/2 CUPS MALT
1/2 CUP OIL
1 1/4 CUPS HOT WATER

MIX SEPARATELY:
1 1/2 CUPS WALNUT PIECES
1 3/4 CUPS COCONUT
1 1/4 CUPS CAROB POWDER
1/2 TSP KELP
3/4 CUP CORNMEAL
3 3/4 CUPS W.W. FLOUR

MIX TOGETHER. SHOULD BE WET ENOUGH TO SPREAD. BAKE 45-60 MINUTES, TEST WITH KNIFE.

COCO-ALMOND COOKIES

~ 35 COOKIES

PREHEAT OVEN TO 335°

MIX: 2 CUPS CORNMEAL
1 1/4 CUPS RYE FLOUR
1 CUP MILLET MEAL
1/8 CUP SOY FLOUR
4 1/2 CUPS COCONUT SHREDS
1 CUP RSTD. ALMOND PIECES
1/2 TSP KELP

MIX SEPARATELY:

2 CUPS MALT
1 1/4 CUPS WATER
1/2 TSP ALMOND EXTRACT

MIX TOGETHER.

SCOOP ONTO COOKIE SHEET WITH SMALL SCOOPER OR SPOON. FLOUR OR WATER MAY HAVE TO BE VARIED SO THAT DOUGH IS SOLID ENOUGH NOT TO STICK TO DRY SCOOPER BUT WET ENOUGH TO SPREAD AND RISE A BIT IN THE OVEN.

BAKE 25-30 MINUTES 'TIL BROWNED ON BOTTOM.

CAROB-MINT COOKIES

~ 25 COOKIES

← SAME

MIX: 2 CUPS CORNMEAL
1/4 CUP RYE FLOUR
1/4 CUP MILLET MEAL
1 TBL SOY FLOUR
1/2 CUP CAROB POWDER
3/4 CUP WALNUT PIECES
1 CUP WALNUT MEAL

MIX SEPARATELY:

1 1/4 CUPS MALT
1/2 CUP WATER
11 DROPS PEPPERMINT OIL

← SAME.

← SAME. ADDITIONALLY, WE PRESS A SMALL WALNUT PIECE INTO THE CENTER OF EACH COOKIE. FOR BOTH THOSE AND THESE, SOY MILK MAY BE SUBSTITUTED FOR SOY FLOUR & WATER.

← SAME. THESE WILL GET VERY DARK ON BOTTOM.

RAW FRUIT BALLS

1 CUP DATES
1 CUP DRIED PEACHES
1 CUP RAISINS
1 CUP COCONUT
1 CUP WALNUTS
LEMON JUICE OR ORANGE JUICE TO TASTE

BLEND DRIED FRUIT FIRST (A MEATGRINDER WORKS WELL.) ADD WALNUTS LAST SO LITTLE PIECES REMAIN USE SMALL SCOOP OR HANDS. DON'T PREHEAT OVEN, REFRIGERATE, THEN PIG OUT.

SCENTED PECAN BALLS

2½ CUPS PECAN MEAL
1 CUP DATES
½ - 1 TBL ORANGE BLOSSOM WATER

BLEND. SHAPE. ROLL IN COCONUT. REFRIGERATE UNTIL YOU GET HUNGRY.

★★★★★ **Rising Star** were unable to send anything about themselves but Wildflour bakers and cookbook co-ordinators Kathy and Mike visited them in late 1980, during a 3 month, 40-bakery tour of North America. They write:

Wonderful as many bakeries and bakers were, Rising Star was our high point. Greeting us with an outpouring of enthusiasm and warmth, the six-person collective put their bakery, storefront and homes at our disposal. Never have we seen such beautiful baked goods. Producing from a tiny baking space, with very little equipment, they filled their bright storefront with a vast selection of mouthwatering pies, cakes, bars, rolls, cookies, granola, nut mixes, pizza and bread. We were urged to sample everthing and we tried valiantly.... As we munched the finest yeasted bread we came across - the wonderful sesame-encrusted peasant bread - Rising Star's bakers described to us the P.S.C. workers co-op, a 3-collective structure which embraced the bakery, the Oasis Café collective in downtown Victoria and a warehouse collective. It had been started up 2 years previously and seemed to be booming.

Unfortunately, we heard during the writing of this book that Rising Star had run into financial difficulties and in early 1981 the bakery was sold to a partnership of 2 former collective members. We hope the future will see a return to a collective structure, but we are glad that Rising Star and its fine products have not been lost to the world!

Victoria, B.C. Canada

Peasant Bread

2 x 1½ pound loaves

This is a unique and wonderful bread. Deliciously flavored with the subtle and very nutritious flax seeds and encrusted with toasted sesame seeds, it's a delight for eye and palate.

1¼ cups warm water
1 Tbl. molasses
1 Tbl. yeast

* Mix the yeast, water and molasses, letting it sit a moment.

½ cup sunflower seeds
¼ cup flax seeds
⅔ cup water

* Soak sunflower and flax seeds in water.

¼ cup whey powder or milk powder (optional)
1 Tbl. oil
1 tsp. salt
5-6 cups hard whole wheat flour
¼ cup dates, chopped or whole

* Mix in the whey/milk powder if used, the oil, salt and flour and knead the dough well. When the dough is smooth and stretchy work in the dates.

* Let the dough rise, punch down and shape into 2 loaves. Dip each loaf completely in warm water and roll in sesame seeds until crusted over. Let rise in pans. Bake at 350°-375° for 40-45 minutes.

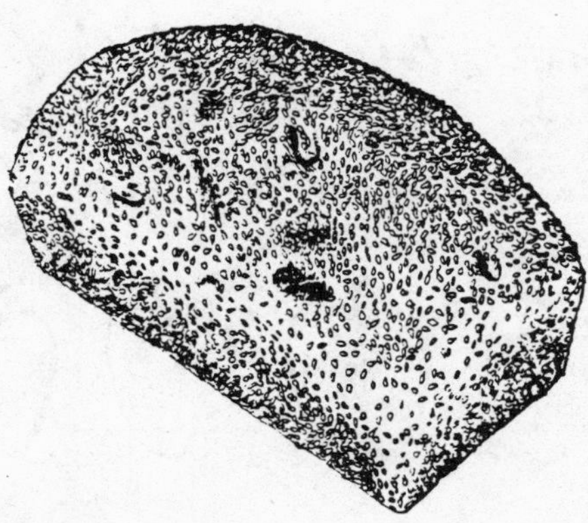

Apple Kuchen

1 lb. sweet bread dough makes 1 - 9" x 13" pan

One of Rising Star's most popular treats - fragrant and so delicious. Serve cooled and cut as a pastry or warm and freshly baked for an irresistible dessert.

Crust: 1 lb. sweet bread dough (see p. 116 or 126)

Roll out to about ½" thickness to fit oiled pan. Lay in pan.

Filling: about 4 medium apples, sliced or chopped
¼ cup honey (optional)

Spread apples over dough and drizzle honey over it desired. OR make a blended or cooked pureé with apples and honey and spread on dough.

Streusel topping
¼ lb. butter, cold
2 cups whole wheat pastry flour
2 Tbl. cinnamon
½ cup honey
vanilla to taste (optional)

Work butter into flour and cinnamon, with finger or fork until like fine breadcrumbs. Lightly work in honey and vanilla. Sprinkle streusel topping over fruits.

Proof in a warm place for 30 minutes. Bake at 350° for 30-40 minutes, until top starts to brown. Needless to say, it works with other fruits! Peaches, blueberries, apricots... a mixture...

Carob Cake

2 - 8" round pans

What a texture! Cloud soft. No eggs or dairy in this amazing cake.

3 1/4 cups whole wheat pastry flour
2 tsp. soda
3/4 cup oil
1 2/3 cups water
2 Tbl. vinegar
2 tsp. vanilla
1 3/4 cups honey
6 Tbl. carob powder

Blend dry ingredients.

Mix wet ingredients.

Combine dry with wet.

Bake for 35 minutes at 350°.

Carob Icing

not dairyless

6 Tbl butter
1 cup milk powder
1 cup carob
1/2 cup honey
1 tsp. vanilla
1/4 cup sour milk, buttermilk or yogurt.

Allow butter to soften. Sift the carob powder. Cream the carob, milk powder and butter (it will be a bit dry). Add remaining ingredients and blend to a smooth consistency. Ice cake after it cools.

Honey Cake and Fruit Upside-Down Cake

1- 9"x 13" cake

The honey cake alone is rich and delicious. The simple addition of fruit slices makes it a luscious and elaborate looking dessert treat.

Honey Cake

1 cup coconut oil, melted *
1½ cups honey
1 cup milk or sour milk
4 eggs, beaten
½ Tbl. vanilla
3½ cups whole wheat pastry flour
2 tsp. baking powder

Cream together oil and honey. Blend in milk, eggs and vanilla. Stir in flour and baking powder 'til blended.

Pour batter into greased or oiled pan. Bake at 350° for about 45 minutes or until tester comes out clean.

* Try margarine if you can't get coconut oil.

for Fruit Upside-Down Cake

In the bottom of an oiled pan spread slices of apple and/or pear with chopped walnuts, raisins, currants, etc. as desired (don't make this too thick a layer!)

Spread cake batter over fruit.

Bake at 350° for about 50 minutes until brown on top.

Let cool somewhat, then carefully turn out cake onto tray or plate so fruit is on top.

Spread a little extra honey over it for a nice glaze, if desired. Looks beautiful!

Devil's Carob Cake

1 x 9" cake

You won't believe how light, moist and rich this cake is. A top favorite with the recipe testers. 'A real devil's food texture.' 'Would make great cupcakes'.... 'Wonderful for a birthday party' 'Would even appeal to non-carob lovers.'

6 Tbl. butter
3/4 cup honey
1 egg
1 1/2 cups whole wheat pastry flour
1 tsp. baking soda
6 Tbl. carob powder
1 cup milk
1 tsp. vanilla

Preheat oven to 350°. Cream butter and honey. Beat in egg. Mix in remaining ingredients as listed. Pour in greased pan and bake for 35-45 minutes, until a knife inserted in the center comes out clean.

Poppy Seed Loaf

Makes 2 loaves or cakes.

A lovely, rich but light cake.

1 cup poppy seeds
1 cup milk

Soak together for 1-2 hours

½ lb. butter
1 cup honey

Cream together well. Combine with milk and poppy seeds.

2 cups ww pastry flour
4 tsp. baking powder

Add these to liquid mixture and mix in.

4 egg whites, beaten stiff.

Fold in egg whites.

Pour batter into greased pans and bake at 350° for 45 minutes or until cake pulls away from sides or knife comes out clean.

Gingerbread Muffins

24 muffins

2 cups whole wheat pastry flour
½ cup dry milk powder
1 tsp. baking powder
1 tsp. baking soda
1 Tbl. ground ginger
1½ tsp. cinnamon
½ tsp. ground cloves
⅔ cup molasses
⅓ cup honey
⅓ cup oil
1 egg
1 cup water

Heat oven to 350°. Stir dry ingredients together. Combine molasses, honey, oil, egg and water. Stir dry ingredients into wet (the secret to muffins is not to overbeat them).

Bake for 12-15 minutes until they test done. Let them cool halfway then take them out and place on cooling rack.

Blueberry Coconut Muffins

18 muffins

The coconut adds a nice twist to these flavorful muffins.

3/4 cup safflower (or coconut) oil
3/4 cup honey
3 eggs
1 1/2 tsp. lemon rind
3 tsp. vanilla

Blend wet ingredients together with a whisk or beat well with a wooden spoon.

4 cups whole wheat pastry flour
1 1/8 cups shredded coconut
1 1/2 tsp. baking powder
1 1/2 cups blueberries, fresh frozen or defrosted

Mix together the flour, coconut and baking powder. Blend into the wet ingredients. Lightly stir in the blueberries. The batter will be thick-this makes a delicious muffin. You can add milk, however, if you desire a runnier batter.

Spoon batter into greased muffin pans and bake at 350° for about 30 minutes until a knife comes out clean.

Eggless Cheesecake

Elegantly fills a 10" springform pan. You can put any fresh fruit topping on this one or just savor it plain.

<u>Crust</u>:
- 1/4 lb. butter, melted
- 1 2/3 cups whole wheat flour
- 1 cup wheatgerm
- 1/8 cup honey

Mix crust together by hand and press into place.

<u>Filling</u>: you can run all of these ingredients through a blender or cream very well starting with the cream cheese alone, either by hand or mixer.

- 2 lb. cream cheese
- 4 Tbl. arrowroot
- 2 cups yoghurt
- 1 cup honey
- 2 tsp vanilla
- 1 banana mashed
- lemon juice to taste

Pour filling into crust and bake at 350° for about 1 1/2 hours. The cake will set as it cools.

Almond Crescents

Makes about 20 3" long crescents.
Wheatless, dairyless. Pretty and rich.

1 cup coconut oil (solid)
1/3 cup honey
2 Tbl. water
2 tsp. vanilla
2 cups oat flour (blend oats in blender)
1/2 cup ground almonds
plus a couple of extra Tbl. of ground or finely slivered almonds

Cream together the oil and honey. Add water and vanilla. Blend in flour and ground almonds. Chill the dough. Shape into logs 1" in diameter and 6" long. Cut in half and shape into crescents. Place on oiled cookie sheet. Brush with oil and sprinkle with ground or slivered almonds. Bake at 325°-350° for 12-15 minutes until lightly browned around edges. Leave on the tray to cool and firm up.

15 macaroons

Wheatless, dairyless. Very pretty. A big hit with the recipe tasters!

1 cup raw grated carrot
1/8 cup water
3/8 cup honey
3/8 cup safflower or mild oil*
3/4 tsp. almond extract
1 tsp. or more grated lemon rind

Mix together the wet ingredients.

1 1/2 cups shredded coconut
3/8 cup soy flour
1 tsp. arrowroot

Mix together the dry ingredients, then add to the wet. The mixture should stay firm. Add more coconut if necessary. Scoop or spoon out small mounds onto oiled cookie sheet.
Bake at 350° for 30 minutes, until lightly golden-browned on top.

* Rising Star used coconut oil. The recipe would probably be fine with less oil altogether—experiment to your taste.

Papaya Squares

20 × 2" squares

A Canadian baker's fantasy! Outrageously rich and sweet.

1¼ cups dried papaya chunks
1 or more cups water

Preheat oven to 350°. Put papaya and enough water to cover in a pan or double boiler and cook slowly until papaya is tender (15-30 minutes.)

Shortbread crust:
¾ cup butter
⅜ cup honey
⅜ cup wheatgerm
1½ cups w/w pastry flour

Cream butter and honey and mix in wheatgerm and flour. Spread in pan and bake for 5 minutes at 350°. Use an 8" × 10" pan or 10" round pan.

Topping:
3 eggs
1 cup honey
¾ tsp. baking powder
⅜ cup w/w pastry flour
¾ tsp. vanilla
¾ cup chopped cashews

Beat eggs and whisk in remaining ingredients. Stir in the papaya and pour over the baked crust. Bake at 350° until firm and browned on top - about 40 minutes.

Walnut Shortbread Cookies

18 generous cookies

Easy. Luscious. Impressive.

½ lb. butter
½ cup warm or melted honey
2½ cups whole wheat pastry flour
½ tsp. vanilla
1 cup finely chopped walnuts

Preheat oven to 350°. Cream the butter, add the runny honey and vanilla and cream well. Blend in the flour and walnuts. Scoop or spoon onto greased cookie sheet and press down with wetted fingers, fork or cookie press (you can vary the cookie size as you wish). Bake at 350° for 15 minutes or until lightly golden brown around the edges and on top.

Lemon Coconut Pie

1 8"-9" pie.

Dairyless, eggless. Unusual and interesting!

1 baked pie crust (see recipes in section on pies)

½ Tbl. agar-agar flakes
½ cup boiling water

Boil together for one minute.

3 cups water (or part pineapple juice)
1 cup shredded coconut
6 Tbl arrowroot
3 Tbl lemon rind
⅔ cup cashew butter (or almond butter)
¾ cup honey

Blend till smooth with first mixture.
Heat 'til very thick, stirring constantly.

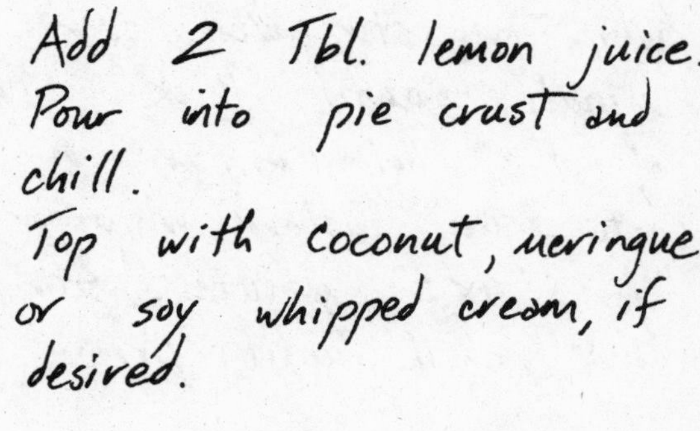
Add 2 Tbl. lemon juice.
Pour into pie crust and chill.
Top with coconut, meringue or soy whipped cream, if desired.

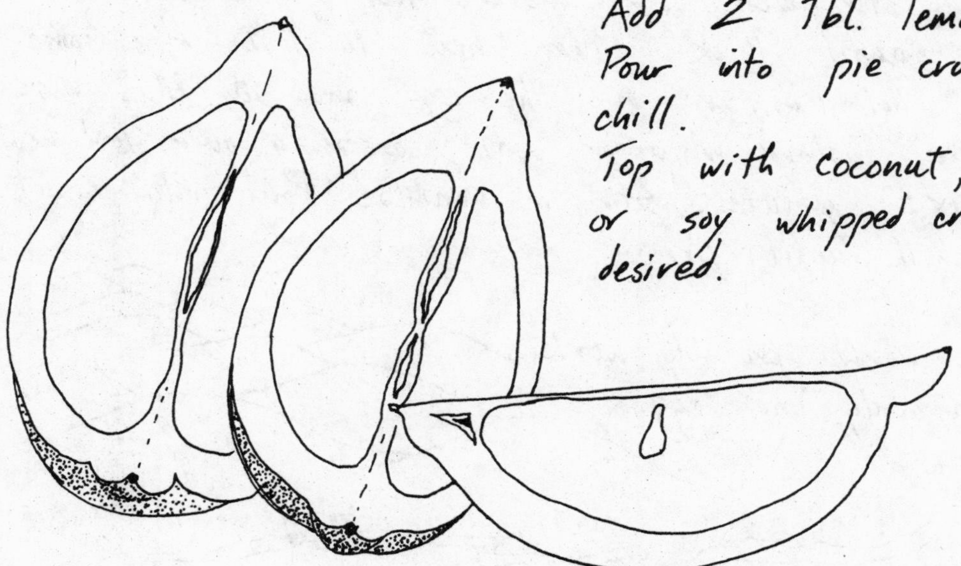

Carob Cream Pie

1-9" pie

Rich. Chocolatey.

1 baked pie crust (see recipes in section on pies)

3 cups milk
1/4 cup carob powder
1/2 cup honey
6 Tbl. arrowroot
5 Tbl. whole wheat flour
2 eggs, beaten *
1 Tbl. vanilla

Scald 2 1/2 cups milk. Blend carob, honey, arrowroot and flour with remaining milk. Stir into scalding milk and whip or stir well over medium heat for about 8 minutes until thick. Turn heat to low. Mix some of the hot mixture into the eggs and add this back into the custard. Whip or stir constantly over low heat for 4-5 minutes. Stir in vanilla. Pour into crust and chill until firm.

* this would probably work with only one egg.

Banana Cream Pie

1-9" pie

"Very good." "Smells and tastes great."

1 baked pie crust (see recipes in section on pies)

- 3½ cups milk
- ¾ cup pureéd banana
- ½ cup honey
- 6 Tbl. arrowroot
- ⅓ cup whole wheat flour
- 2 eggs, beaten
- 1 Tbl. vanilla

Scald 3 cups milk. Blend banana, honey, arrowroot and flour with rest of milk. Stir into scalding milk and follow remaining instructions as for carob cream pie.

Pumpkin Pie

1-9" pie

Dairyless, eggless. Soft and creamy filling with a nice flavor.

1 unbaked pie crust
(see recipes in section on pies)
3¼ cups mashed pumpkin or winter squash
1½ cups thick soy milk or nut milk*
¼ cup arrowroot
¼ cup cashew or almond butter
½ cup honey
1½ Tbl. molasses
1 Tbl. vanilla
1 Tbl. cinnamon

Blend all ingredients together until smooth. Pour into crust and bake at 350° for 30-40 minutes until lightly firmed and brown on top.

* Make nut milk by soaking nuts in water, preferably overnight then blending with water as needed until smooth and creamy. Strain if desired. Cashews or almonds work especially well; cashews need not be soaked.

Suggested variations: 1) add lemon and/or orange rind to filling
2) omit nut butter and use 2 Tbl. ground pumpkin seeds

At the Slice-of-Life Bakery—Cambridge, Ma.

Loaves of freshly-baked bread
Sit in the window of the bakeshop
In the mid-afternoon sun,
Round and content like cows
In the meadow of their own existence,
Its raisins like boulders and
Its warm smell rising like the soul from the body
In which I indulge.
But the bread pays no attention to me:
Immersed in being merely bread;
It loves the baker who created it,
Rises to meet him on his terms.
Ah, but bread does not live
By man alone.
Instead it sits still with itself,
While I am somewhere else, beside myself
Entangled foolishly with its misty vapors,
Which in one moment are serious
And in the next completely ludicrous.
The loaves seem to know
What I have suspected all along.
I turn away for a moment dreaming
And then turn back, ready to join the flock
Of customers, and be on my way.
I imagine that the loaves have winked.

One loaf follows me home in a brown paper bag
Like a dog following a stranger trustfully,
Taken with his smell.
Somewhere between this moist vapor
And the human smell of my work-a-day sweat,
We meet, this loaf and I,
Balanced in the bread-and-butter
Of the simple, the good life.

Ed Cates

Christmas Stollen

2 12" braided loaves

1½	cups	warm water	Dissolve honey in warm water and add yeast.
⅓	cup	honey	
1	tbl.	yeast	
1	lge.	egg	When yeast is bubbling, mix in egg, butter, nutmeg, salt, and lemon juice.
3	tbl.	melted butter	
½	tsp.	nutmeg	
1	tsp.	salt	
4	tsp.	lemon juice	
5½-6	cups	whole wheat flour (hard)	Knead in flour, saving ½ cup to add if needed for smooth and elastic consistency.
½	tsp.	orange rind	Knead for 5 mins., then add remaining ingredients and finish kneading. Let rise in warm place till doubled (about 1 hour).
½	tsp.	lemon rind	
⅓	cup	walnuts	
⅓	cup	dates	
⅓	cup	raisins	

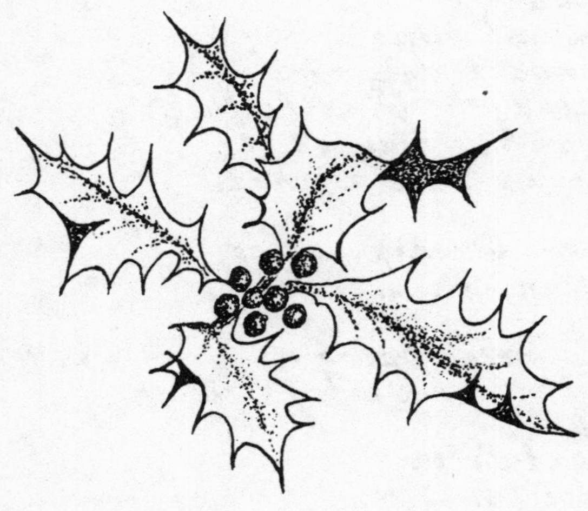

Punch down and split into 2 loaves. Divide each loaf into 3 equal ropes (about 18" long) and braid. (See section on HOW TO BAKE).

Let braided loaves rise till doubled. Bake at 350° till done (about 45 minutes).

Anadama Bread

"Very tasty" 2 1½ lb. loaves

2	cups	warm water
⅓	cup	molasses
1	tbl	yeast
4	cups	w/w flour (hard)
⅓	cup	soy flour
⅔	cup	cornmeal
1½	tbls	corn oil
1	tsp	salt

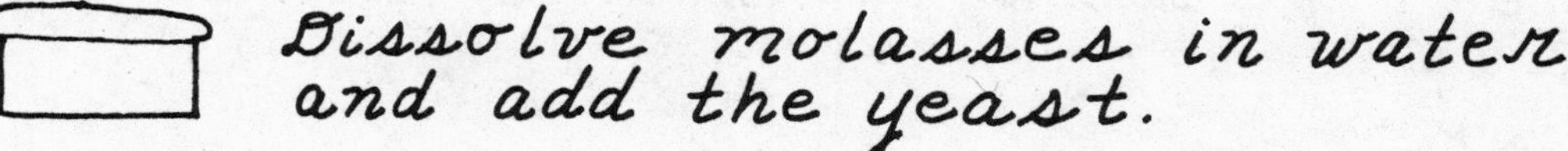

Dissolve molasses in water and add the yeast.

When yeast is bubbling, mix in the remaining ingredients. Knead well.

Cover dough and let rise in a warm place till doubled.

Shape into loaves and let rise again in the pans. Bake at 350° for 45-50 minutes.

You may increase the amounts of cornmeal and soy flour (reducing the w/w somewhat) for a richer, denser loaf.

Cranberry Muffins

18 small muffins

Dry

2 cups w/w flour
½ cup non-instant dry milk
1 tsp. baking powder
1 tsp. baking soda
} mix together well.

Wet

¾ cup honey
⅜ cup oil
1¼ tbl. lemon juice
¾ tbl. lemon peel
1 beaten egg
} Combine thoroughly.

6 ozs. cooked cranberries (boil 5 minutes)

Pour wet ingredients into the dry and fold gently.

Then stir in the cranberries.

Fill oiled muffin tins about ⅔ full.

Bake at 350°— about 15 minutes.

Festive appearance

. . . . .

Pleasingly tart flavor

. . . . .

Not overly sweet

. . . . .

Can be baked as a loaf

Spicy Apple Muffins

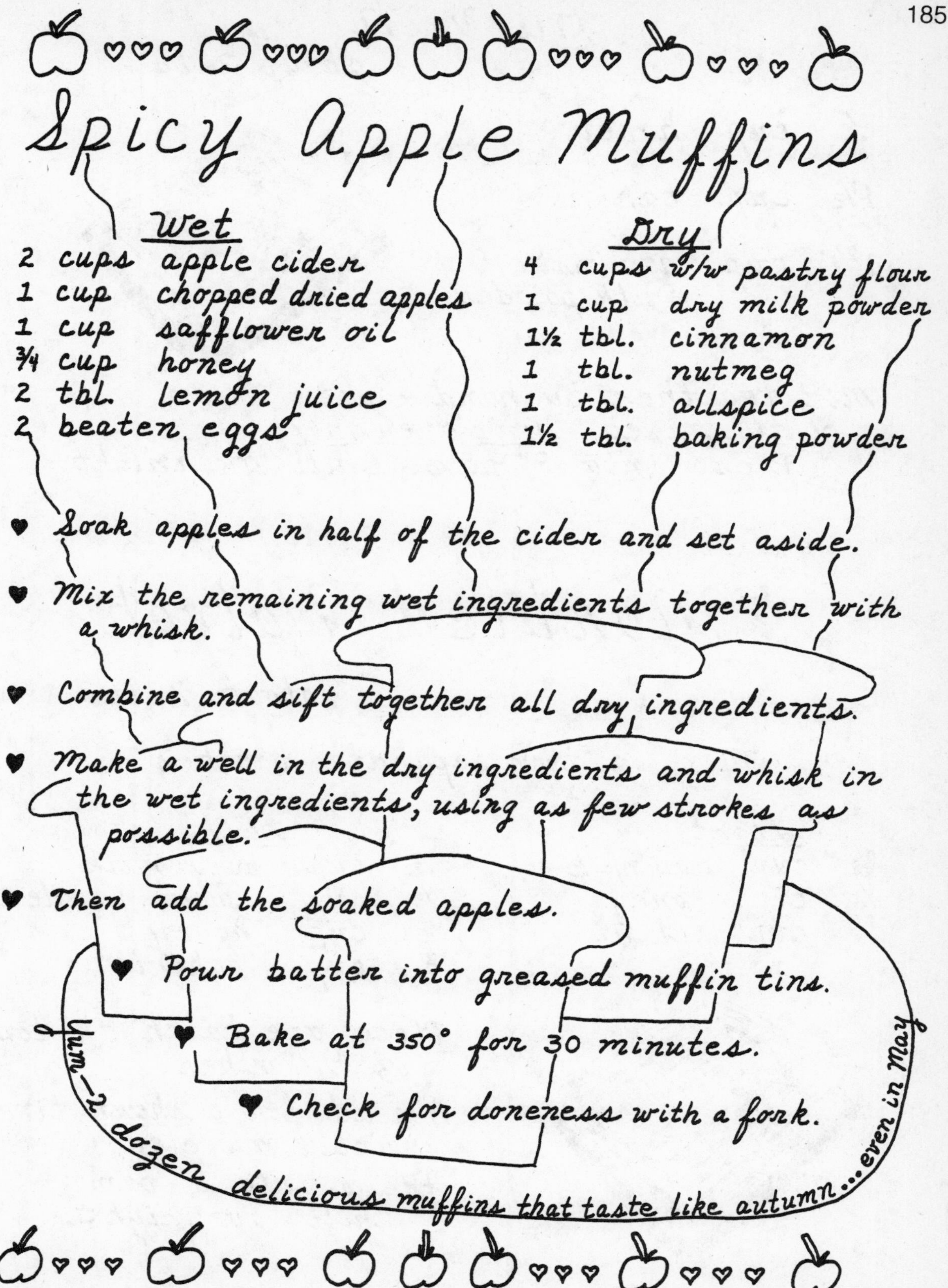

Wet

2 cups apple cider
1 cup chopped dried apples
1 cup safflower oil
3/4 cup honey
2 tbl. lemon juice
2 beaten eggs

Dry

4 cups w/w pastry flour
1 cup dry milk powder
1½ tbl. cinnamon
1 tbl. nutmeg
1 tbl. allspice
1½ tbl. baking powder

- Soak apples in half of the cider and set aside.
- Mix the remaining wet ingredients together with a whisk.
- Combine and sift together all dry ingredients.
- Make a well in the dry ingredients and whisk in the wet ingredients, using as few strokes as possible.
- Then add the soaked apples.
- Pour batter into greased muffin tins.
- Bake at 350° for 30 minutes.
- Check for doneness with a fork.

Yum—2 dozen delicious muffins that taste like autumn... even in May

Halvah

about 2 lbs.

2/3 cup honey

1½ cup tahini

1⅔ cup non-instant milk powder

Mix together by hand – just until mixed. Don't over-mix! Press into 8" pan. Chill overnight.

Marbled Halvah

about 2 lbs.

Mix in two separate batches.

Light

- 7/8 cup dry milk
- 1/3 cup honey
- 3/4 cup tahini

Dark

- 1/2 cup dry milk
- 1/3 cup carob powder
- 1/3 cup honey
- 3/4 cup tahini

Place one batch on top of the other.

Knead for a short time until marbled.

Press into 8" pan. Chill overnight.

small planet bakery

TUCSON, ARIZONA

SMALL PLANET BAKERY IS A COLLECTIVE CONSISTING OF 3 WOMEN AND 4 MEN. WE USE ORGANIC WHOLE WHEAT FLOUR IN OUR BREADS WHICH WE BAKE THREE TIMES PER WEEK.

WE STRIVE TO KEEP OUR PRICES DOWN WHILE AT THE SAME TIME PAYING OUR COLLECTIVE DECENT WAGES. IT'S A TOUGH BATTLE, BUT WE STILL SELL OUR 1½ LB. LOAVES OF WHOLE WHEAT BREAD FOR UNDER ONE DOLLAR. (80¢ WHOLESALE, 1981)

WE BEGAN IN 1974, AND HOPE TO CONTINUE SERVING THE PUBLIC NATURAL FOODS SUCH AS GRANOLAS AND WHOLE GRAIN BREADS.

apple bread

2 x 1½# LOAVES

1 TBL. YEAST
1½ CUPS LUKEWARM WATER
6 CUPS HARD WW FLOUR
¼ CUP HONEY
2 TBL. OIL
1 TSP. SALT

¾ CUP APPLE JUICE
1 MED. APPLE- CHOPPED
3 TBL. SUNFLOWER SEEDS
2 TSP. CINNAMON
SCANT ½ TSP. NUTMEG
(FRESHLY GROUND IS NICEST)

ADD YEAST TO WATER, STIR LIGHTLY. ADD ABOUT 1½ CUPS FLOUR AND HONEY (ENOUGH FLOUR TO MAKE PANCAKE BATTER).

LET STAND FOR ABOUT ½ HOUR.

MIX REMAINING FLOUR, NUTMEG, CINNAMON AND SALT, SET ASIDE. MIX HONEY, APPLE JUICE, CHOPPED APPLE, SUNFLOWER SEEDS, AND 1 TBL. OIL.

ADD ENOUGH FLOUR MIXTURE TO YEAST BATTER, UNTIL DOUGH PULLS AWAY FROM SIDES OF THE BOWL, ADD APPLE MIXTURE TO DOUGH.

MIX FOR A FEW MINUTES AND THEN ADD REST OF FLOUR MIXTURE. WHEN DOUGH COMES TOGETHER ADD REMAINING TBL. OF OIL.

KNEAD UNTIL SMOOTH AND ELASTIC.

ALLOW TO RISE IN COVERED OILED BOWL 40 MIN. - 1 HOUR UNTIL DOUBLED IN SIZE. SHAPE INTO LOAVES AND PUT IN 2 OILED LOAF PANS. LET RISE AGAIN. BAKE AT 350° FOR 40 MIN.

orange-date surprise bread

2 × 1½ # LOAVES

SWEET AND FRUITY- SPECKLED WITH POPPY SEEDS- MOST APPEALING!

2½ CUPS WARM WATER
1 TBL. YEAST
6 TBL. HONEY
5½–6 CUPS HARD WW FLOUR
2 TBL. OIL
1½ TBL. POPPYSEEDS
3 TBL. OATS
1 TSP. SALT
JUICE OF 1 ORANGE
1 TBL. ORANGE RIND
½ CUP CHOPPED DATES

MIX TOGETHER WATER, YEAST, HONEY AND 2 CUPS FLOUR, LET THIS SPONGE SIT UNTIL BUBBLY, ABOUT 30 MINUTES.

MIX IN REMAINING INGREDIENTS AND KNEAD WELL ADDING FLOUR, AS NEEDED, TO MAKE SOFT SPONGY DOUGH.

LET DOUGH RISE IN COVERED OILED BOWL UNTIL DOUBLE IN SIZE, ABOUT 30 MINUTES.

SHAPE INTO TWO LOAVES AND LET RISE AGAIN IN OILED PANS.

BAKE AT 400° FOR ABOUT 35 MINUTES.

sunseed bread

2 × 1½# LOAVES

¼ CUP HONEY
⅛ CUP OIL
2 CUPS WARM WATER
1 TBL. YEAST
5 CUPS HARD WW FLOUR
½ CUP SUNFLOWER SEEDS
½ TBL. SALT

MAKE A SPONGE FROM THE HONEY, OIL, WATER, YEAST & 2 CUPS FLOUR, MIXING IT TOGETHER UNTIL IT RESEMBLES PANCAKE BATTER.

LET STAND FOR 30 MINUTES.

ADD REMAINING FLOUR, (RESERVE SOME TO MIX IN AS YOU'RE KNEADING) SALT AND SUNNIES. STIR UNTIL WELL MIXED, THEN TURN OUT AND KNEAD UNTIL DOUGH IS SPRINGY TO TOUCH, ABOUT 10 MINUTES.

PLACE IN OILED BOWL, COVER, AND LET RISE. SHAPE AND LET RISE AGAIN FOR ABOUT 45 MIN. UNTIL LOAVES' TOPS HAVE RISEN ABOVE THE EDGES OF THE PANS.

DURING THE LAST OF THE RISING TIME, PREHEAT OVEN TO 400°. PLACE LOAVES IN OVEN AND IMMEDIATELY TURN TO 350°. BAKE FOR 50 MINUTES, UNTIL THUMPED BOTTOM SOUNDS HOLLOW.

granola

EITHER RECIPE YIELDS 2 LBS.

TRY USING THICK CUT OATS IF YOU CAN GET THEM!

CASHEW DATE

5½ CUPS OATS
⅓ CUP WHEAT GERM
⅓ CUP SAFFLOWER OIL
⅓ CUP HONEY
3 TBL. SESAME SEEDS
1 CUP CASHEWS
½ TSP. VANILLA
1 CUP DATE PIECES *

COCONUT ALMOND

5½ CUPS OATS
⅓ CUP WHEAT GERM
⅓ CUP SAFFLOWER OIL
⅓ CUP HONEY
2½ TBL. SESAME SEEDS
⅓ CUP CHOPPED ALMONDS
⅓ CUP SUNFLOWER SEEDS
½ CUP COCONUT Δ
½ TSP. ALMOND EXTRACT

FOR BOTH RECIPES, BEGIN BY MIXING OATS, WHEAT GERM AND SESAME SEEDS. ADD CASHEWS, OR ALMONDS, SUNFLOWER SEEDS AND POSSIBLY THE COCONUT. IN ANOTHER BOWL, MIX THE OIL, HONEY AND WHICHEVER EXTRACT YOU'RE USING TOGETHER, THEN POUR THE LIQUIDS INTO THE OTHER BOWL. MIX THEM ALL TOGETHER, THEN SPREAD THE GRANOLA OUT ON A COOKIE SHEET IN A LAYER THAT IS ABOUT AN INCH THICK. BAKE AT 325° FOR 25-30 MIN.

* IF YOU'RE MAKING THE CASHEW DATE GRANOLA, WAIT TO ADD THE DATES UNTIL AFTER THE GRANOLA HAS BAKED AND COOLED.

Δ IF YOU'RE MAKING THE COCONUT ALMOND, YOU CAN ADD THE COCONUT BEFORE OR AFTER YOU BAKE THE GRANOLA, DEPENDING ON WHETHER OR NOT YOU LIKE IT TOASTED.

Eugene, Oregon.

Solstice Bakery is a worker-owned, worker-operated business in Eugene, Oregon. We make whole grain breads, pastries and granolas, using _only_ whole grains without any artificial additives or preservatives. All our products are both eggless and dairyless and use organically grown ingredients whenever possible.

We make 8 types of yeast bread, 3 types of essene bread, and two kinds of granola.

Sprouted Wheat Bread
A MAGICAL BREAD YOU GROW YOURSELF!

HARD Spring Wheat berries; dried fruits, nuts, seeds.*

- Select hard spring wheat berries for sprouting. The softer strains will not make a firm loaf. Soak berries overnight (12 HRS.), drain the next morning. Continue as you would sprouting any seed: rinse and drain twice daily.
- The sprouts are ready for bread when the white sprout hairs (usually there are two) are 1½ – 2 times the length of the berry. TASTE it. Is it sweet?
- The sprouting process usually takes about 3-4 days, but changes a lot according to season, temperature, humidity, moon phase, etc.. The sprout length is the best guide and the moment of ripeness passes quickly. Experience is the surest guide to what's best in your area.

> SPROUTED berry: If the hairs are too long, there is too much moisture and the bread WILL NOT BAKE UP. If they are too short, the natural sweetness will not yet have developed.

- Skip the last rinse before baking to dry the berries out – DO NOT RINSE them in the evening before the morning you want to bake them.
- When ready to bake, simply grind the sprouted berries in a "meat grinder" getting a dough that almost looks like hamburger. *fruits, nuts, seeds, may be added to taste.
- Divide dough into approximately 1 lb. balls and shape by hand into ROUND, somewhat flat loaves. A bowl of water to lightly moisten hands aids in handling. Place on oiled sheet.
- That's it. No kneading or rising required. Bake in a 250° oven for 2½ hrs., until the loaves are firm. Keep extra loaves in a refrigerator. ENJOY!

Cinnamon Date Bread

2 loaves

1 Tbl. yeast
2 cups water
4 Tbl. malt
1 Tbl. cinnamon
3 Tbl. honey
1 tsp. salt
4 Tbl. oil
4-6 cups hard w.w. flour
1 cup date pieces.

Dissolve yeast in water, then add malt, cinnamon and honey to make a sponge. (You can also add a little flour to help the yeast in its activating process.) Let it sit for 20 minutes.

Add the salt and oil and stir briskly making sure all the ingredients thus far are thoroughly mixed. Slowly start adding flour until the bread can be kneaded in your hands. (depending on your flour, it will probably take 4-6 cups). Knead the dough well, about 10 minutes, then add the dates. Knead 5 minutes more then shape into a blob and let rise, covered, in an oiled bowl until double in size. Punch dough down, shape into loaves and let it rise a second time in the pans. When it has risen above the lip of the pan put it in the oven (preheated at 350°) for about 45 minutes. (The dough will not pop up much in the oven - it will look almost as it does when first put in).

Test it - put on a rack to cool and enjoy it warm.

Coco Short Bread

2 dozen 2½" squares

A fairly simple recipe that results in a luscious light treat, almost like French pastry.

1 lb. soy margarine
1½ cups honey
1 tsp. almond extract
1 tsp. vanilla
4 cups w.w. pastry flour
4 cups coconut (shredded)
4 cups oats

Cream margarine and honey. Mix in the extracts. Combine flour, coconut and oats. Add to creamed mixture. Press evenly into 8½" x 24" pan. Poke fork holes every 2 inches or so. (Maybe make a nice pattern.)
Bake at 350° for 35 minutes. Cut into squares while still warm.

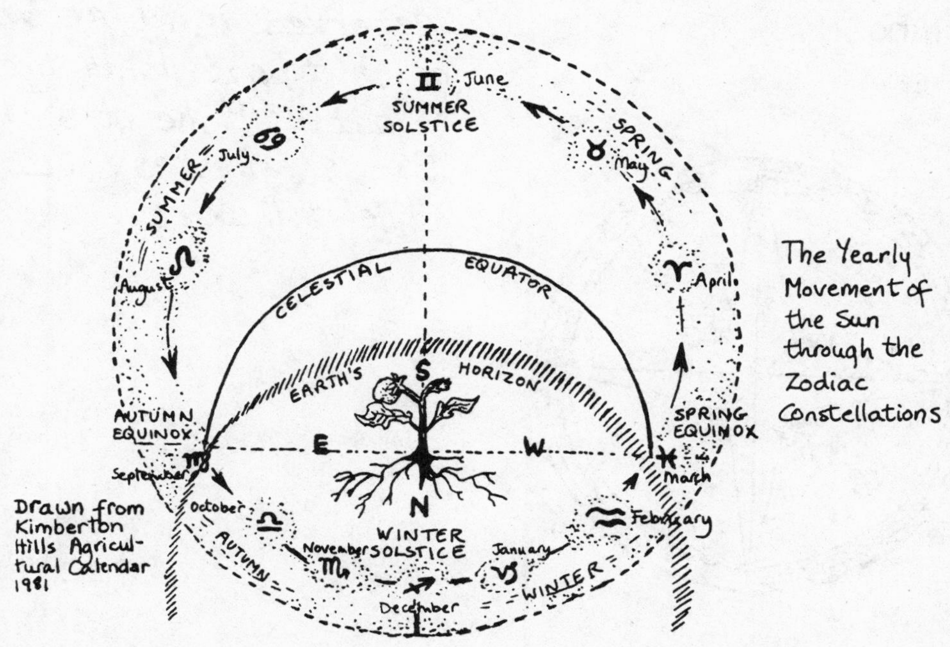

Drawn from Kimberton Hills Agricultural Calendar 1981

The Yearly Movement of the Sun through the Zodiac Constellations

DATE BARS

8" x 12" or 7" x 11" pan

2 1/4 cups date pieces

Soak the date pieces in enough hot water to not quite cover them, stir, let sit for 2-3 hours.

1/2 cup safflower oil
3/8 cup honey
1/6 cup malt
2 cups oat flour
1/3 cup soy flour
2 1/2 cups rolled oats

Mix oil, honey and malt together.
Combine flours and add to wets. Add the oats. Mix them in with your hands.
Pat/press thinly onto bottom of oiled 8"x12" or 7"x11" pan – something close to that. (Save some to sprinkle on top.)
Spread date filling evenly on crust. Crumble reserved mixture on top of that; pat lightly to even it out. Bake at 350° for 35-45 minutes. Cut while still warm.

Optional:
add walnuts to crust
add apples, raisins, or cinnamon to filling.

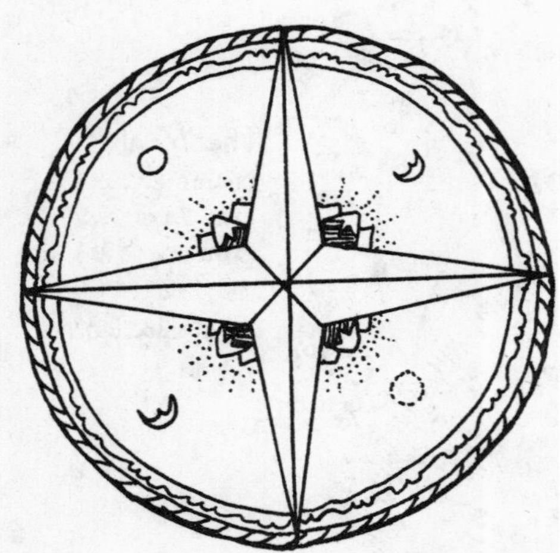

Hello.

We are a collective of ± 15 people who run a natural foods bakery and granary in Ithaca, N.Y.

Somadhara was originally started by a group of Ananda Margas as a community bakery and tearoom. Eight years and many changes later, we've grown into what we are today — a center for natural, unadulterated, healthy foods and wares. In addition to baking our own whole grain and honey breads and pastries we operate a retail store where we sell bulk foods, deli items (tabouli, tofu salad, hummus ect.), housewares, books, vitamins, produce, herbs and a variety of packaged goods ~ all with peace and the planet in mind ....

Coconut Macaroons

24 macaroons

These look and taste good.

1/4 cup butter
1/2 cup honey
1 egg
2 cups coconut
1 cup w.w. pastry flour

Cream the butter
add honey & mix well.
beat in 1 egg
add coconut & flour; mix well.

Drop by tablespoons onto greased cookie sheet & bake at 350° for 12 minutes or until golden brown on bottoms.

variations:

add 1-2 tsp. cinnamon
add 1-2 Tbl. carob powder
add 1 tsp. almond extract

Best Butter Batter

We call this best because this is the kind of recipe that can be as changeable as you feel. Follow the basic recipe and drop by tablespoons onto a greased cookie sheet and it's the beginning of a cookie.

- press the cookie down & sprinkle nuts on top for a butternut cookie.
- press a hole in the top of the cookie and fill with apple butter for an apple drop cookie.
- etc.

Best Butter Cookie Batter

½ cup butter
2 Tbl. safflower oil
¼ cup honey
2 cups w.w. pastry flour
½ tsp. vanilla
½ tsp. baking powder (optional)

Cream butter
add oil, honey & vanilla
mix in flour & baking powder

* For a **Molasses butter cookie** substitute either blackstrap or unsulphured molasses for honey.

You could also add up to a ½ cup more flour to make a slightly stiffer dough to be used as a pie crust of sorts. Just press the dough into a floured pan (using a floured rolling pin or your imagination), to a crust depth of ⅛" or less. Use any left over goo to be used as a topping for whatever it is you're making. Apple pie, fig bars etc..

For Apricot Almond Bars: 350°, for 35 min.

Press this dough into a 10" circular pan or large brownie pan. Precook crust for 10 minutes or until golden brown. Meanwhile make a mixture of apricots (cooked till soft or soaked overnight) and some almond extract if desired. Mix up; spread this mush on dough & sprinkle with chopped almonds. (and any left over dough if desired.)

Tahini-Raisin-Oat Cookies

35 small cookies

~no wheat~

1 cup tahini
3/4 cup honey
3/4 cup sunnies
2 1/4 cups rolled oats
1 cup raisins

Preheat the oven to 350°. Soak the raisins in hot water. Mix the tahini and honey together (over heat for easier mixing). Add sunnies and oats; mix. Drain and add the raisins, then mix-up the whole mess. Drop by tablespoonful onto greased cookie sheets and press the cookies down with a wet fork. Bake for 15-20 minutes or until the bottoms are light brown.

Butter Sesame Cookies

Pretty to look at, pretty quick to make; these cookies are very rich and delicate.

12 large flat cookies

1/4 lb. butter

1/2 cup honey

1 cup sesame seeds

7/8 cup w. w. pastry flour

optional: some grated lemon or vanilla

Cream the butter. Add the honey and mix, then add the sesame seeds and the flour.

Bake at 350° until the edges are browned, and the middle is golden brown. Don't press these cookies down. Just drop them by teaspoonfuls and they'll spread themselves.

Carob Nut Fudge

8"x8" pan

VERY rich! Each piece is a whole, delicious dessert.

2/3 cup peanut butter
2/3 cup honey
2/3 cup carob powder
1/3 cup cashews or walnuts
2/3 cup sunnies
1/3 cup sesame seeds
1/3 cup raisins, soaked
1/3 cup coconut

Mix peanut butter and honey together. (it's easier if you heat them). Stir in the carob powder, then add the rest of the ingredients. Mix them all up, and then press the mixture into an oiled 8"x 8" pan. Cut into small pieces. The fudge is good with or without the raisins.

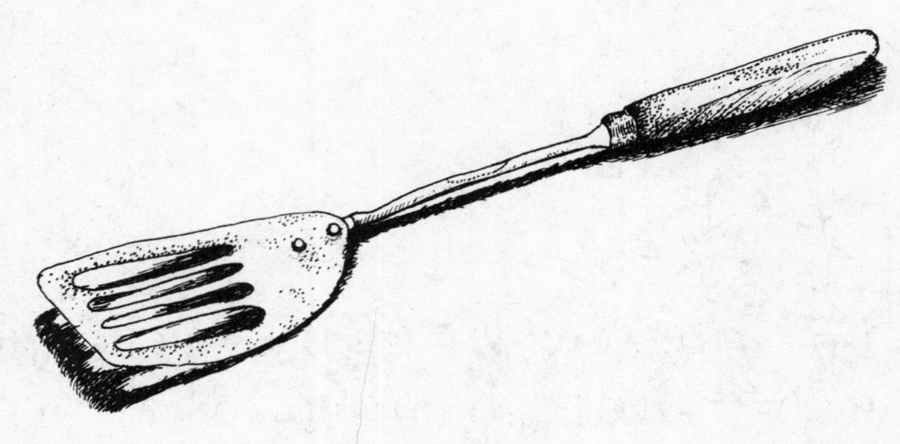

SUMMERCORN

FAYETTEVILLE ARKANSAS

Summercorn Bakery and Soyfoods is a worker-owned, collectively managed state non-profit corporation started in 1974. We have a small retail trade and also distribute wholesale to stores, coops and buying clubs in a seven state region. Stone-grinding our flour fresh before each bake, with organically grown grain from neighboring Kansas, makes for some wonderful aromas coming out of our bakery. We buy direct from local growers whenever possible. Our focus is producing for and educating the public about whole grains and the urgency of making use of plant sources of protein.

Old World Rye Bread

3~1 lb. loaves

"This recipe came to us from a Scandinavian lady who grew up in a bakery family. The only changes we made are the substitution of carob for roasted, ground coffee beans and an addition of slippery elm & Kelp powder."

"Sponge Ingredients"

3 cups water - 1/4 cup unsulphured molasses
2 tbl. yeast - 3 1/2 cups hard whole wheat flour

4 tsp corn or safflower oil - 2 tsp Kelp powder
1 tsp salt - 2 tsp slippery elm powder
1/4 cup dark roast carob powder - 1 1/2 tbl. caraway seed
3 cups rye flour - 2 cups (approx.) hard whole wheat flour

Develop sponge, allow to rise 20 minutes & add remaining ingredients. Knead well. Allow to rise once, divide into 3 rounds and allow to rise again for 20 minutes before placing in preheated 350° oven for 1 hour.

"A dense, winter bread to go with a bowl of soup."
Very rich, flavorful & moist with a thick, chewy crust.

Cinnamon Currant Bread

2-1½ lb loaves

We bake this bread in a two piece cylindrical strap bread pan. The round slices with a swirling of cinnamon & honey in the currant whole wheat bread dough makes great morning toast. It works fine in regular pans too. Make a basic whole wheat bread dough, such as the one from Nature's Bakery, Madison.

To 3 LB. whole wheat bread dough add: 1 cup currants (or you can substitute raisins) that have been soaked in 3 TBL. boiling water to soften, and 3 TBL. whole wheat flour to balance this added moisture from adding the soaked currants. Allow to rise once, punch down, rise again (this 2nd rising may be omitted, but what's the hurry) and cut into 2 loaves, flatten this out into a rectangle and spread approx. 2½ TBL. of honey (or more) evenly over the flattened dough leaving one edge without honey. Shake cinnamon generously over this same area leaving one edge clean. This is our future "seam."

honey & cinnamon
no honey & cinnamon

Turn ½" edge on either side in to enclose honey & cinnamon. Roll up leaving unhoneyed edge to seal the outside edge. Pinch all seams well to stop honey oozing out while baking. Bake for 50 minutes at 350° F.

start rolling this end
unhoneyed edge
fold in

Ozark Barley Bread

2 - 1½ lb loaves

(unleavened) This is a favorite in Fayetteville. The recipe is an adaptation from the Tassajara Bread Book, (The "Bible" of basic bread baking.)

2 cups roasted barley flour - 1 tbl. oil - 1 tsp. salt
3½ cups hard whole wheat flour - 1 tsp. kelp powder
½ cup cornmeal - 3 tbl. sesame seed
⅓ cup corn oil - 3 cups boiling water

Roast barley flour in 1 tbl corn oil, stir continually. Mix flours, meal, salt + kelp. Add oil and mix with hands, rub through well. Add boiling water, knead well. Allow to rest briefly covered with a damp towel before cutting + shaping into rounds. Cutting shallow slits (¼" deep) in tops will prevent cracking while in oven. Cover + proof 4-8 hours. Re-moisten if necessary during proofing. Bake at 350° for 2 hours.

Peanut Butter Cookies

45-2" cookies

2/3 cup oil - 1 2/3 cups peanut butter
1 3/4 cups honey - 2 tsp. vanilla
1 1/2 tsp. baking powder - 4 cups w.w. pastry flour

Blend wet ingredients. Add dry ingredients and mix well. Spoon onto oiled cookie sheet and press to 1/4" with a spatula. Make a crisscross design with a fork if desired. Bake at 350° for 10-12 minutes.

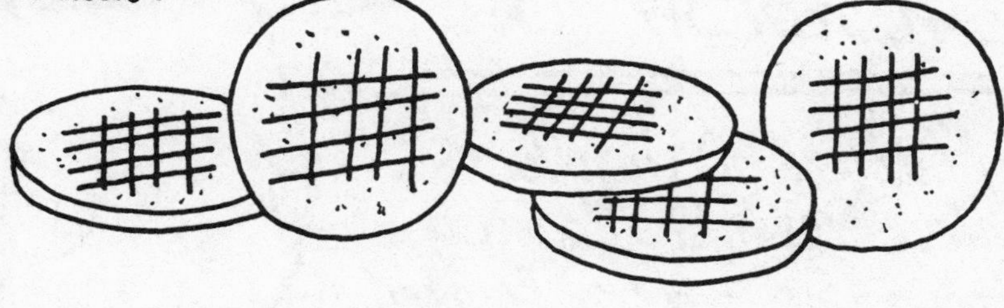

Carob Nut Brownies

9 brownies, - an 8"×8" pan or equivalent

1/2 cup safflower oil - 1 cup honey
1/4 cup egg replacer + 1/2 cup water (mix well)
1 1/2 tsp. vanilla
2 cups whole wheat pastry flour
2 tsp. baking powder - 1/2 cup carob powder
1/2 cup chopped nuts (save some to sprinkle on top)

Blend liquid ingredients well. Add dry ingredients and mix. Pour into a pan that has been oiled and floured. Press evenly into pan. Bake 25 minutes at 350° Allow to cool before cutting.

Egg Replacer
1 tbl. dry + 1-2 tbl. water = 1 egg
Mix together well:
2 parts arrowroot powder
1 part tapioca flour
1 part slippery elm powder

SUNFLOUR BAKERY

Bloomington. Ind.

One feature of Sunflour is its close ties with Bloomingfood Cooperative Grocery. Located in a small room in Bloomingfood's building, it is hard for Co-op shoppers to avoid smelling the bakery's presence. Sunflour first was established as a private business connected with the Earth Kitchen Restaurant. When the restaurant burned in 1977, the non-profit organization that runs Bloomingfoods bought the bakery and turned it into a worker's collective. Although there have been hard times, Sunflour has benefited from the strong support of the Co-op and both businesses look forward to expanding into new locations in the near future.

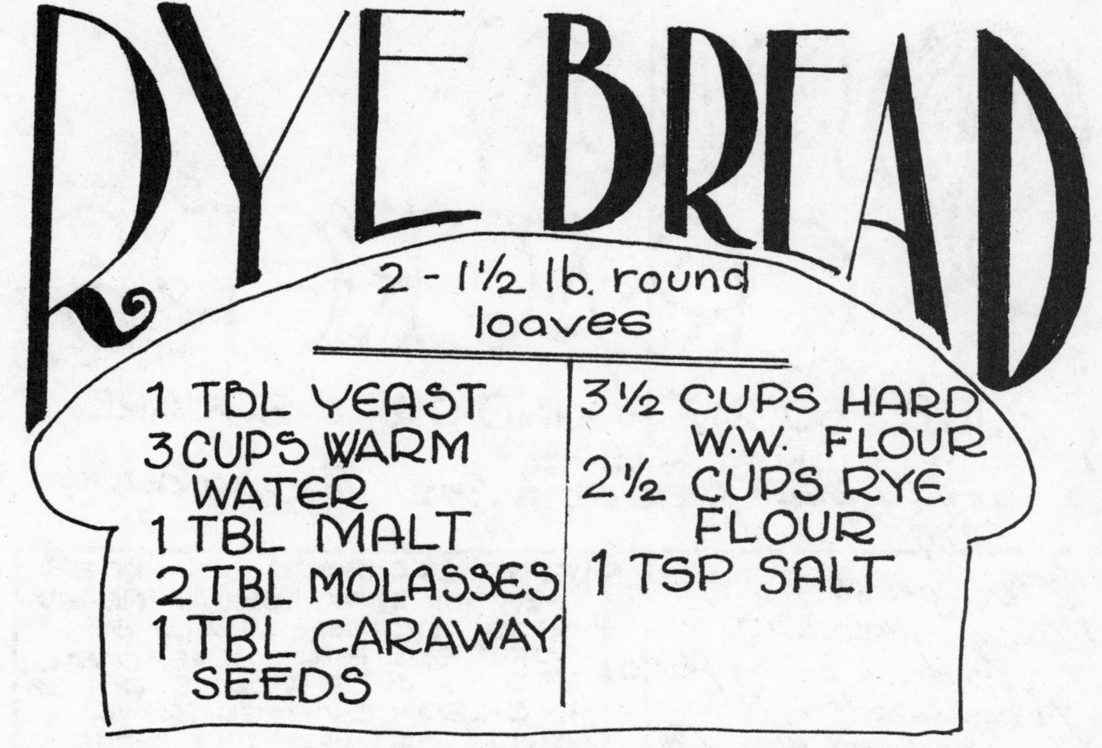

· LET YEAST DISSOLVE IN WATER FOR A FEW MINUTES. THEN MIX-IN MALT, MOLASSES AND SEEDS. STIR IN A CUP OF W.W. FLOUR (OR MORE) & LET SIT ABOUT 10 MINUTES. OR MIX IT ALL UP RIGHT AWAY AND PROCEED TO: STIR IN THE FLOURS, AND SALT, ADDING A LITTLE MORE FLOUR IF NECESSARY TO GET A LIGHT BUT NOT STICKY TEXTURE. KNEAD WELL, (10 MINUTES, OR MORE, IF YOU GET INTO IT!) SET DOUGH IN OILED BOWL AND COVER. LET IT RISE TIL PUFFED UP TO ABOUT DOUBLE IN SIZE. PUNCH DOWN, SHAPE INTO TWO ROUND LOAVES DIP BOTTOMS IN RYE FLOUR BEFORE PLACING ON BAKING SHEET. LET RISE AGAIN. YOU CAN SCORE A SHALLOW CROSS, VERY GENTLY ON THE TOPS BEFORE BAKING, AT 400° FOR 30-35 MINUTES.

ONION CRACKERS

YIELD: 80 2½" ROUND OR 2" SQUARE CRACKERS

pretty white flecked crackers with a nice oniony tang.

- ½ Tbl. yeast
- 1¼ cups warm water
- ¼ cup dried onion flakes
- 1½ cups oats
- 1½ cups hard w.w. flour
- ½ tsp salt (can be left out, or try kelp instead)

- LET YEAST DISSOLVE IN WATER THEN MIX IN REMAINING INGREDIENTS. DOUGH SHOULD BE SOFT BUT FIRM. KNEAD WELL, 5-10 MINUTES. PLACE DOUGH IN OILED, COVERED BOWL AND LET RISE TILL DOUBLED. PUNCH DOWN AND KNEAD BRIEFLY.

- TO MAKE ROUND CRACKERS _ ROLL OUT DOUGH ON FLOURED SURFACE TO ABOUT ⅛" THICK, CUT CRACKERS WITH COOKIE CUTTER OR DRINKING GLASS AND PLACE ON BAKING SHEET THAT'S BEEN OILED OR DUSTED WITH CORNMEAL.
- FOR SQUARE CRACKERS - ROLL OUT DOUGH DIRECTLY ONTO BAKING SHEET, CUT WITH A PASTRY WHEEL OR KNIFE, FOR SQUARE CRACKERS TO BE BROKEN APART AFTER BAKING & COOLING.
- BAKE AT 375° FOR 15-20 MINUTES UNTIL HARD BUT NOT OVER BROWN. THEY'LL "CRISP-UP" MORE AS THEY COOL.

* SHORTER BAKING & THICKER DOUGH = CHEWY CRACKERS
LONGER BAKING & THINNER DOUGH (1/16") = CRISPER CRACKERS

* YOU CAN LET THE CRACKERS RISE A LITTLE BEFORE BAKING, IF YOU WISH.

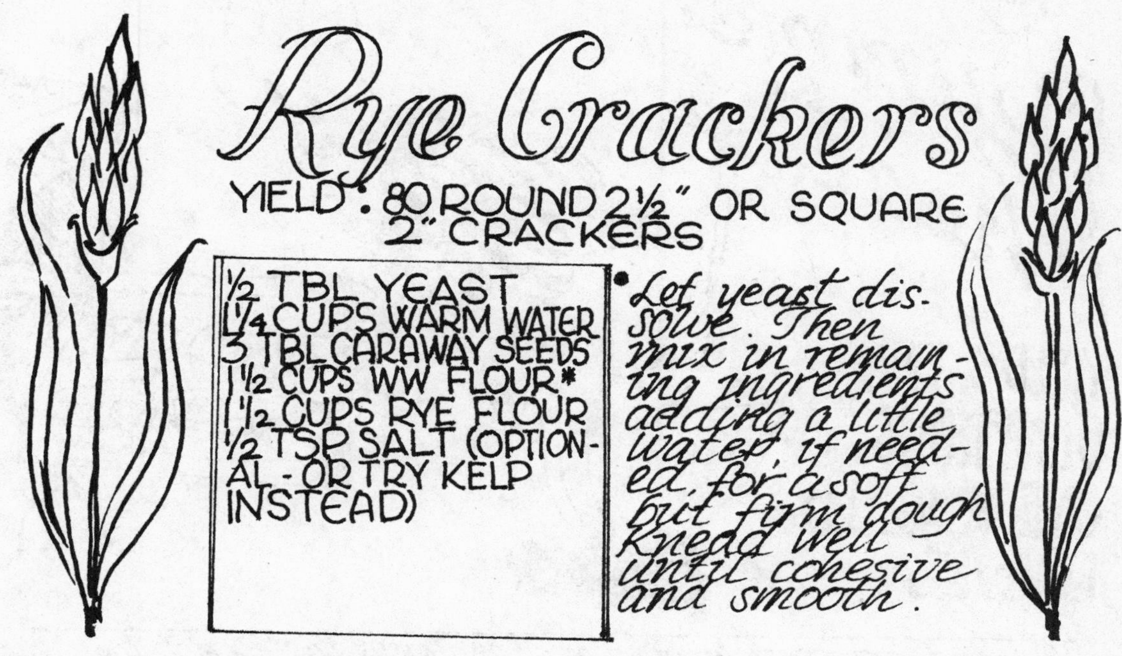

Rye Crackers

YIELD: 80 ROUND 2½" OR SQUARE 2" CRACKERS

½ TBL YEAST
1¼ CUPS WARM WATER
3 TBL CARAWAY SEEDS
1½ CUPS WW FLOUR*
1½ CUPS RYE FLOUR
½ TSP SALT (OPTIONAL - OR TRY KELP INSTEAD)

• Let yeast dissolve. Then mix in remaining ingredients adding a little water, if needed, for a soft but firm dough. Knead well until cohesive and smooth.

• Place dough in oiled, covered bowl and let rise til doubled. Punch down and knead briefly. Make round or square crackers as described for Onion Crackers on previous page.

Bake at 375° for 15-20 minutes until hard but not charred! They crisp up as they cool.

* SEE NOTES for Onion Crackers for varying cracker texture. When we tested rye crackers, <u>if left to sit for 15-20 minutes</u> before baking, the Round Crackers puffed up like little pita breads in the oven - fun.

* You can use w.w. pastry or hard w.w. flour in this recipe, or a blend. Apparently, pastry flour tends to make a crisper cracker.

Summer Wheat

YIELD: TWO GENEROUS ONE & 1/2 LB LOAVES

Nice and crunchy, with a rich molasses taste - not too much, though. (Reduce it if you prefer.)

1 TBL YEAST
2 1/2 C. WARM WATER
5 TBL MOLASSES
2 C. HARD WW FLOUR

Mix together, and let sponge sit until risen and bubbling.

3/4 C. CRACKED WHEAT OR BULGUR
1/2 C. SUNFLOWER SEEDS
3 1/2-4 C. HARD W.W. FLOUR
1 TSP. SALT

Add to sponge, mix well, adding flour to get soft but kneadable, consistency. Knead well until dough is elastic. Let rise in oiled, covered, bowl until doubled in size. Punch down and shape into two loaves. Let rise again in oiled pans. Bake at 350° for 45° minutes.

RAISIN BRAN BREAD

YIELD:
2~1½ LB LOAVES

A quick bread that is great warm, for breakfast. Can be made as muffins, too, of course.

- 3/4 cup-1 cup molasses
- 2 2/3 cups milk
- 1 1/2 Tbl vinegar
- 2 1/2 cups bran
- 3 1/4 cups w.w. flour
- 1 tsp baking soda
- 2/3 cup raisins

MIX WET INGREDIENTS; MIX DRY INGREDIENTS. COMBINE THEM, STIRRING TIL JUST MIXED IN. POUR BATTER INTO OILED PANS. BAKE RIGHT AWAY AT 350° FOR 50-60 MINUTES, UNTIL KNIFE INSERTED IN CENTER COMES OUT CLEAN.

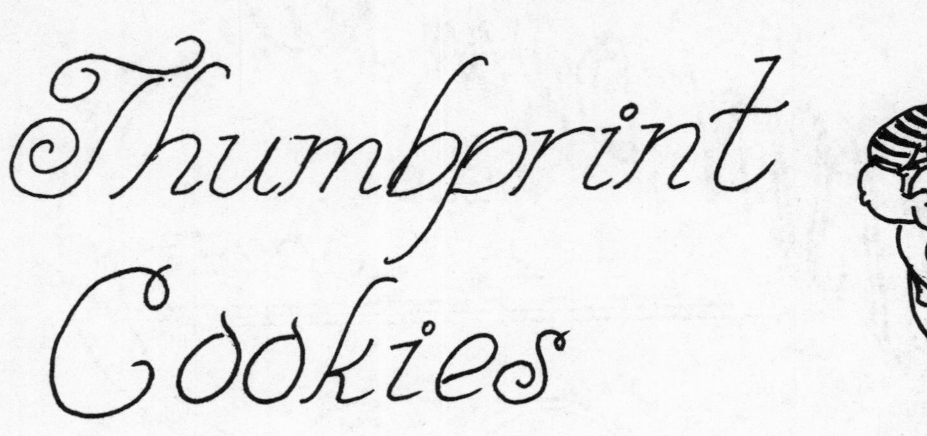

RICH LITTLE MOUTHFULS OF SHORTBREAD...
These would be nice to serve to friends.

3/4 cup (6 oz.) butter	1/8 tsp vanilla
1/2 cup honey	1 egg
1/8 tsp. almond extract	2 1/2 cups ww pastry flour.

- Cream butter, honey, extract and vanilla til smooth and light. Mix in the egg. Stir in the flour. Drop cookies onto oiled sheet. Press your thumb in the middle of the cookies.
- Try putting a walnut, or strawberry jam in the thumbprint.
- Bake at 350° for 10-15 minutes.

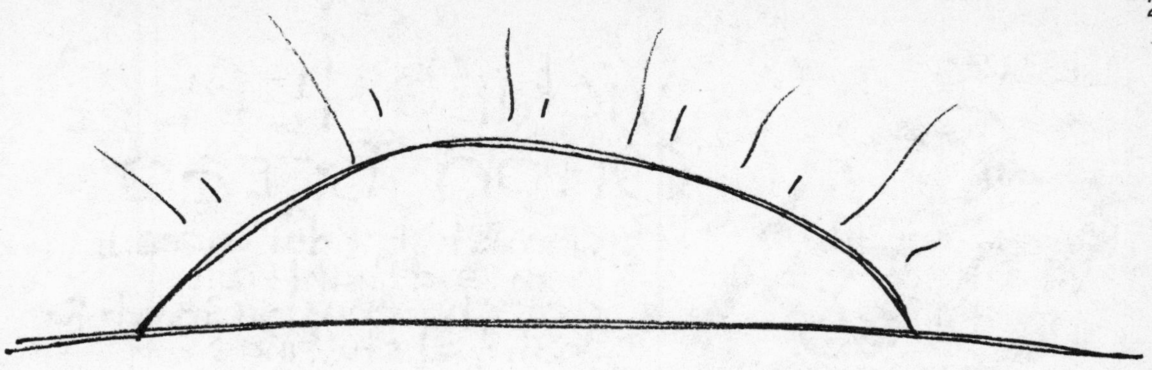

sunrise bakery

tallahassee, florida

sunrise bakery was the dream of a group of Tallahassee "coopers", who for a long time baked out of their own kitchens, providing great bread for the co-op community. This is the way many of our bakeries started off, working out of peoples' ovens at home.

The co-op in Tallahassee is a strong one and has produced a fine recipe book — "The Leon County Food Co-op Cookbook". Now it seems as if Sunrise Bakery as such may not come together, but we dont want you to miss their unusual + highly nutritious recipes. One note: for potato water recipe, see On The Rise Bakery

2 loaves

Vickie's Herb Onion Bread

a moist tender bread with a delightfully crunchy crust. Great for holiday stuffings

Sponge

1 tbl baking yeast
2 c. potato water
2 tbl honey
3 c. hard w.w. flour

Combine: all of the sponge ingredients and mix thoroughly. Let rise in covered bowl for 20. minutes

1/4 c. oil
2 tbl. lecithin (opt.)
1 med. onion
2 tbl nutritional yeast
1 tsp salt (opt.)
1/2 tbl. oregano
1 tbl basil
2 tsp thyme
1/2 c. soy flour
2-3 c. hard w.w. flour

Dice onion + sautee in 2 tbl oil until transparent. Then add sauteed onions + all remaining ingredients (except the w.w. flour) to the sponge, and mix well. Slowly add the w.w. flour as you go.

Knead thoroughly til elastic, then let rise in covered, oiled bowl til doubled. Punch down, shape two loaves, and place in oiled loaf pans. Let rise for 15-20 minutes in a warm place, then bake at 350° for 40-50 minutes

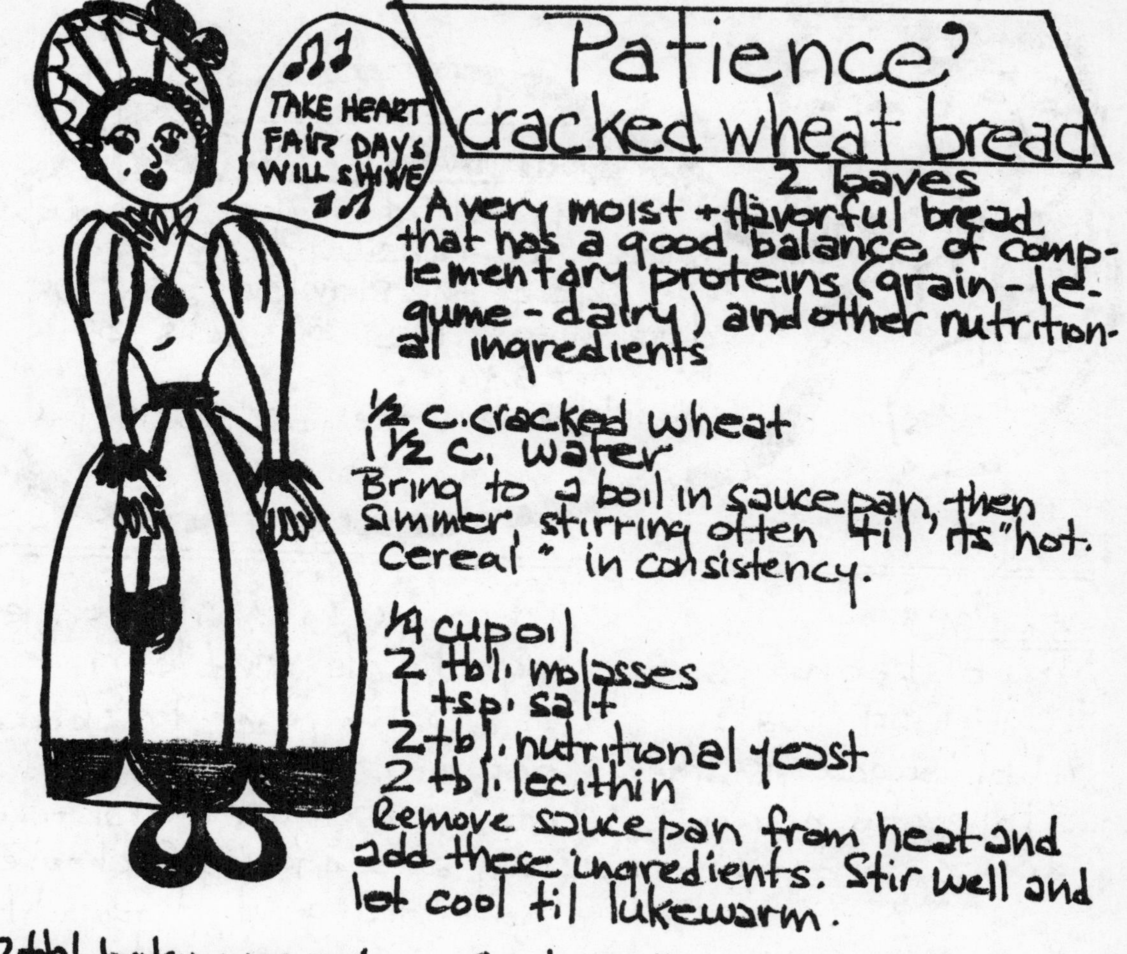

Patience' cracked wheat bread

2 loaves

A very moist + flavorful bread that has a good balance of complementary proteins (grain-legume-dairy) and other nutritional ingredients

½ c. cracked wheat
1½ c. water

Bring to a boil in sauce pan, then simmer, stirring often til its "hot cereal" in consistency.

¼ cup oil
2 tbl. molasses
1 tsp. salt
2 tbl. nutritional yeast
2 tbl. lecithin

Remove sauce pan from heat and add these ingredients. Stir well and let cool til lukewarm.

2 tbl. baking yeast
⅓ c. warm water

Combine these 2 ingredients in separate bowl + mix slightly let set until yeast begins to foam.

1½ c. potato water
3 c. hard w.w. flour
¼ c. honey

Mix with the now foamy yeast mixture, beat 2-3 minutes, let rise 20 minutes. Then add to cool cereal mixture.

¼ c. milk powder
½ c. soy flour
2-3 c. hard w.w. flour

Now add milk + soy + mix well. Then add w.w. flour. Knead til springy. Let rise til doubled in oiled bowl. Then rise in oiled pans til just over the top of the pans. Bake at 350° for about 40 minutes.

Sourdough W.W. Bread

a very fine light enriched sourdough bread with a chewy taste + crust. The age of the starter largely determines the sourness of the bread. The older it is the more sour it is

Sponge:

- 1½ Tbl baking yeast
- 1 cup warm water
- 6 Tbl sourdough starter
- 3 Tbl nonfat dry milk
- 2 cups hard w.w. flour

Thorougly mix all sponge ingredients, and let rise in a warm place for about one hour. (Note: the sourdough starter reacts with metals - causing an odd taste. So choose non-metal bowl, if possible)

- 2 Tbl molasses
- 2 Tbl honey
- 2 Tbl butter/margarine (melted)
- 1 tsp salt
- 1½ cups hard w.w. flour

add remaining ingredients and mix well. Knead then place in oiled bowl (covered) and let rise in a warm place til doubled. Punch down, shape 2 loaves and place in 2 separate loaf pans. Let rise again for about 45 minutes, then bake at 375° for about 35 minutes.

Pumpkin Clouds

30 mediumsized cookies

A light, delicious favorite!

½ c. honey
¼ c. butter
2 eggs
½ c. cooked pumpkin
1½ C. (pastry) w.w. flour
½ tsp baking soda
⅛ tsp. cinnamon
⅛ tsp. ginger
½ C. walnuts

Mix wet ingredients well. Then add the combined dry ingredients to the wet.
Mix until dry disappears. Then drop by spoonfuls onto oiled cookie sheet.

Bake at 350°
for 12 minutes or until lightly (pumpkin) browned!

PAW PAW, MICHIGAN

GRAIN DANCE IS THE NEW NAME FOR THE "AND BAKERY" PART OF THE PAW PAW FOOD CO-OP AND BAKERY, A NATURAL FOODS GROCERY AND BAKERY UNDER THE SAME ROOF. PAW PAW IS A SMALL TOWN (3 TRAFFIC LIGHTS) IN THE FRUIT BELT REGION OF SOUTHWESTERN MICHIGAN. WE ARE A NON-PROFIT CORPORATION, MEMBER OWNED AND RUN. THE BAKERY AND STORE EACH HAVE ONE FULL TIME WORKER AND ONE TO TWO PART TIME WORKERS. ALTHOUGH THERE IS CO-OPERATION IN OUR ORGANIZATION, THERE ARE ALSO MANY STRUGGLES AND WE ARE LOOKING TOWARDS A STRONGER DEFINITION OF CO-OPERATIVE PROCEDURE, A CLARIFICATION OF GOALS AND MISSION, AND AN INCREASED KNOWLEDGE OF BUSINESS SKILLS.

GRAIN DANCE SELLS ITS GOODS THROUGH CO-OPS AND RESTAURANTS IN KALAMAZOO (19 MILES AWAY) AS WELL AS THROUGH THE PAW PAW FOOD CO-OP. WE GET GREAT ORGANIC FLOURS AND OTHER INGREDIENTS FROM THE MICHIGAN FEDERATION OF FOOD CO-OPS.

OUR FRIENDS AT WILDFLOUR IN ANNARBOR GET MANY CALLS AND VISITS FOR ADVICE, INFORMATION, AND MORAL SUPPORT AS WE TRY TO HELP OUR BAKERY GROW IN THE RIGHT DIRECTION. THEY AND THE C.W.G.E.A. HAVE BEEN A GREAT INSPIRATION TO US AND A POSITIVE CONTACT WITH MATURE COLLECTIVES.

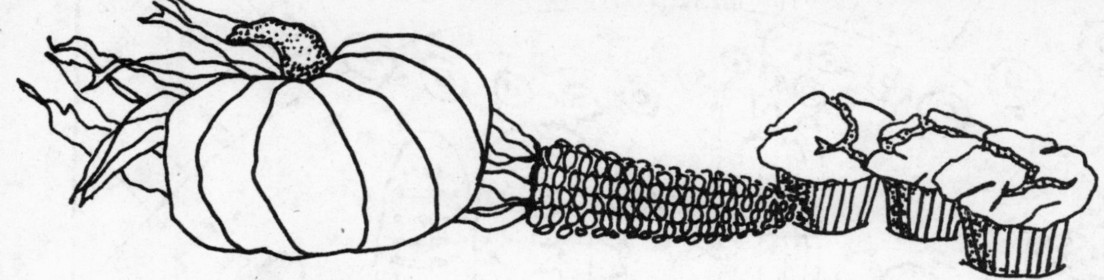

Pumpcorn Muffins

makes 12

½ cup safflower oil ½ cup honey 1½ cups pumpkin puree 1 cup water	Beat together with a wire wisk until smooth.
2¼ cups whole wheat pastry flour 1 cup cornmeal 1 Tbl. baking powder 1 tsp. cinnamon ½ tsp. ginger ¼ tsp. cloves ¼ tsp. nutmeg	Stir together drys. Add to wets, blend in quickly with wisk. (do not overbeat) Scoop into papered muffin tins. Bake at 375° about 30 minutes or til done.

Uprising Breads Bakery
Vancouver, B.C.

Uprising Breads Bakery is a part of Collective Resources and Services Workers Co-operative

CRS WORKERS' CO-OP

which developed out of the co-operative movement in British Columbia. CRS is currently composed of three collectives; a bakery, a food wholesaling business, and a bookeeping collective.

At the bakery we make both bread and goodies for retail and wholesale. We see ourselves as part of the diverse urban community in which we live and work, so we try for a broad appeal in attempting to increase people's awareness of nutritional and economic alternatives

Uprising tries to operate a viable business ~ worker controlled and non-sexist ~ practicing collective management and making good bread and treats, of course!

Peanut Butter Cookies with carob chips or raisins

Yield: 3 doz. good size cookies
Oven: 350°

1. Cream together wet ingredients.
2. Combine dry ingredients.
3. Mix the dry into the wet just until dryness disappears.

2 cups w.w. pastry flour
1⅛ cups oats
1⅓ cups sunflower seeds
1 tsp. baking soda
1 tsp. cinnamon
1⅔ cups carob chips or raisins

6 ounces butter (1½ sticks)
1⅓ cups honey
2 cups peanut butter

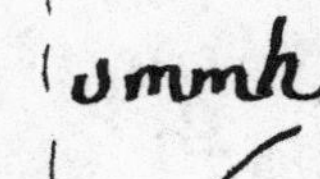

4. Drop by spoonsful onto oiled cookie sheet and bake about 15 minutes 'til golden. Let cool on sheet before removing, as they are quite soft.

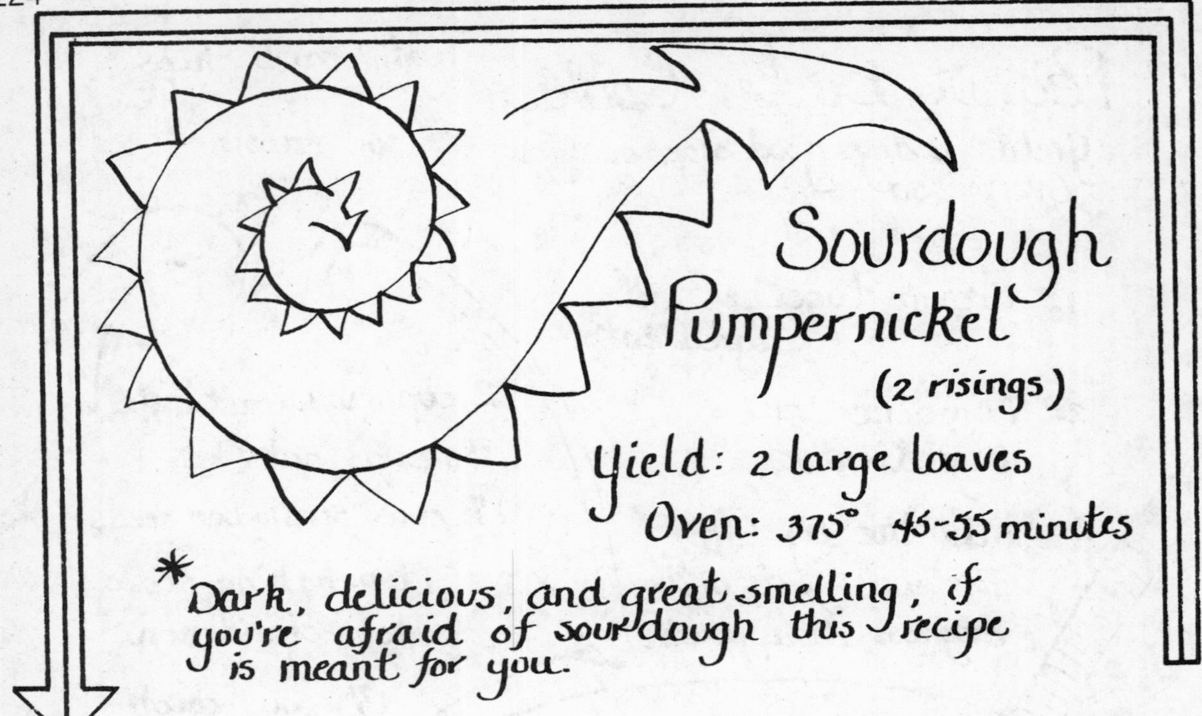

Sourdough Pumpernickel

(2 risings)

Yield: 2 large loaves

Oven: 375° 45-55 minutes

* Dark, delicious, and great smelling, if you're afraid of sourdough this recipe is meant for you.

The STARTER is a pleasure to make! It's ALIVE!

Mix ½ cup of rye flour and ½ cup of cold water. Let this sit, open to the air, or loosely covered, 24 hours.

Now you FEED THE STARTER the next day by adding a little more flour and a little more water, about half and half. Continue to feed every day 5-7 days depending on temperature of environment. A sour, bubbly concoction is achieved as the starter grows, picking up yeast organisms in the air, and will later give the bread a rise.

When you make sourdough bread, ALWAYS SAVE SOME STARTER for the next time. After using, feed and mix to a loose, but not watery, consistency. After feeding allow starter to remain out for several hours, then refrigerate.

NEXT →

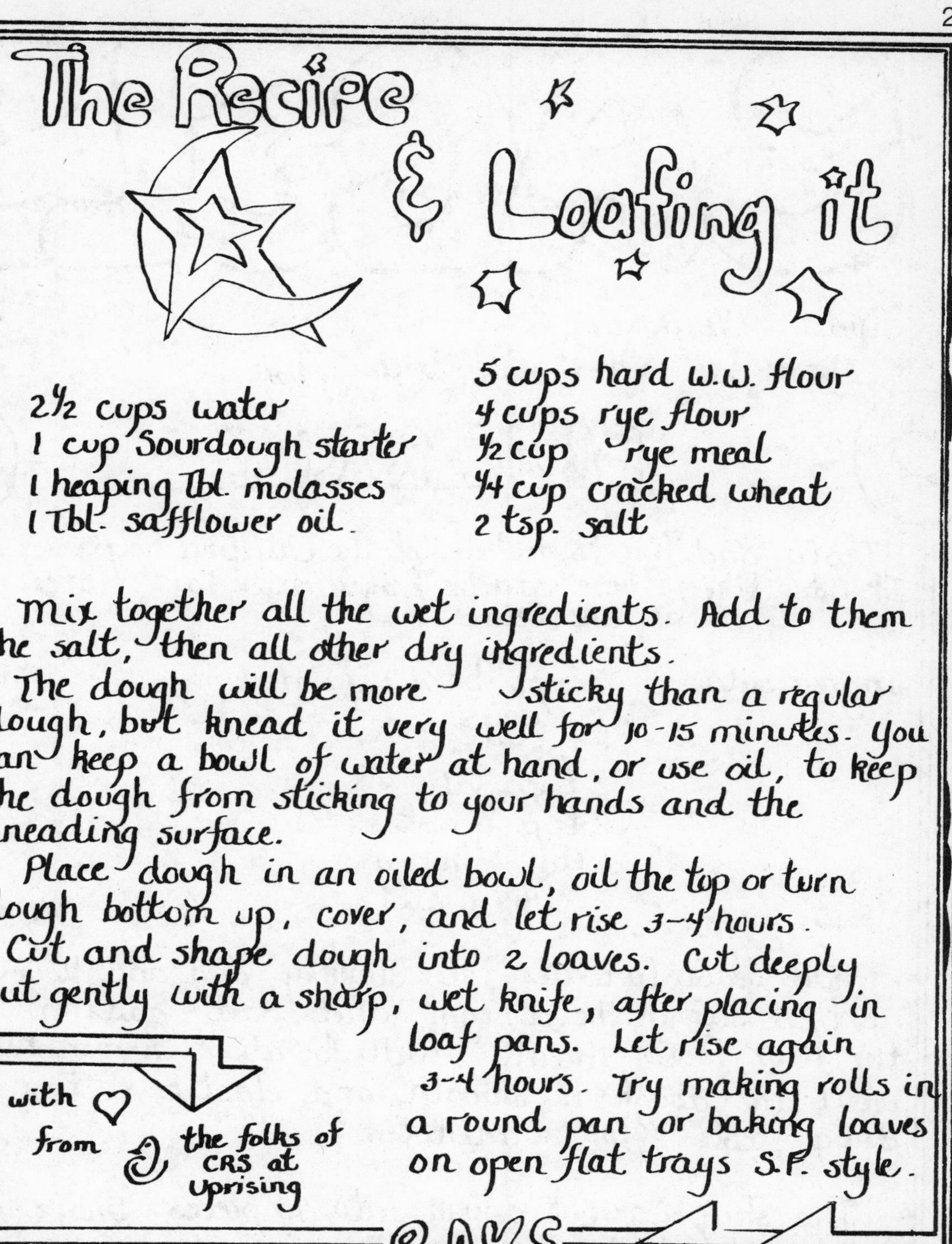

The Recipe & Loafing it

5 cups hard w.w. flour
2½ cups water
4 cups rye flour
1 cup Sourdough starter
½ cup rye meal
1 heaping Tbl. molasses
¼ cup cracked wheat
1 Tbl. safflower oil.
2 tsp. salt

Mix together all the wet ingredients. Add to them the salt, then all other dry ingredients.

The dough will be more sticky than a regular dough, but knead it very well for 10-15 minutes. You can keep a bowl of water at hand, or use oil, to keep the dough from sticking to your hands and the kneading surface.

Place dough in an oiled bowl, oil the top or turn dough bottom up, cover, and let rise 3-4 hours.

Cut and shape dough into 2 loaves. Cut deeply but gently with a sharp, wet knife, after placing in loaf pans. Let rise again 3-4 hours. Try making rolls in a round pan or baking loaves on open flat trays S.F. style.

with ♡ from the folks of CRS at Uprising

BAKE 'til darkest brown

Yield: 1½ dozen
Oven: 350° or 425°; also boiling H_2O.

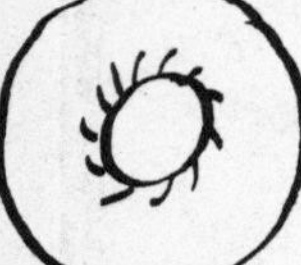

BASIC RECIPE

Tasty and fun to make, let the children help. If you like, these can be frozen raw for later. Directions are below.

Ingredients:
- 7 cups hard w.w. flour
- 2 eggs
- 1 Tbl. oil
- 2 tsp. salt
- 2 tsp. yeast
- 1 Tbl. honey
- 2 cups water

Add yeast to water, stir slightly, and add honey. Next, stir in the oil, eggs, and salt, adding the flour last. Knead well for about 10 minutes until the dough is smooth and elastic. Let dough rest for 30 minutes.

The shaping: Cut dough into 18 pieces. Shape dough into thick cylinder, long enough to wrap around your hand.

Shape pieces into doughnut forms. Have a pan of water boiling. (Honey may be added to the water for a sweeter taste and a nice glazed look.) Drop bagels into water for 30-60 seconds. Lay bagel on oiled tray and sprinkle with poppy or sesame seeds.

Bake: 425°/20 min or 350°/30m

If frozen, allow about 1½ hrs. for thawing, then prepare as above.

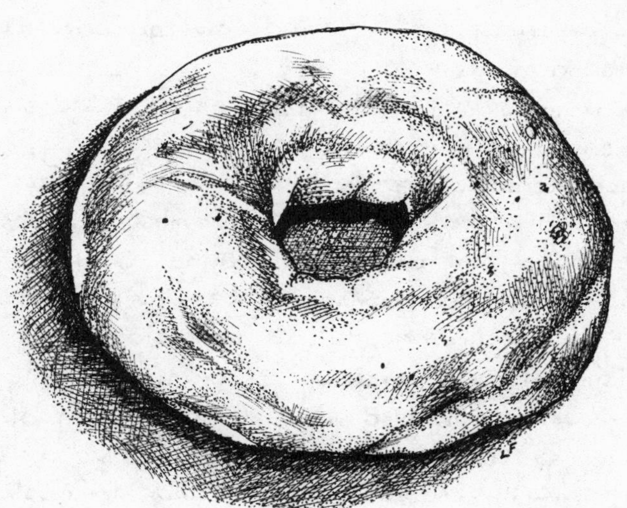

BAGEL (bā'gəl) n:

A ring-shaped roll with a tough, chewy texture made from a plain yeast dough that is dropped briefly into boiling water and then baked;

From the Yiddish 'beygel' and Middle High German 'bouc', meaning ‹ ring or bracelet ›, and the Indo-European root 'bheug' meaning ‹ to swell › related to bent, pliable, or curved objects.

Berkeley, Ca.

Uprisings Baking Collective is a worker-run whole grain bakery located in Berkeley. Established in 1975, Uprisings produces naturally baked goods made with organic whole grain flours, fresh fruits and vegetables, and never with white or brown sugar. The fifteen workers here turn out over 2000 loaves of bread each week plus thousands of cookies and hundreds of pounds of granola every week. We deliver our baked goods all over Berkeley, and at our storefront sell a variety of baked goods and groceries at the lowest prices around.

There is no boss here—all decisions are made by the workers. Conflicts are solved co-operatively, and major decisions are made at regular workers' meetings. All workers participate in most aspects of the bakery—from sales and baking, to clean-up and bookkeeping. We emphasize the development of each worker to their fullest potential.

Uprisings is very much a community bakery, with its workers involved in a cross-section of progressive causes and groups. The bakery as a whole periodically endorses benefits and demonstrations and has distributed hundreds of thousands of label-sized inserts in its bread—publicizing countless solidarity meetings, countercultural institutions, anti-nuclear, anti-racist and anti-imperialist events and campaigns. We are well aware that an Uprisings Bakery constructed on our principles will only survive in the long run if we encourage uprisings in every phase of society.

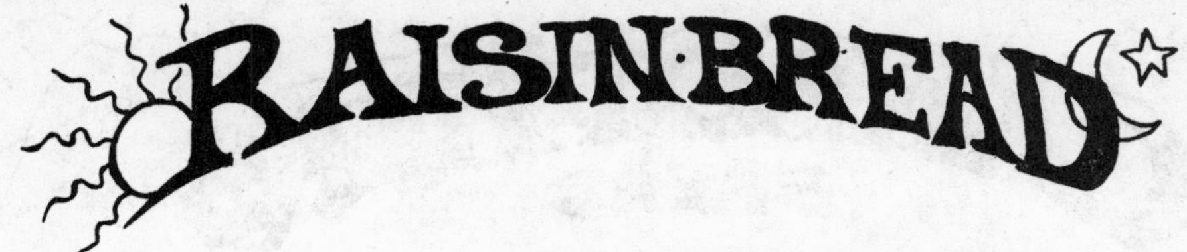

2 - 1½ lb. loaves

A light spicy, medium-sweet loaf with juicy raisins. The kids will love it - and so will you. Try it for french toast, using extra-thick slices, and topping with real maple syrup - yum !!

1¼ cups warm water
6 Tbl malt syrup
1 Tbl yeast
2 cups hard w.w. flour

Cream malt with water, stir in yeast until dissolved. Beat flour in well, then let rise till doubled.

½ cup rolled oats
½ cup water

Mix oats with water and let sit 15 minutes.

1 cup raisins
⅓ cup sunflower seeds
1 Tbl cinnamon
½ tsp nutmeg
⅓ cup oil
¼ tsp salt
3 cups hard w.w. flour

Add oat mixture and all other ingredients to sponge. Mix and knead well until dough has a uniform smooth feel. Let rise till doubled, punch down, shape into two loaves. Let rise in oiled bread pans. Bake at 350° for 50 minutes.

2 - 1½ lb loaves

Deliciously flavorful.

SPONGE:
- 1 2/3 cups warm water
- 1/3 cup malt syrup
- 1 Tbl. yeast
- 2 1/2 cups hard w.w. flour

- 1 cup grated carrots
- 2/3 cup finely chopped scallions
- 1 tsp garlic powder
- 1/2 tsp sage
- 2 tsp dill weed
- 2 tsp ground basil
- 2 tsp thyme
- 1 1/2 tsp cumin
- 1 Tbl poppy seeds
- 1/4 cup oil
- 1 tsp salt
- 3 1/2 cups hard w.w. flour

Mix malt and water well, stir in yeast until it dissolves. Beat flour in, then let rise until sponge is doubled in size.

Add all remaining ingredients. Mix well, then knead dough until it's pliable and elastic. Let rise, covered, in warm place, till doubled. Punch down. Let rise a second time, if desired, or shape into two loaves and place in oiled pans. Let rise again in pans. Bake at 350° for 50 minutes.

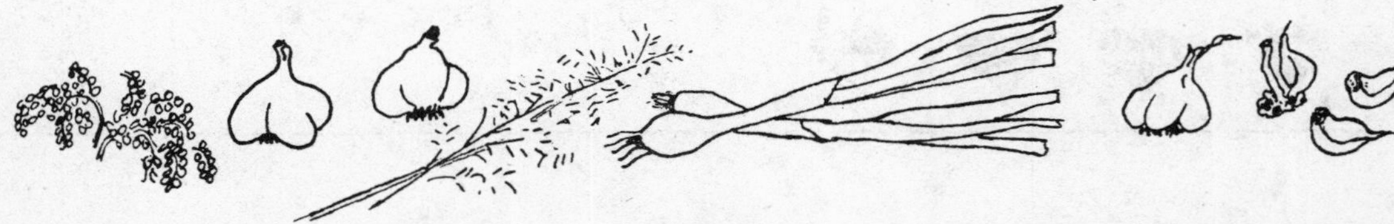

2 x 1½ lb loaves

A delicious lemon-flavored yeasted bread.

1⅔ CUPS WARM WATER
3 TBL MALT SYRUP
1 TBL YEAST
1⅔ CUPS HARD W.W. FLOUR

Cream malt with water, stir in yeast till dissolved. Beat flour in well, then let rise till doubled.

1 CUP CHOPPED DATES OR DATE PIECES
⅓ CUP LEMON PEEL + JUICE
½ CUP SESAME SEEDS
¼ CUP OIL
½ - 1 TSP SALT
4 CUPS HARD W.W. FLOUR

Add all remaining ingredients. Mix and knead the dough well, till it's smooth and elastic. Let rise, covered, in oiled bowl till doubled in bulk. Punch down.

Shape into two loaves. Let them rise in oiled bread pans. Bake at 350° for 45-50 minutes.

U.S. Agribusiness out of the 3rd World!

no eggs
no wheat

2 x 8" pans
or 1 bundt pan

A particularly delicious moist cake. Just smelling it - especially warm from the oven - transports you back to some wonderful childhood memory. At least, that's how it affected the recipe testers. See what it'll do for you!

- 3/4 cup butter, melted or very soft
- 1 cup honey
- 4 Tbl oil mixed with } = 4 eggs
- 4 Tbl garbanzo flour }
- 1½-2 cups buttermilk
- 2½ cups rice flour
- 2 tsp baking powder

spices:
- 1 Tbl cinnamon
- 1 tsp nutmeg
- 1 tsp cardamon

add last:
- 1 cup coconut
- 1/4 cup poppy seeds
- rind of lemon, grated
- 2 tsp vanilla

Cream butter and honey together. Add garbanzo/oil mixture and beat well. Combine flour, baking powder and spices. Add in stages to creamed mixture, alternating with buttermilk, stirring each time. Now add last four ingredients; stir in gently. Pour into oiled pans. Bake 350° - 35 minutes (50-60 for bundt)

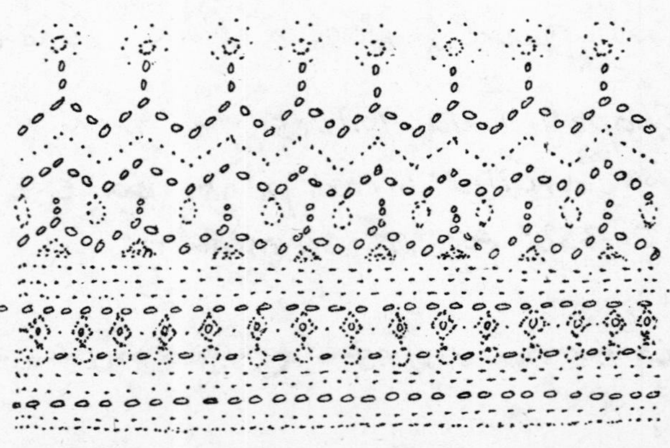

Carrot Cake

"Most Toothsome"

2~8" cakes

~no egg~
~no dairy~

~This sweet rich cake will melt in your mouth. You'll agree it's very fine just as it is, but if your fancy has it, besmear it with the dairy-free frosting on page 158 or this Cream Cheese Frosting:
~1¼ lb cream cheese, ⅜ cup honey, 1 Tbl vanilla, juice of lemon or orange ~ beaten till smooth~

1 cup light oil
1½ cups honey
⅓ cup raisins
1 Tbl lemon peel

Combine these ingredients well~

4 cups grated carrots (pref. organic)

Mix in the delectable orange mound of grated carrots~

1 cup walnuts
4 cups w.w. pastry flour
1 Tbl baking soda
1 Tbl Cinnamon
1 tsp nutmeg
½ tsp cardamon
½ tsp allspice
½ tsp coriander

Combine dry ingredients together and stir them into the wet~

~Oil the pans, pour in the batter. Bake at 350° for 45 minutes or until fork comes out clean. Cool before removing from pan.

Coconut Cake

2 x 8" cakes

Divine.

1 cup butter
1 cup honey
4 beaten egg whites
1 cup milk
1 tsp vanilla
1 tsp almond extract

2 cups w.w. pastry flour
1½ cups shredded coconut
1 Tbl baking powder

Cream together butter + honey. Beat in milk, vanilla + extract.

Combine dry ingredients and mix them into the creamed mixture. Now fold in the egg whites, beaten till white and stiff.

Bake in oiled pans at 350° for 25 minutes, or until fork or knife tests clean.

Frosting (if the cake's not rich enough for you...)

1½ lb. cream cheese
⅓ cup honey
1 cup coconut
1 Tbl vanilla
1 tsp almond extract
juice of one orange

Let cream cheese soften and beat in honey, then remaining ingredients.

Let cake cool before frosting.

Fans of this sweet rich cookie pay a higher price, which Uprisings donates to People Against Nuclear Power, a San Francisco anti-nuclear group.

5 dozen medium cookies

Dry:

- 1 Tbl nutritional yeast
- 1 cup chopped cashews
- 1 cup date pieces
- 1 cup shredded coconut
- 3⅝ cups w.w. pastry flour
- 1½ tsp baking powder

Wet:

- 2 cups maple syrup
- 1 Tbl vanilla
- 1 cup oil

Combine dry ingredients. Combine wet ingredients. Mix them together until batter has the consistency of thick peanut butter. Drop spoonfuls onto oiled cookie sheet. Bake at 325° for about 17 minutes.

Cookies should be crispy.

Simple Scones

About 3 dozen small scones

Put the kettle on - it's time for an English teatime treat!

2 cups coarse w.w. flour, or mix of w.w. flour with rye or cornmeal

2 cups flour ~ any combination of w.w., rice, soy, rye or fine ground corn flour.

4 tsp baking powder
6 ounces butter, melted
2 Tbl maple syrup
1 cup milk

Mix together butter, maple syrup and dry ingredients. Mix in milk to make a soft rolling consistency. Roll out on lightly floured surface. Cut into shapes (rounds, triangles, squares). Bake on oiled pan for 10-15 minutes at 325°. Eat them warm or cool, with or without butter and jam (the English way!)

Rich Currant Scone ~ rich ain't kidding....

4 generous rounds, 7 inches across (=16 triangular scones).

- 2/3 cup butter
- 4 cups w.w. pastry flour
- 1 cup oatmeal
- 3 tsp baking soda.
- 4 eggs
- 1 cup buttermilk
- 1/4 cup honey
- 1 cup currants

Cut butter into mixed dry ingredients until well blended. Save currants to add later.

Beat eggs and add to rest of wet ingredients.

Make a hole in the center of flour mixture and pour in wet mixture. Mix in gently, until all is moistened.

Stir in currants. Don't knead.

On floured surface, shape dough into 4 round patties, about 1" thick. Cut into four (see picture). Brush with melted butter + honey glaze or milk, if desired. Bake on oiled sheet at 350° for about 20 minutes, till lightly browned and a little firm on top. Serve hot or cooled.

SESAME CRUNCH BARS

Makes about 30 2inch squares.

Use an 8"x 14" pan, or similar.

5/8 cup peanut butter
1¼ cups honey
2 tsp vanilla
1¼ cups oats
1¼ cups cashews
1 cup wheat germ
6¼ cups sesame seeds
5/8 cup sunflower seeds

Cream together peanut butter, honey and vanilla. Add the rest of the ingredients and mix well with your hands – it works best and saves on dishes. With wet hands or rolling pin, flatten mixture to uniform thickness on oiled pan. Dough will be stiff – be patient. Bake at 350° for about 25 minutes. Let cool.

A selection from Uprisings' Talking Bread inserts.

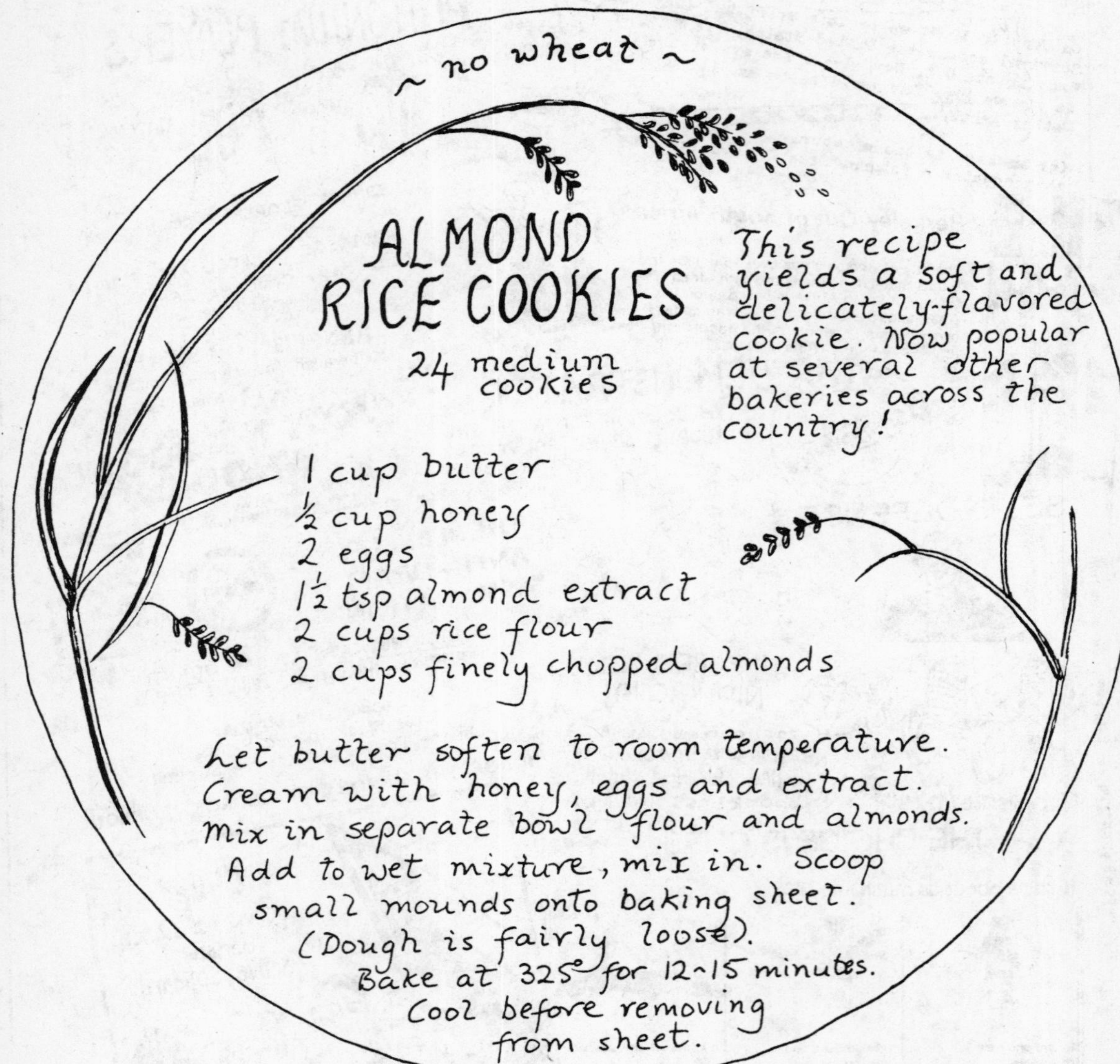

~ no wheat ~

ALMOND RICE COOKIES

24 medium cookies

This recipe yields a soft and delicately-flavored cookie. Now popular at several other bakeries across the country!

1 cup butter
½ cup honey
2 eggs
1½ tsp almond extract
2 cups rice flour
2 cups finely chopped almonds

Let butter soften to room temperature. Cream with honey, eggs and extract. Mix in separate bowl flour and almonds. Add to wet mixture, mix in. Scoop small mounds onto baking sheet. (Dough is fairly loose). Bake at 325° for 12-15 minutes. Cool before removing from sheet.

Carob Mint Balls

Makes about 3 dozen 1" balls

Very fudgy and nicely flavored. No bake.

1 cup sesame seeds
1 cup sunflower seeds, finely ground (in blender or grinder)
1 cup carob powder
1 cup chopped walnuts

1⅓ cups honey
½ Tbl vanilla
1½ Tbl water
1 cup peanut butter
¼ tsp peppermint oil

optional~ coconut for rolling balls

Combine dry ingredients. Combine wet ingredients and mix well with dry, adding a little extra water if needed. Shape dough with hands and roll in shredded coconut, if desired, to make balls. Chilling dough before shaping may help create a firmer texture for rolling.

CREAM CHEESE CAROB CHIP COOKIES

~ 24 large cookies ~

Rich, soft, always a hit. Reduce or omit lemon for a less tangy taste.

1 cup butter
6 oz cream cheese
} Warm to room temperature. Cream together.

1 cup honey
2 large eggs
1½ Tbl lemon peel
1½ Tbl vanilla

Add honey, eggs, lemon and vanilla. Beat until smooth.

4 cups w.w. pastry flour
½ cup carob chips

Add flour and carob chips. Mix until uniform.

Scoop onto oiled cookie sheet, flatten and bake at 325° for 25 minutes. Let cool. (Can add ⅔ cup chopped walnuts.)

WILDFLOUR COMMUNITY BAKERY

Ann Arbor, Michigan

MILT KEMNITZ

Wildflour Community Bakery sits nestled between People's Food Co-op and Al Dente Pasta Shop, one block from Ann Arbor's colorful Farmer's Market. Wildflour is a whole grain, non-profit co-operative bakery, managed by a collective of six members. Decision-making is on the consensus model.

There is little specialization of labor at Wildflour. Work shifts are shared equally (we all do some of the baking and some of the cleaning), and the other operational responsibilities are rotated.

However, Wildflour is more than a bakery managed by a production collective, it is also a community bakery. People of all ages come to volunteer their labor in return for a discount, (which applies to all the local food co-ops), and a "free" loaf of bread. These volunteers are an essential part of the bakery – the only machines we use are the mixer, oven, and bread slicer. The bakery depends on people power to scoop its cookies, shape its dough, and bag its loaves.

Wildflour is also a co-operative. Although there is no official membership, input is sought from concerned users, both around the kneading table, in the store, and at Community Involvement Meetings, held every few months. At these meetings, repricing, co-ordinator pay and other policies affecting the bakery's future are discussed.

Going hand in hand with involvement of the community is Wildflour's concern with education. For seven years the bakery has sponsored its "Rolling in Dough" program, through which co-ordinators become guest teachers once a week in the Ann Arbor Elementary Schools. Showing the students stalks of wheat, we talk about the relationship between the land and agriculture and a healthy society. Then in small groups, the children make dough right on top of their desks. This brings up some of the dynamics of working collectively. Later, each child has his or her unique bread sculpture, baked in the school ovens, to take home and enjoy.

The bakery also participates in the State and County Deferred Sentencing programs. This allows first offenders to erase the record of the offense by working a required number of hours at a non-profit organization of their choice. This often brings people to the bakery who have never been exposed to a democratic work environment or to whole grains. Time and again, the process of working with bread, in an atmosphere where people are enjoying themselves and have control over their lives, provides an enriching experience. Many people continue to volunteer at the bakery long after completing their hours.

Wildflour is now more than ten years old. We who work there know this would never have come about without the loyal support of the Ann Arbor community. That is why at Wildflour Bakery "Community" is our middle name!

Seven Grain Bread

Yields 2 loaves

This is an exciting loaf, even for the skilled baker to make. It needs a little preparation that can be done even a day ahead.

Gather: 1/4 c. cooked rice (about 3 Tbl. raw)
1/3 c. cooked millet (" 2 Tbl. ")
1/3 c. cooked barley (" 2 Tbl. ")
(These grains can be cooked together in the same pot)

Sponge (mix & sit a bit):
1 1/2 Tbl. yeast
2 c. warm water
3 c. hard w.w. flour
1 1/2 Tbl. molasses
1 Tbl. honey
1/3 c. rolled oats

Then add:
1 1/2 Tbl. oil (safflower)
1 tsp. salt
2 Tbl. vinegar
1/2 c. rye flour
1/4 c. cornmeal

Work in: 3 c. hard w.w. flour

Knead until elastic, about 100 times

Finally, add your cooked grains, cooled to at least room temperature, kneading until fully mixed.

Place in an oiled bowl. Cover with a damp cloth. Let rise to double. Divide in 2 and shape in loaves. Place in oiled bread pans. Let rise to double. Bake at 350° for 45 minutes, or until done.

DATE NUT BREAD

Yields 2 loaves

This is not a sweet bread but a nice variety of whole wheat. Just right for a home-warming gift. The best loaves are made with organic dates

Sponge: ½ c. whole dates
2¼ c. warm water
1 Tbl. yeast
2¼ c. hard w.w. flour

Then add & mix: 1 Tbl. tahini (ground sesame seeds)
1 tsp. salt
2¼ - 2½ c. hard w.w. flour (just enough to make a firm, moist, elastic dough)

After kneading well, mix in: ½ c. whole dates
⅔ c. walnuts (whole or chopped; of course the whole nuts are easier to see)

Place in an oiled bowl. Cover with a damp cloth. Let it rise to double its size. Punch down.
Shape into loaves and let it double again in oiled pans.
Bake at 350° for 45 minutes or until done.

JUST RYE

Yields 2 loaves

Especially for those who want to eat bread but shy away from wheat. No sweetener.

The day before boil in 1 3/4 c. water
- 1 medium potato
- 8 dried apricot halves

till very soft

Mash and sit overnight. Then mix 1 c. warm water (or juice) and 1 1/2 Tbl. yeast with potato mixture to form a sponge. Let sit a bit til foamy.

Then add:
- 2 Tbl. oil (safflower)
- 1/2 Tbl. salt
- 1 Tbl. vinegar

Mix in • 4 1/2 – 5 1/2 c. rye flour, so dough is not too sticky to knead. It will be quite sticky, but don't add too much flour. Knead well.

Because of the absence of wheat (gluten), this dough is not the usual, elastic type. You may want to try it a few times just to get the feel of it.

Place in an oiled bowl and cover. Let rise. (It may not double.) Punch down. Shape into 2 round loaves and place on an oiled cookie sheet. Let rise about 1 1/2 times in bulk. This may take 3-5 hours, so paint the tops with oil. Bake at 350° for 45 minutes.

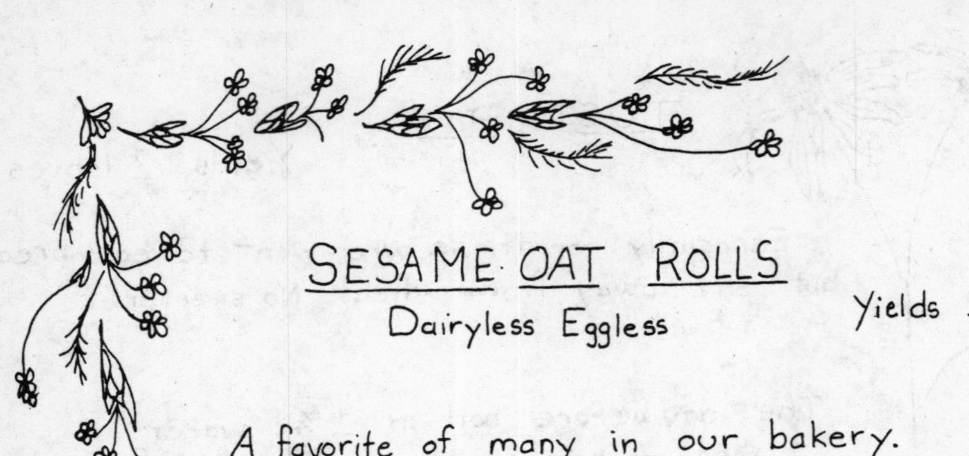

SESAME OAT ROLLS

Dairyless Eggless

Yields 1 dozen

A favorite of many in our bakery.

Sponge (mix & sit a bit):
- 2 c. + 2 Tbl. warm water
- 1 c. oats
- 1½ Tbl. yeast
- ½ c. honey

Then add & mix:
- 3½ Tbl. oil
- ½ Tbl. salt
- 5½ - 6 c. hard w.w. flour

Add the least amount of flour for a soft, light dough. Just mix until the dough is thoroughly combined.

Lastly add • ⅔ c. sesame seeds

Place in an oiled bowl. Let double Punch down. Divide into 12 pieces, shape some what as you do for bread, keeping the roll goal in your mind. Try rolling the ball in a small circle to smooth & round it. These will rise a lot so give them plenty of room. Bake at 350° for 25 - 35 minutes, till golden on bottom.

ONION ROLLS

Dairyless Eggless

Yields 1 dozen large rolls

Sponge:
- 1 ½ c. warm water
- 1 Tbl. yeast
- ¼ c. honey
- 2 c. hard w.w. flour

Then add and knead briefly:
- 2 Tbl. oil (safflower)
- 1 ½ tsp. salt
- 1 ½ c. rye flour
- 2 ⅓ - 3 c. hard w.w. flour (add as needed)
- 1 lb. fine chopped raw onions

As you add the onions, your dough will moisten up. So aim for a drier dough - it will also make roll forming easier.

When ingredients are fully combined, place in an oiled bowl. Let rise, not quite to double. Punch down.

Divide into 12 pieces and knead as you would bread dough, turning in the sides, keeping a smooth surface down.

Dip the smoothest side into a bit of water, then into a bowl of poppy seeds.

Arrange on oiled pan, poppy seed side up. Give them plenty of room to rise.

When they are not quite doubled, bake at 350° for 30-40 minutes til browned on bottom.

PIZZA

Yields 2, 12 inch pies

There are five basic steps to our pizza:
(1) Cheese grating, (2) Vegetable cutting, (3) tofu cooking, (4) Sauce, and (5) Dough. If you'd like, you can cook the sauce a day ahead of time. (In fact, tomato sauce flavors are said to blossom with a day or two of early preparation.)

The Dough – will take 45-60 min. so give yourself time.

Sponge (mix & sit):
- 1 ½ c. warm water 3/4 c 3/4
- 1 Tbl. honey 1/2 tbl.
- 2 Tbl. yeast 1 tbl
- 2 c. hard whole wheat flour 1 c.

Then add:
- 1 Tbl. oil (safflower) 1/2 tbl.
- ¼ Tbl. salt 1/8 Tb.
- 1 Tbl. oregano 1/2 Tbl.
- ½ tsp. cayenne 1/4 tsp
- ½ Tbl. basil 1/4 Tbl

Knead in until elastic:
- 1 ½ c. 3/4 c hard whole wheat flour

This dough should not be quite as stiff as regular bread dough. Set aside in an oiled bowl. Cover with a damp cloth. Let double.

Cheese grating – Grate a total of 1 lb. of cheese. We mix mozzarella, provolone & a hot pepper cheese. Set aside.

Pizza - Continued

Sauce - this recipe will give you enough for 6 pies (it keeps well in the fridge, or freeze it)

Boil for 5 min.
- 3c. water
- 3 1/2 Tbl. oregano
- 2 Tbl. basil
- 1 Tbl. marjoram
- 2 Tbl. dried garlic
- 1 Tbl. honey
- 1 tsp. salt (optional)
- as much fresh garlic as you like

Whisk in • 30 oz. tomato paste

Simmer 20 minutes, stirring often. Set aside.

Tofu - (Ah, tofu!) Begin to sauté 1 onion & 3 cloves garlic. When they look a bit clear, add 1/2 lb. tofu cubed. (If you are a tofu fan, you can use a 1 lb. block). Add 2 Tbl. tamari and stir another minute or until tamari begins to dry. Take off heat and set aside.

Vegetables - can be used according to what is in season and what you like. Generally, we use:
- 1 green pepper, diced
- 1 yam, diced and steamed
- 1/2 bunch broccoli, diced
- 1 small zucchini, diced
- 1 small onion, diced

Set aside.

To begin, divide dough in 1/2, as well as all other steps. Roll out to a 12 inch round. Place on a pizza pan sprinkled with corn meal. Flute edge to keep filling in. Prick all over with a fork and bake for 10 minutes at 350°.

Cover with 1 c. sauce, spread evenly.
Divide tofu and sprinkle evenly over pizza.
Divide vegetables and cover again.
Divide cheese and sprinkle over pizza. Repeat.
Bake at 400° for 20 minutes or until golden on top.

As always, enjoy the fruits of your labor.

AREPAS

EL PAN DE MAIZ VENEZOLANO

INGREDIENTES

1/2 KILO DE MAIZ BLANCO O AMARILLO (PREFERENTEMENTE BLANCO)
AGUA, SAL

PRECOCIMIENTO DEL GRANO

LIMPIE Y LAVE EL MAIZ, HIERVALO HASTA QUE ESTE BLANDO, SAQUELO Y ENJUAGELO CON AGUA FRIA; FINALMENTE DEJELO ENFRIAR

MOLIMIENTO DEL MAIZ

PONGA EL MAIZ PRECOCIDO A TRAVES DE UN MOLINO DE MANO O ELECTRICO HACIENDO QUE SALGA PASTOSO Y FINO

AMASADO

AMASAR LA HARINA CON AGUA Y SAL (AL GUSTO), ENTONCES HAGA UNA ESPECIE DE BOLA, CON, Y DEL TAMAÑO DE LA PALMA DE SUS MANOS PASANDOLA DE UNA A OTRA CON MOVIMIENTOS GIRATORIOS, FINALMENTE LA BOLA DEBE DE QUEDAR APLANADA

VENEZUELAN CORN BREAD

INGREDIENTS

1 Lb. OF WHITE OR YELLOW CORN, SALT, WATER

THE CORN'S FIRST COOKING

CLEAN AND WASH THE CORN, BRING IT TO BOIL, COOK TILL TENDER, RINSE WITH COLD WATER LET IT COOL DOWN

THE CORN'S MILLING

PUT THE COOKED CORN THROUGH A GRINDER. THE DOUGH SHOULD COME OUT SOFT AND FINE

KNEAD

KNEAD THE DOUGH WITH WATER AND SALT TO TASTE MAKE SMALL BALLS, PRESS THEM MAKING A KIND OF FAT PANCAKES

COMO COCINARLA

PONGA LA AREPA EN UNA CHAPA (PARRILLA) CALIENTE (QUE NO PEGUE) DANDOLE LA VUELTA HASTA QUE AMBOS LADOS QUEDEN LIGERAMENTE OSCURECIDOS, ENTONCES HORNEELAS POR 35 O 40 MINUTOS A UNA TEMPERATURA DE 350º

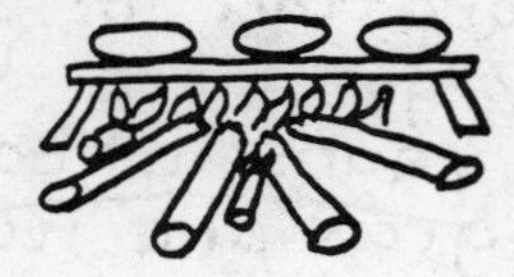

COOKING

LAY THE AREPA ON A HOT GRIDDLE, COOK BOTH SIDES. WHEN THE OUTSIDE IS HARD, PUT THEM IN THE OVEN AT 350°F FOR 35 TO 40 MIN.

OTROS INGREDIENTES

LAS AREPAS SON COMIDAS A DIARIO COMO DESAYUNO (O EN OTRO MOMENTO) LAS PUEDE LLENAR CON MANTEQUILLA, AGREGANDOLE: QUESO, HUEVOS, AGUACATE, TOMATE O CUALQUIER OTRA COMBINACION DE SU GUSTO

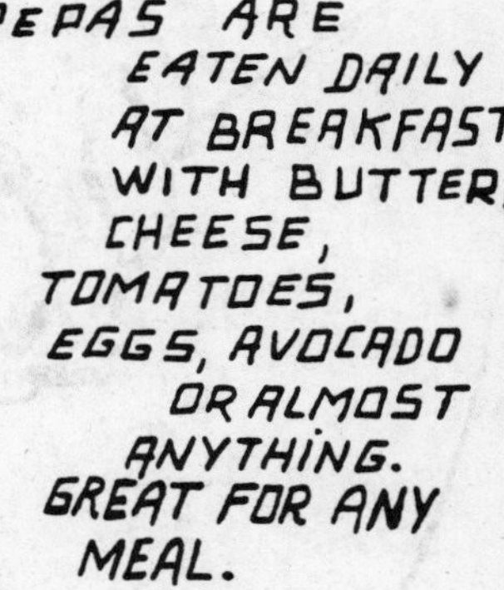

ANOTHER INGREDIENTS

AREPAS ARE EATEN DAILY AT BREAKFAST WITH BUTTER, CHEESE, TOMATOES, EGGS, AVOCADO OR ALMOST ANYTHING. GREAT FOR ANY MEAL.

LLENADO

ABRA LA AREPA CON UN CUCHILLO Y LLENELA CON SU COMBINACION FAVORITA

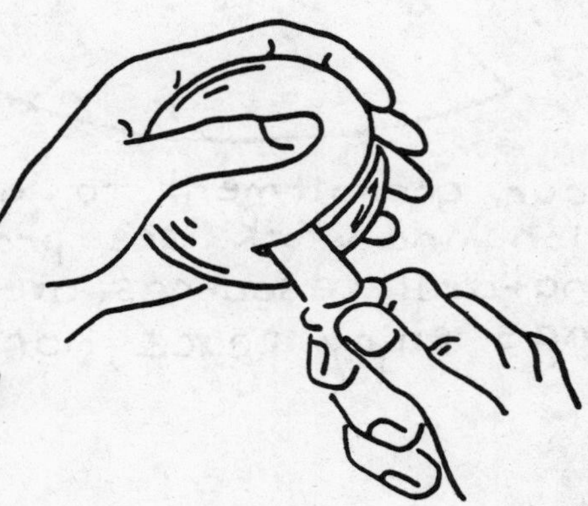

FILLING

OPEN THEM AND STUFF WITH YOUR FAVORITE FILLING, LIKE A PITA BREAD

BUEN PROVECHO

ENJOY THEM

Join us in celebration of Wildflour's 10th anniversary! We know we only got here because we all worked together. In the years ahead, with all our efforts, we will continue to grow and work for the ideals that we all share

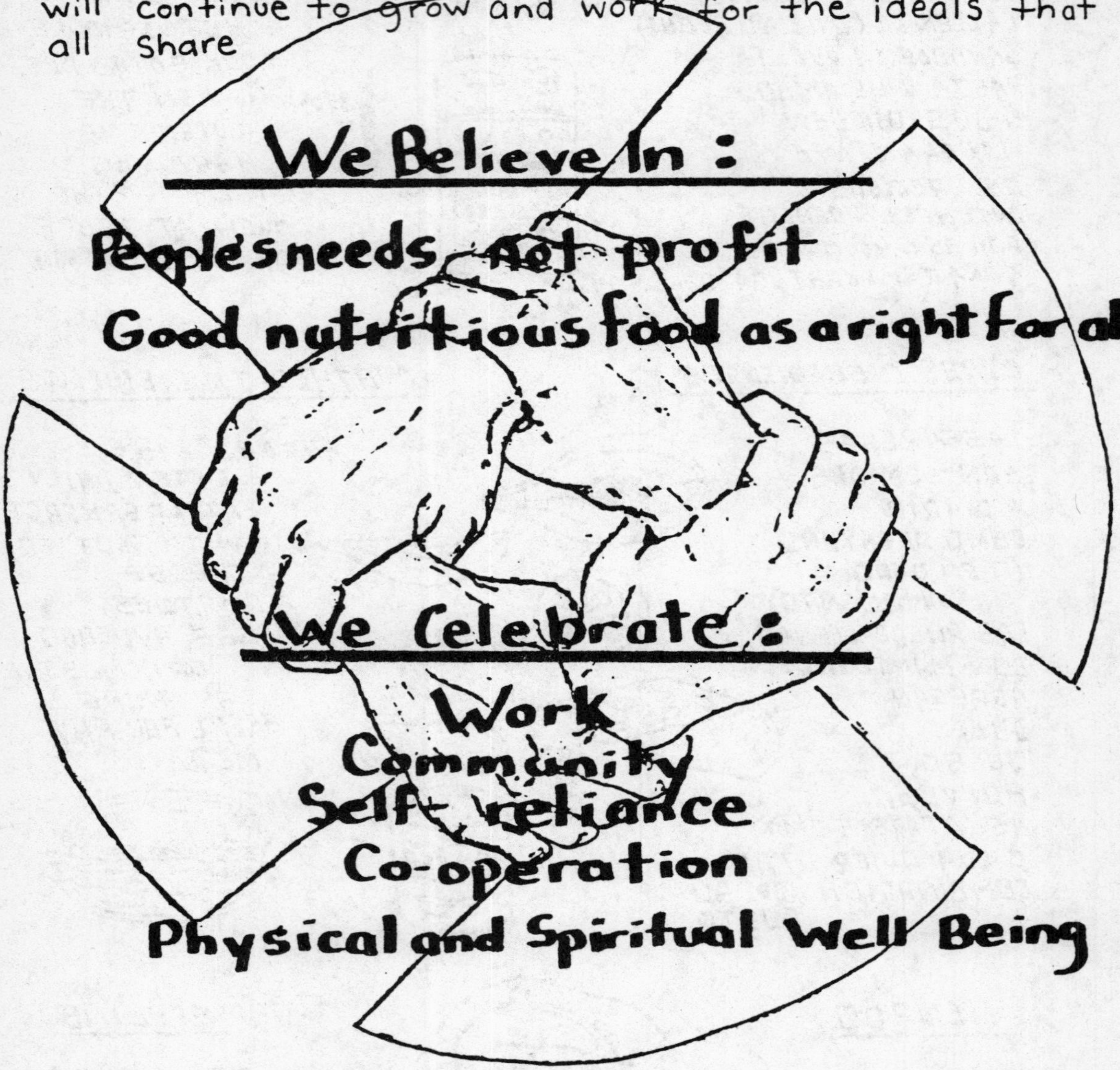

We Believe In:

Peoples needs not profit

Good nutritious food as a right for all

We Celebrate:

Work

Community

Self-reliance

Co-operation

Physical and Spiritual Well Being

We renew our commitment to a world community where education and work are productive and joyful; wealth and natural resources are shared by all, and all living things enjoy peace, harmony, and freedom.

August 1985

DATE CRUNCH

Yeild: 3 1/2 lbs.

A delicious granola or snack that is sweetened only with dates. It contains no oil, wheat, salt, nuts, or dairy.

3 1/4	Cups Date Pieces or Pitted Dates	(1 lb.)
1	Cup Very Hot Water	
9 1/4	Cups Rolled Oats	(2 lb.)
1 1/2	Cups Sunflower Seeds	(1/2 lb.)
3/4	Cup Sesame Seeds	(1/4 lb.)

1. Combine dates with water and let stand until dates are softened. Then beat, blend or puree until a smooth butter is obtained.

2. Add the oats then the seeds and stir gently until well coated.

3. Spread evenly on unoiled baking sheets or pans— not too thick (about 1/2 in.), just so you can't see the metal of the pans.

4. Bake at just above 350° for 20-25 minutes. When cooked, the surface looks golden brown and a rich aroma is given off. It will be soft but crisps up as it cools.

5. You may want to check during baking and rotate the pans in case of darkening around the edges. Crunch can burn easily!

6. Cool on sheet, then store in an airtight containeror plastic bag.

DAIRYLESS

PECAN - RAISIN ESSENE ROLLS

YIELD ~ 12 6 OZ. ROLLS

1. SOAK FOR 8 HOURS OR MORE:
   2 lbs. HARD W. W. BERRIES
2. RINSE THE SPROUTS 2 OR MORE TIMES A DAY UNTIL THE TAILS ARE 1½ TIMES LONGER THAN THE BERRIES.
3. SKIP THE LAST RINSE BEFORE GRINDING THE SPROUTS (OR THE SPROUTS WILL MAKE DOUGH THAT IS TOO WET).
4. GRIND THE SPROUTS IN A MEAT GRINDER USING THE FINEST DYE. OR YOU CAN HOMOGENIZE THE SPROUTS THROUGH A CHAMPION JUICER.
5. KNEAD INTO THE DOUGH:
   2 CUPS RAISINS
   2 CUPS PECANS

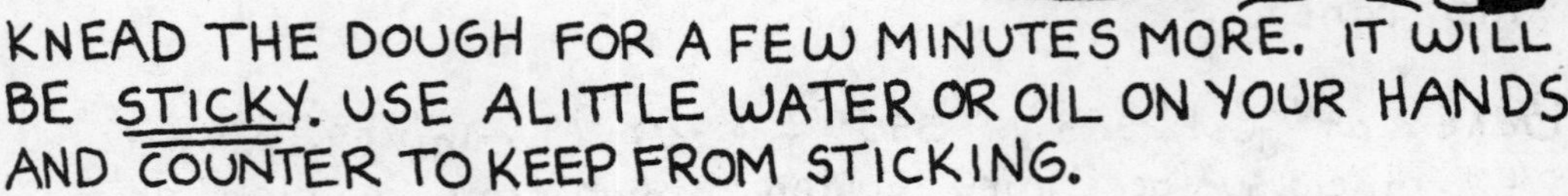

   KNEAD THE DOUGH FOR A FEW MINUTES MORE. IT WILL BE STICKY. USE A LITTLE WATER OR OIL ON YOUR HANDS AND COUNTER TO KEEP FROM STICKING.
6. SHAPE INTO ROLLS & PRESS A PECAN IN THE CENTER OF EACH ROLL. PLACE ONTO A GREASED COOKIE SHEET.
7. BAKE AT 275°F. FOR APPROX. 1 HOUR. THE BOTTOM SHOULD BE BROWNED, MOIST AND SPRING BACK TO THE TOUCH. THESE HARDEN AS THEY COOL.

DAIRYLESS

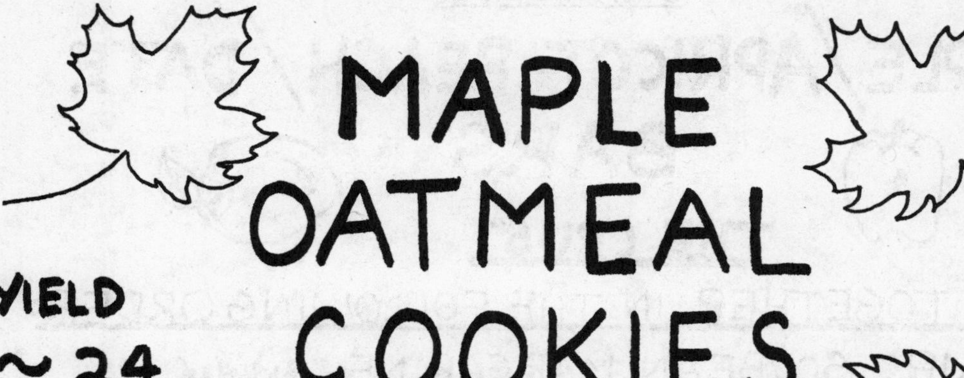

MAPLE OATMEAL COOKIES

YIELD ~ 24

1. CREAM TOGETHER WELL:

1 CUP SOYBEAN MARGARINE

1/3 CUP MAPLE SYRUP

1/3 CUP HONEY

1 tsp. VANILLA

2. THEN ADD TO # 1:

1 CUP WW PASTRY FLOUR

1 CUP WALNUTS

2 3/4 CUPS ROLLED OATS

DROP 1 ROUNDED TBL. ONTO A GREASED COOKIE SHEET. FLATTEN TO 1/2 INCH WITH A WET COOKIE PRESS. BAKE AT 350°F FOR APPROXIMATELY 15 MINUTES, OR UNTIL GOLDEN BROWN.

DAIRYLESS

APPLE/APRICOT-PEACH/DATE BARS

THE CRUST

1. MIX TOGETHER IN THE FOLLOWING ORDER:

   1 CUP SOYBEAN MARGARINE
   1/2 CUP HONEY
   1 3/4 CUPS W.W. PASTRY FLOUR
   1/2 CUP SOY FLOUR
   3 CUPS ROLLED OATS
   3 Tbl. SESAME SEEDS

2. FIRMLY PRESS HALF OF THE CRUST INTO A GREASED 8" x 8" PAN. RESERVE THE REMAINDER FOR THE TOP.

THE FILLINGS

3. MIX FOR 5 MIN. WITH AN ELECTRIC MIXER ON LOW SPEED:

   A. APPLE – 2 1/2 lbs. FINELY CHOPPED APPLES
   2 Tbl. CINNAMON

   OR:

   B. APRICOT-PEACH – 3 CUPS DRIED APRICOTS, 2 3/4 CUPS DRIED PEACHES } SOAKED OVERNIGHT
   1 Tbl. CINNAMON

   OR:

   C. DATE – 3 1/2 CUPS PITTED DATES, 1 1/4 CUPS RAISINS } SOAKED FOR 1/2 HOUR
   1 Tbl. CINNAMON

4. SPREAD THE FILLING OVER THE BOTTOM CRUST. PRESS THE REST OF THE CRUST ON TOP OF THE FILLING.
5. BAKE AT 350°F. UNTIL GOLDEN (20 to 30 MIN.)

PECAN SANDIES

YIELD~24

WILDFLOUR'S MOST POPULAR COOKIE!

1. CREAM TOGETHER WELL:

(IT HELPS TO HAVE INGREDIENTS AT ROOM TEMPERATURE)

3/4 CUP BUTTER
5 Tbl. MAPLE SYRUP
1 tsp. VANILLA

2. IN ANOTHER BOWL, STIR TOGETHER:

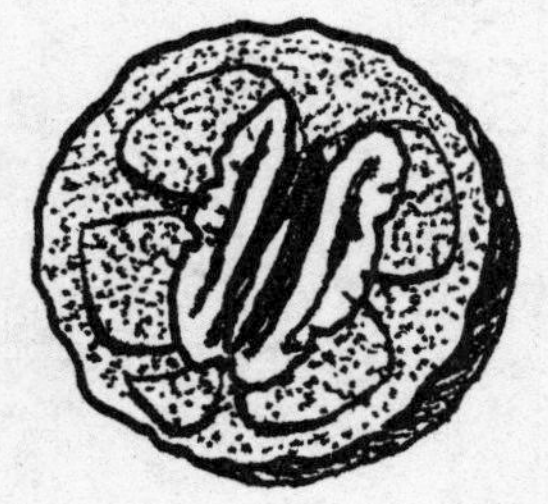

1½ CUPS WW PASTRY FLOUR
3/4 CUP PECAN MEAL

3. STIR #2 INTO #1

DROP 1 ROUNDED TBL. ONTO A GREASED COOKIE SHEET FLATTEN TO ½ INCH WITH A WET COOKIE PRESS. PRESS A PECAN IN THE CENTER. BAKE 350°F FOR APPROX. 20 MIN. THE PECAN WILL LOOK REDDISH-BROWN WHEN DONE.

WHEATLESS DAIRYLESS FRUIT-SWEETENED

FRUIT & NUT DROPS

YIELD ~ 2 DOZEN

1. **SOAK OVERNIGHT:**

[A] 2 CUPS DARK FIGS + 2 CUPS LIGHT FIGS OR [B] 2 CUPS DATES + 2 CUPS LT. FIGS

OR

[C] 1 CUP DRIED PEACHES + 1 CUP DRIED APRICOTS + 1½ CUP DATES + ½ CUP DRIED PINEAPPLE

2. HOMOGENIZE THE FRUIT IN A BLENDER; THROUGH A CHAMPION JUICER; OR USE AN ELECTRIC MIXER.

3. **THEN ADD:**

2 CUPS ROLLED OATS

1 3/4 CUPS COCONUT OR SESAME SEEDS OR PECAN MEAL

½ CUP SUNFLOWER SEEDS

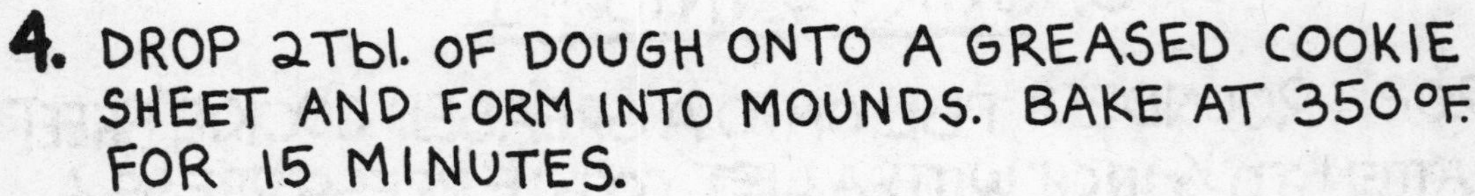

4. DROP 2Tbl. OF DOUGH ONTO A GREASED COOKIE SHEET AND FORM INTO MOUNDS. BAKE AT 350°F. FOR 15 MINUTES.

5. THESE COOKIES CAN ALSO BE SERVED RAW, JUST REFRIDGERATE INSTEAD OF BAKE THEM.

WHEATLESS

CAROB COCONUT CLUSTERS

YIELD ~ 18

1. CREAM TOGETHER WELL:
   - 1/2 CUP BUTTER
   - 5/8 CUP HONEY

2. THEN ADD TO #1:
   - 1 EGG, LIGHTLY BEATEN
   - 1 tsp. VANILLA

3. STIR TOGETHER & ADD TO #1 & #2:
   - 2 CUPS SHREDDED COCONUT
   - 2 CUPS ROLLED OATS
   - 3 Tbl. SIFTED CAROB POWDER

DROP 1 TIGHTLY PACKED Tbl. ONTO A GREASED COOKIE SHEET. BAKE AT 350°F FOR 20 MINUTES, TIL COOKIES ARE BROWN ON THE BOTTOM & STILL MOIST. ALLOW TO COOL ON THE SHEET.

DREAM COOKIES

YIELD ~ 24

1. CREAM TOGETHER WELL:

1½ CUPS BUTTER

½ CUP HONEY

3 drops of ALMOND OIL
OR
¼ tsp. ALMOND EXTRACT

2. IN ANOTHER BOWL STIR TOGETHER:

2½ CUPS WW PASTRY FLOUR

1 tsp BAKING POWDER

2 Tbl. CAROB POWDER

STIR # 2 INGREDIENTS INTO # 1 INGREDIENTS

3. THEN FOLD IN EACH ITEM SEPARATELY:

½ CUP SOURCREAM
1 CUP CHOPPED ALMONDS
1 CUP UNSWEETENED CAROB CHIPS

DROP 1 ROUNDED Tbl. ONTO A GREASED COOKIE SHEET. BAKE APPROX. 20 MIN. AT 350°F. COOKIES SHOULD BE GOLDEN BROWN ON BOTTOM.

Wolfmoon was a community bakery that produced wholesome breads, natural goodies, pizzas and vegitarian deli items. At 7:00 most mornings one could find a varied group of volunteer workers around the large wood table kneading bread and sharing their experiences and thoughts. But Wolfmoon Natural Co-operative Bakery closed its doors permanently in June 1981, despite its often-complimented products, and being a medium for exchange of thoughts and energy.

Wolfmoon closed because of a lack of clearly defined goals in the co-op store and the bakery, no regular formal discussion between store and bakery staff, and an unwillingness by many to come to terms with the necessity of utilizing business tools. A sad, reluctant crew gave the bakery its final cleaning the first few days of June. But let us hope we all have learned to work out our goals and keep them in mind despite our differences, and to seek and use the tools necessary to attain those goals. And, hopefully, people in other co-operatives can learn from our experience without suffering the same fate.

WOLF MOON BAKERY

EAST LANSING, MICHIGAN

Oatmeal Sunflower Millet Bread

yields 2×1 1/2 # loaves

Looks pretty & tastes good. A Wolfmoon favorite.

① Mix together & let sit until lukewarm

1/2 cup millet
1/2 cup sunflower seeds
1 cup oats
2 tsp soy margarine
3 cups boiled water

② Mix together & let sit a few minutes, until soaked grains cool. Mix the two mixtures together & let this sit until bubbly.

1/2 cup warm water
1 tbl. yeast
3 tbl molasses

③ Add to sponge and knead well, adding flour as needed, to get a nice elastic texture.

1 tsp salt
3-3 1/2 cups hard ww flour

Let dough rise until doubled in bulk in oiled covered bowl. Shape into 2 loaves, & let rise again in oiled pans. Bake 350° for 45 minutes.

Hi-Protein Bread

yields 2 × 1½# loaves

Lots of protein and delicious flavor in this light brown, close-textured loaf. Very popular with the testers. Many variations possible, with the different optional ingredients. Think up your own too!

① Mix together + let cool.
1 cup boiling water
1/4 cup oats
1/4 cup rice flakes

② Mix well with whisk.
1 3/4 cups warm water
1 tbl. yeast
1/4 cup milk powder

③ Add to yeast mix and mix well. Let this sponge sit until bubbly.
3 tbl. honey
1 1/2 tbl. safflower oil
2 cups hard whole wheat flour

④ Add these to sponge.
1/4 cup soy flour
1/4 cup bran (optional)
1/4 cup wheat germ (optional)
1/8 cup sesame seeds (opt.)
1/8 cup nutritional yeast (opt.)

⑤ 1 1/2 - 2 cups hard whole wheat flour (more if options are omitted.)

Then add mix of oats and rice flakes. Mix together well, adding rest of ww flour as needed. Dough works best if a little dry. Knead until good and springy. Let dough rise in oiled covered bowl till double in size. Shape into 2 loaves. Let rise again in oiled pans. Bake at 350° for 45 minutes.

Halvah

~eggless, dairyless~
1×10" round pan, or brownie pan

Quick, nutritious & tasty

2 1/4 cups tahini
1/2 Tbl. vanilla
1 1/2 cups bran
1/2 cup honey
1 1/2 cups soy (or soya) powder
1/2 cup sesame seeds

Mix well together. Press into lightly oiled pan. Refrigerate to firm up (doesn't take long). Cut into small pieces - its rich! Alternatively, press into small cups, eggcups or muffin pan lined with wax paper or plastic wrap. Refrigerate and up end for appealing dome-like treats.

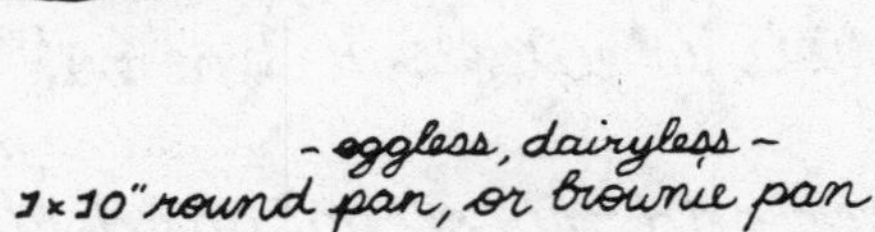

Carob Halvah

~eggless, dairyless~
1×10" round pan, or brownie pan

Rich & Fudgy

2 3/4 cups tahini
2/3 cup honey
1/2 tbl. vanilla
1 1/2 cups bran
1 1/2 cups soy (or soya) powder (not flour)
1/2 cup sesame seeds
1/2 cup carob powder
1 tbl. sesame oil (safflowers Ok)

Mix ingredients together well. Press into lightly oiled pan. Refrigerate to firm up. Cut into little pieces - a little goes a long way. See alternative serving idea under halvah, above, for round carob candies.

Women's Community Bakery

Washington, D.C.

We are a ten member womens collective who operate a non-profit consumer owned bakery. Our aim is to provide good whole foods to people at the lowest possible prices. We place an emphasis on selling to consumer groups, food coops and non-profit stores. We encourage people to organize with their co-workers, in their apartment buildings, and with their neighbors to buy food collectively at non-profit prices.

We choose to be a women's collective in order to provide opportunities for women to accept responsibility, develop self esteem, acquire business skills, learn to work co-operatively with other women, and to trust one another.

Being a women's group does not mean that we are separatists or sexists. We find roles for women in our society oppressive. We are trying to break out of those roles and to help others to do the same.

Onion Rye Bread

2 x 1½ lb loaves

One of the testers' favorites.
Smells enticing and has a wonderful blend of flavors.

1 1/3 cups warm water
1 TBL. yeast
1 1/2 TBL. molasses
1 1/2 tsp. malt
1 1/2-2 cups hard W.W. flour

Dissolve yeast in water. Add molasses and malt, then mix in the flour. Let sit until bubbly.

2 1/2-3 cups hard W.W. flour
1 3/4-2 cups Rye flour
1 1/2 TBL. vinegar
1 1/2 TBL. safflower oil.
1/4 cup buttermilk
2 tsp caraway seeds
1 small onion chopped
1 tsp salt (optional)

Add the liquid ingredients and then the remaining dry ones. Adding in flour as needed to obtain a good springy texture.
Let dough rise in a bowl until doubled. Punch down and shape into 2 round loaves. Let rise again on an oiled sheet. Bake at 375° for 35-40 min.

Taste Real Bread Again!

Warm Morning Cinnamon Granola Bread

2 loaves

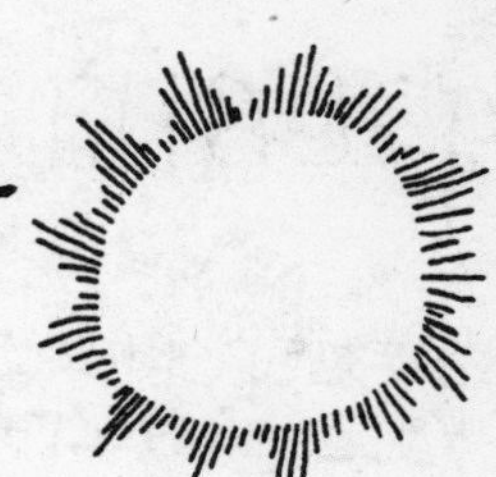

Soak 6 ounces of Granola
in 3/4 cup water for 1 hour.

Dissolve 1 TBL yeast
in 1½ cups warm water.
Stir in ¼ cup honey,
and 2 cups hard w.w. flour.
Let this rest until bubbly.

mix in 3 TBL. Soy oil,
1½ TBL. Vinegar,
2 TBL. cinnamon,
1 tsp. salt.

Now knead in about
3½ - 4 cups hard w.w. flour.
Work the dough until it is
smooth and elastic, adding
the granola last.

Let rise in an oiled bowl until
it has doubled in size. Punch
down and let rise again. Punch
down once more and shape into
two loaves. Let rise in oiled bread
pans, then bake 35-40 minutes
at 375°.

Sandwich Rolls

plain

makes 8 rich 5 oz rolls

2 tsp yeast
1/2 cup warm water
2 TBL honey
1 cup hard w.w. flour

mix together and let sponge sit until bubbly.

1/2 cup MILK
1 Small egg
4 TBL soy oil
1 tsp. salt
2 - 2 1/4 cups hard w.w. flour

add these ingredients and mix, then knead until the dough is elastic.

Let rise in an oiled bowl until doubled in size. Divide into 8 pieces and shape into rolls. Brush the tops with eggwash or water and dip them in sesame or poppy seeds if you like. Let rolls rise on an oiled pan until puffy.

onion

1 chopped onion
1 clove garlic crushed
1/2 tsp. rosemary
1 TBL. poppy seeds
Just enough oil to moisten

mix half of this in with the dough towards the end of kneading. after shaping the rolls, smush the rest of the onions on top. Let rise.

Bake at 375° for 15-20 minutes.

Breakfast Bran muffins

makes 2 dozen

Very Light and Very Good, not too sweet.

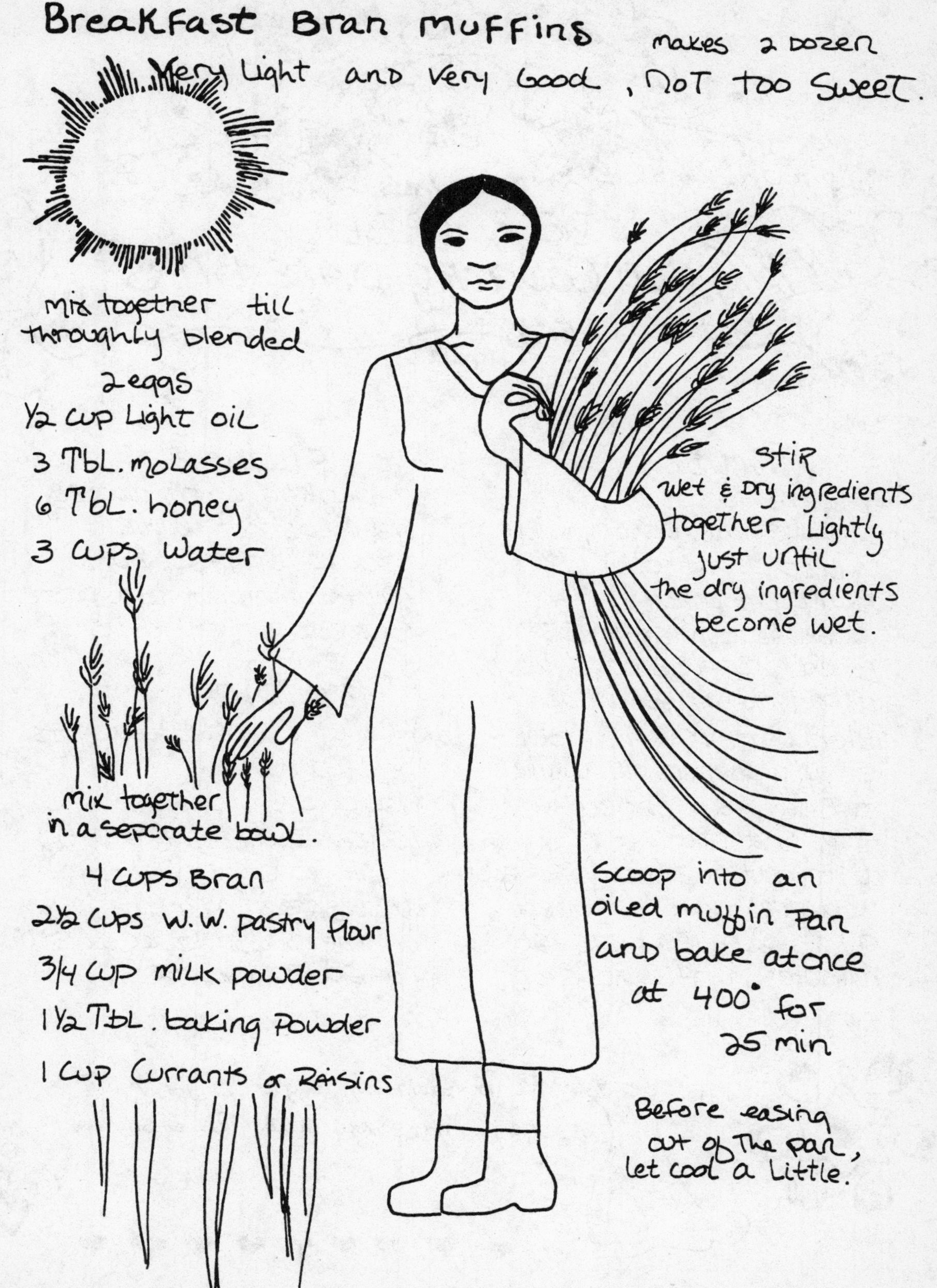

mix together till throughly blended

- 2 eggs
- 1/2 cup Light oil
- 3 TbL. molasses
- 6 TbL. honey
- 3 cups Water

mix together in a seperate bowl.

- 4 cups Bran
- 2 1/2 cups W. W. pastry flour
- 3/4 cup milk powder
- 1 1/2 TbL. baking powder
- 1 cup Currants or Raisins

Stir wet & dry ingredients together Lightly just until the dry ingredients become wet.

Scoop into an oiled muffin pan and bake at once at 400° for 25 min

Before easing out of the pan, let cool a Little.

DINGWALL'S DELECTABLE OLD COUNTRY DATE BARS

Crust

4 cups oats
2 cups w.w. pastry flour
1 cup light oil
1/2 cup honey

preheat oven to 350°

Break up the oats with a rolling pin, or in a blender. mix in flour. Slowly pour in oil while mixing. Add honey and stir just until it is distributed evenly. Spread and press into an oiled 9 x 13 pan. Bake 15-20 minutes, until golden.

Filling

4 packed cups dates
1 1/2 cups hot water.

Soak for 1-2 hours. Mash or blend to a paste. Spread on the crust.

topping

1/4 cup crushed walnuts
1/4 cup honey
1 1/2 cups coconut
1 cup eggwhites (about 5)

mix together lightly, and spread over the filling on the crust. Bake at 350° for 20-30 minutes.

Are you saving the egg yolks for me? They'll make my coat nice & shiny.

Julia's favorites

Raisin oatmeal cookies

makes 40 2½ inch drops

1 cup light oil,
⅔ cup barley malt,
½ cup honey,
2 tsp. vanilla,
2 large eggs.
1 tsp almond extract.

½ cup chopped walnuts,
½ cup sunflower seeds,
1¼ cups raisins,
1 cup wheat germ,
½ cup non instant milk powder,
1¼ cups ww. pastry flour,
2 cups rolled oats.

First cream the wet ingredients together, and then add the premixed dry ingredients. Stir until the dry stuff disappears. Add a little water if necessary so that the cookies drop off your spoon onto the cookie sheets with ease. They will spread some on the trays so leave room for them to grow.

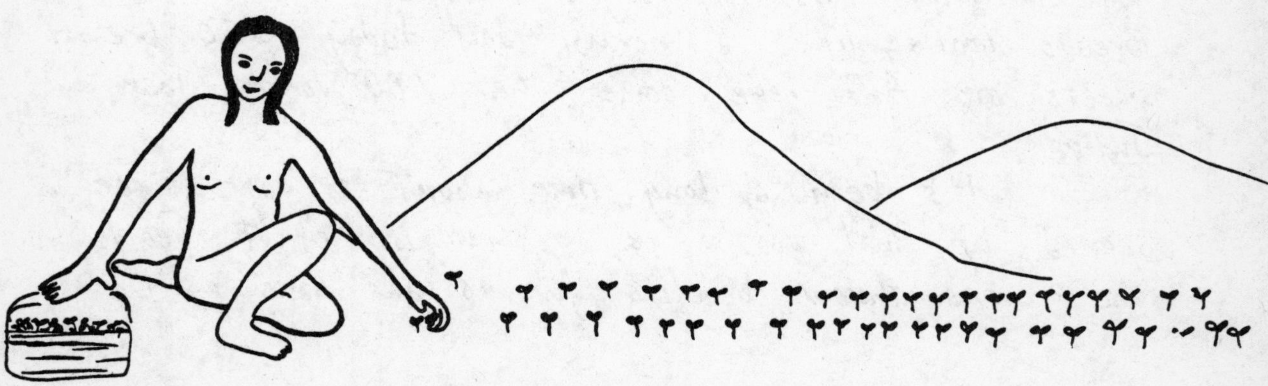

Buffalo, New York

The alarm rings. Stretch - wow is it dark. The ride to work is quiet and peaceful. The air is chilly but clear. I get there at 5:45, turn on the lights and the ovens. I start the first batch of bread in the mixer. Got to make sure the water temperature is right since the mixing bowls got pretty cold overnight. Hey, the late shift did a good job cleaning up and making sure everything's set up for today. The six of us have been working well together lately and some of the volunteers are getting to be strong workers too. I'll have to remember to bring that up at the meeting. Positive criticism is just as important as negative.

Let's see, what are we making today? It's pizza day - should be lots of retail customers. Ooh, and we get to make some of those mint carob chip cookies that Wildflour Bakery taught us. And Cinnamon Raisin Breads. Looks like a normal day today - 250 breads, sweets, etc. And here come the 7:00 workes, Josh and Julius.

It's been a long time - about 4 years since we opened up - that was a real community effort. People in the coops threw benefits for us and gave us the support we needed. Buffalo's co-op community is great. At this point we're starting to sell well in the supermarkets, but the co-ops will always be our strongest base and our first allegiance.

Where was I? Time for the third batch to go in the mixer. The cookies are coming out really good today. It's nice working with whole wheat and without sugar or preservatives. I like being able to stand behind what we make. When we were using white flour in the pita bread it threw me off a bit. I'm glad we discontinued it.

Here comes Debbie, she's doing deliveries today—and here's Peter, he's on the 8:00 shift. He'll stay an hour later than everyone else and mop the floor at the end of the day. Three men and one woman working inside the bakery again today. Ever since Mar took off on one of our patented, unlimited, unpaid vacations our sexual balance has been thrown off. We all like having an equal number of men and women and when she gets back things will be back to normal.

Well, the day is rolling now. It's time to loaf the bread. It's my job to watch the ovens. Then we'll bag up the sweets and wrap the pizza. I get to take off early while the others slice the bread, bag it and clean up. We have some bad days, but I'd say this is another good day in the life of the Yeast West Bakery.

Hard flour = Bread Flour
Pastry flour sub = 1¾c ap flour + ¼ c Cornstar

Buttermilk Dinner Rolls

2 dozen rolls

These are light, delicious rolls perfect for an elegant dinner or special company. For different shapes see <u>Shaping</u> in <u>How to Bake</u>.

4 Tbl. honey
1½ cups buttermilk
½ cup butter

Combine buttermilk, butter and 4 Tbl. honey in saucepan. Heat gently until butter melts.

⅜ cup warm water
1 Tbl. yeast
1 Tbl. honey

Stir water and 1 Tbl. honey in bowl. Add yeast and let sit a few minutes to proof.

3 cups hard ww flour
2 cups ww pastry flour
½ tsp. salt
1 tsp. baking soda

Sift together the flours, salt and soda. Using large bowl combine buttermilk mixture, foamy yeast water and ½ of flour mixture. Beat well and let rise 30 minutes.

Add rest of flour mixture and knead until smooth. Let rise in oiled, covered bowl 30 minutes, punch down and shape the rolls. Allow to rise in oiled pan. (covered) for about 15 mins. then bake at 400° for 20 mins.

Apple Cake

2 x 9" round pans

Fruity, moist and fragrant, this cake was a big favorite with the recipe testers. Dot the top with a few pecans, walnuts or almonds, before baking, for a beautiful coffeecake.

½ lb butter
1½ cups honey
5 eggs, beaten
3 Tbl. vanilla
1 cup yoghurt (or buttermilk)

Cream butter and honey together. Add beaten eggs, vanilla and yoghurt.

4½ cups ww pastry flour
2 tsp. baking powder
2 tsp. baking soda
1 tsp. nutmeg
4 tsp. cinnamon
3½ cups chopped apples

Combine flour, powder, soda and spices in a separate, large bowl. Add the wet ingredients and the apples and stir in. Pour into greased pans and bake at 350° for about 45 minutes until a knife comes out clean.

Ginger Cookies

about 3 dozen 3" cookies

Just like Grandma used to make--even better if you used freshly grated ginger. These cookies are quite sweet, however, and the amount of honey can be adjusted to suit individual tastes.

½ cup oil
½ cup molasses
1 egg, beaten
½ cup honey

Combine wet ingredients in medium bowl and mix well.

1 tsp cinnamon
1½ Tbl. dry ginger or
3 Tbl freshly grated ginger
2 tsp baking soda
½ cup dry milk
¼ cup wheat germ
2 cups whole wheat flour

In a separate large bowl, combine all dry ingredients and mix well. Pour the wet ingredients into the dry, and combine thoroughly -- but do not overmix. The resulting batter will be quite thick. Drop by the spoonful onto greased cookie sheet and bake at 350° for 15-20 minutes.

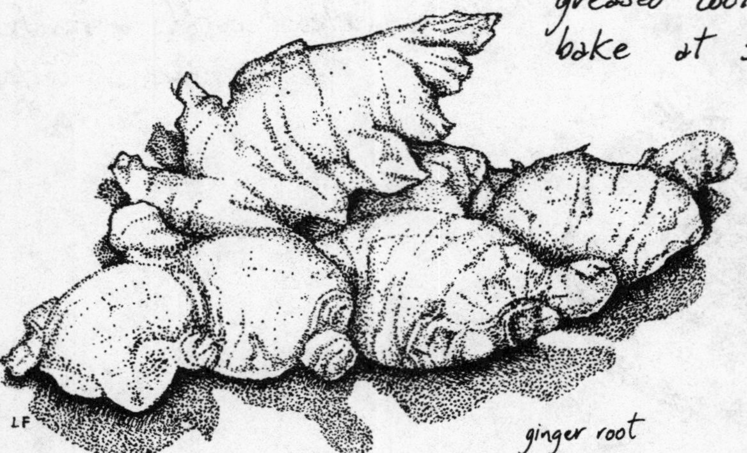

ginger root

Oatmeal Sunflower Cookies

3 dozen 2"-2½" cookies

Yeast West's trademark - one of our very first recipes.

Mix together	½ cup tahini ¼ cup water
Add, and mix well	¾ cup safflower oil 1 cup honey 1 Tbl. lecithin 2 tsp. vanilla ¼ tsp. almond extract
Mix together and add to wet ingredients	7 cups oats 1½ cups sunflower seeds 1 cup ww flour ¾ tsp. nutmeg ¾ tsp. cinnamon ¼ tsp. allspice

Scoop or spoon cookies onto oiled cookie sheet and press with cookie press, jar lid or fingers. Bake at 350° for 20-25 minutes until brown. Let cool before taking off sheet.

Yeast West Familia

Makes about 10 cups or 2½ lbs.

A tasty mix. Vary the fruits and nuts as you like. Good with milk, juice or even hot water, say Yeast West.

oats

Heat oven to 350°. Toast ①, ② and ③ on separate cookie sheets until lightly browned and smelling toasty.

① 5 cups rolled oats
1 cup rye flakes
1 cup sunflower seeds
2 tsp. cinnamon

② 1¼ cups wheatgerm

③ ¼ cup almonds
¼ cup cashews

When cooled mix all 3 together and add ④

④ ¼ cup date pieces
½ cup raisins

Starting a Bakery

"The spiritual high is great. The conference has recharged my collective spirit and reaffirmed the purpose of continuing that spirit. The conference reaffirms the unity we have as one family to help, share, and give guidance to one another. We are a positive force in the struggle for unity of all peoples. A seed is planted each year at these conferences. Let us nourish these thoughts in a fertile collective environment so that existing collective bakeries may continue to exist and new ones may sprout."

(Thoughts on the 1981 CWGEA conference by a participating baker)

One of the goals in writing ***Uprisings*** was to contribute to the growing consciousness about good food and self-reliance by encouraging people to bake for themselves at home. Another effect we hope for is that by conveying the unique satisfaction we get from being cooperative whole grain bakers, we may promote the establishment of more production collectives.

Every bakery in ***Uprisings*** has a different history. Many of the earlier ones grew out of the cooperative baking efforts of a few people, often involved with the local food coop. People who enjoyed baking their own whole grain bread at home found themselves being asked to bake for friends or coop members unable to obtain freshly-made natural baked goods anywhere else. From there on the scale of operations grew until a whole grain collective bakery evolved into being. Some of the more recent bakeries, on the other hand, have been founded specifically by people wishing to create a collective work environment and meet the growing demand for fresh, wholesome food. There are now many areas where the demand would easily support a locally-based baking collective. Instead, bread is shipped in from outside, usually from the larger companies in the "natural foods business".

Should the dream of starting a bakery be or become yours, we offer the following very basic suggestions, gleaned from our collective experience.

Contact or visit an existing whole grain collective bakery. We invite you to write to the Cooperative Whole Grain Educational Association with questions and requests for help. Attending a CWGEA conference will give you a wealth of information and inspiration.

Use cheap space to start with. If local codes about kitchen certification permit, bake at home. A common arrangement is to use the kitchen of a local restaurant, pizza place, or bakery during the hours when they are closed.

Develop a reliable, small selection of products at first. You may start by supplying the food coop and then be able to expand production. A few good wholesale accounts can keep a bakery going—for example, natural food stores, or a local restaurant with a steady order for rolls. You may also be able to sell directly to the public, for instance at farmers' markets. Getting your own storefront can be a goal reserved for the future.

You'll need some equipment. Bakeries have started production with not much more than bread pans and an oven, hand-mixing and kneading ten- or twenty-loaf batches. Pretty soon, though, a mixer becomes desirable. Most bakeries have a proof box too, though you can manage without one, especially in a humid climate; you can build a proof box fairly easily. Good sources of used equipment are close-out sales of restaurants, pizza places, and bakeries. There are also some regional suppliers who accumulate such stock; check with the CWGEA or nearest bakery.

The operating details—everything from pricing to group process—won't be so important at first, but ultimately they can be crucial to your bakery's success or failure. Some basic guidelines can be obtained from the CWGEA or existing bakeries, and are quite simple to initiate. Meanwhile, common sense and respect for others will get you far.

Good luck and stay in touch!

References

Ballentine, Rupert, M.D.: ***Diet and Nutrition*** (Himalayan International Institute, PA;1979)

Blauer, Stephen: ***Rejuvenation*** (Green Grown Publications, P.O. Box 661, Santa Monica, CA 90406; 1980)

Brewster, Letitia & Michael Jacobson, Ph.D.: ***The Changing American Diet*** (Center for Science in the Public Interest—see CSPI for address; 1978)

Brown, Edward Espe: ***The Tassajara Bread Book*** (Shambhala Publications, Berkeley; 1970)

Center for Science in the Public Interest: ***Midget Encyclopedia of Food and Nutrition***, and other publications, posters, etc. (1755 S Street NW, Washington, D.C. 20009)

Co-op Food Fact Sheets (Food Learning Center, [ACA Food Research Committee], 114½ East Second Street, Winona, MN 55987; and ICC Education Project, 953 Jenifer Street, Madison, WI 53703)

Dufty, William: ***Sugar Blues*** (Warner Books, NY; 1976)

East West Journal, Vol. 10, #4 (April 1979): (P.O. Box 970, Farmingdale, NY 11937)

Erewhon: ***The Salt Story*** and other informational leaflets (Erewhon, 8454 Stellar Drive, Culver City, CA 90230)

Essene Gospel of Peace of Jesus Christ, Book I (International Biogenic Society, Apartado 372, Cartago, Costa Rica; 1978)

Gabel, Medard, with the World Game Laboratory: ***Ho-Ping: Food for Everyone — Strategies to Eliminate Hunger on Spaceship Earth*** (Anchor Press/Doubleday, NY; 1979)

Hightower, Jim: ***Eat Your Heart Out: How Food Profiteers Victimize the Consumer*** (Vintage Press, NY; 1976)

Hunter, Beatrice Trum: ***Consumer Beware***, and other publications (Simon & Schuster, NY; 1971)

Institute for Food and Development Policy: several publications (see Lappe) and resource center on agriculture, world hunger, and social justice (IFDP, 2588 Mission St., San Francisco, CA 94110)

Inter-Cooperative Council Education Project: see ***Co-op Food Fact Sheets***

Jacobson, Michael, Ph.D.: ***Eater's Digest: The Consumer's Factbook of Food Additives*** (Doubleday, NY; 1976)—available from CSPI.

Kervran, Louis C., Ph.D.: ***Bread's Biological Transmutations*** (Happiness Press, P.O. Box D.D., Magalia, CA 95954; 1978)

Kulvinskas, Viktoras, M.Sc.: ***Sprout for the Love of Everybody: Nutritional Evaluation of Sprouts and Grasses*** (1978), ***Survival into the 21st Century*** (1981), and other publications (21st Century Publications, 401 N. Fourth St., P.O. Box 702, Fairfield, IA 52556)

Lappe, Frances Moore: ***Diet for a Small Planet*** (Ballantine Books, NY; 1982)

Lappe, Frances Moore & Joseph Collins: ***Food First*** (Ballantine Books, NY; 1978)

Leon County Food Coop: ***Leon County Food Coop Cookbook*** (Leon County Food Coop, 649 W. Gaines St., Tallahassee, FL 32304; 1979)

Lyons, Gracie: ***Constructive Criticism*** (Issues in Radical Therapy, P.O. Box 5039, Berkeley, CA 94705; 1976)

Morgan, Dan: ***The Merchants of Grain*** (Penguin; 1980)

National Nutritional Food Association: leaflets, information and movie for loan on School Lunches and Nutritional Education in Schools, including details of the pioneering Fulton County, Georgia's Nutra School Lunch Program (NNFA, 7727 South Painter Ave., Whittier, CA 90602)

Organic Gardening Magazine (Rodale Press, Inc., 33 E. Minor St., Emmaus, PA 18049)

Phillips, David A.: ***From Soil to Psyche*** (Woodbridge Press, CA; 1977)

Robertson, Laurel, Carol Flinders, & Bronwen Godfrey: ***Laurel's Kitchen: A Handbook for Vegetarian Cookery & Nutrition*** (Bantam Books, NY; 1978)

Saratoga Community Garden: ***Newsletter #19*** (Summer 1982) on amaranth (Saratoga, CA 95070)

Sekules, Veronica: ***Friends of the Earth Cook Book*** (Penguin; 1980)

Senate Select Committee on Nutrition and Human Needs: ***Dietary Goals for the United States*** (Government Printing Office, Washington, D.C.; 1977)

Simon, Arthur: ***Bread for the World*** (Paulist Press, 400 Sette Drive, Paramus, NJ 07652; 1975)

Sproutletter, The (P.O. Box 10985, Eugene, OR 97440)

U.S.D.A.: ***Agricultural Handbook #8: Handbook of the Nutritional Contents of Foods*** (Dover, NY; 1975)

Wigmore, Ann, D.D.: ***Why Suffer?***, ***Naturama Living Textbook***, and other publications (Rising Sun Publications, Boston; 1976)

Yudkin, John, M.D.: ***Sweet and Dangerous*** (Bantam Books, NY; 1973)

Index

Additives....5-6, 7, 26
Addresses of bakeries....48-9
Advertising, Food....7
Agribusiness....6-8
Allergies....16, 27
Almond crescents....173
Almond rice cookies....240
Amaranth....17
Anadama bread....183
Apple bars....258
Apple bread....188
Apple cake....277
Apple kuchen....164
Applesauce cake or muffins....60
Apricot almond bars....199
Apricot-peach bars....258
Arepas....252
Aunt Louise's coco-date granola....106
Auntie Nuke's nuggets....235

Bagels....226
Bagels, sesame garlic or plain....95
Baking powder....23, 42, 43
Baking soda....23, 42, 43
Banana creme cake....80
Banana cream pie....179
Banana muffins....134
Barley....17
Beer....22
Berry....2, 17
Best butter cookie batter....199
Blueberry coconut muffins....171
Blueberry muffins....128
Braiding breads....35-6
Bran, see also Wheat....17
Bran muffins....157
Bran wheat germ bread....141
Breakfast bran muffins....271
Brownies, How to make....40-1
Brownies, Carob....159
  Carob coconut....62
  Carob nut....207
Buckwheat....17
Buckwheat bread....118
Bulgur....21
Butter....26-7, 43
Butter sesame cookies....201
Buttermilk....22, 27
Buttermilk dinner rolls....276

Cakes, How to make....30, 40-1
Carob....29
Carob brownies....159
Carob cake....165
Carob chews....104
Carob chip bars....76
Carob chip chews....87
Carob coconut brownies....62
Carob coconut clusters....261
Carob cream pie....178
Carob halvah....266
Carob icing....165
Carob mint balls....241
Carob-mint cookies....160
Carob nut bars....122
Carob nut brownies....207
Carob nut fudge....202
Carob tofu bars....85
Carrot cake....233
Carrot cake or muffins....59
Carrot cake with tofu frosting....158
Carrot celery bread....52
Carrot herb bread....230
Cashews....8, 28
Cashew date granola....191
Challah....131
Cheddar cheese bread....149
Cheese....27
Cheesecake....73
Cheesecake, Eggless....172
Chemicals....5, 7, 8, 26, 29
Chickpeas, see Garbanzo
Christmas stollen....182
Cinnamon currant bread....205
Cinnamon date bread....194
Cinnamon granola bread....269
Cinnamon rolls....74
Coco shortbread....195
Coco-almond cookies....160
Coco-date granola, Aunt Louise's....106
Coconut....8, 28
Coconut almond granola....191
Coconut cake....234
Coconut dream bars....76
Coconut frosting....234
Coconut macaroons....198
Coffee cake, Tahini....67
Collectives....9-10
Colorings, Natural....29-30
Commercial bread....5-6, 15
Competition....9-10
Containers for baking....31-2
Cookies, How to make....41-2
Cooperative Whole Grain Educational Association. ii, 8, 282
Cooperatives....9-10, 44
Corn....17-18
Corn-benne muffins....157
Corn muffins....127
Corn muffins....135
Corn rye bread....144
Corn syrup....25
Costs, Keeping down....44
Cracked grains....18, 29
Cracked wheat....18, 21
Cracked wheat bread, Patience'....217
Crackers, onion....210
Crackers, rye....211
Crackers, Wheat sprout....121
Cranberry muffins....184
Cream cheese carob chip cookies....242
Cream cheese cookies....152
Cream cheese frosting....233
Crunch, Date....255
Currant-raisin sourdough....110

Daily bread....126
Dairy products....27, 42
Date bars....196
Date bars....258
Date butter....24, 43
Date-cashew ultimate oatmeal cookies....77
Date crunch....255
Date nut bread....246
Date sugar....24, 43
Dates....24
Decorations for cakes, Natural....30
Devil's carob cake....168
Diet, American....3, 6-7, 12-13
Diet for a Small Planet....7, 43
Digestion....2-4, 13
Dingwall's delectable old country date bars....272
Dinner rolls, Buttermilk....276
Dough, Making the....33
  Punching down....34
  Rising of....34, 36-7, 44
Dream cookies....262

Eggless cheesecake....172
Eggs....27, 42
Endosperm....2, 18
English weights and measures....46
Equivalents of weights and measures....46
Essene bread....16, 19, 38, 43
  How to make....39-40
Essene Gospel of Peace....38
Essene rolls, Pecan-raisin....256
Evolution....12-15
Exercise....14

Familia, Yeast West....280
Farina, farinha....17
Fats....13, 26-7, 43
  Hydrogenated....26, 29
  Saturated....14, 26, 27
  Unsaturated....26, 28
Fertilizers, Chemical....6, 8
Flavorings, Natural....29-30
Flaxseed egg replacer....124
Food First....7, 8
Food industry....6-7
Freezing breads....37,40

Freezing dough . . . 44
Fructose . . . 25
Fruit bars . . . 79
Fruit, dried . . . 24-5, 28
Fruit and nut drops . . . 260
Fruit juice . . . 22
Fruit upside-down cake . . . 167
Fruits . . . 24-5, 28-9
Fudge, Carob nut . . . 202

Garbanzo beans . . . 27, 42-3
Germ, See also Wheat . . . 18
Ginger bears . . . 98
Ginger cookies . . . 278
Ginger snaps . . . 151
Gingerbread muffins . . . 170
Gluten, in grains . . . 16, 20, 21
Gluten flour . . . 21
Golden macaroons . . . 174
Grains . . . 16-21
Grandpa's farm bread . . . 89
Granola, Applesauce . . . 80
  Aunt Louise's coco-date . . . 106
  Cashew date . . . 191
  Coconut almond . . . 191
  Date crunch . . . 255
  Holy . . . 106
  Maple . . . 105
  Peanut cashew crunch . . . 106
  Toasted all grain cereal . . . 153
Granola cookies . . . 151
Grits . . . 19, 27, 29
Groats . . . 17, 18

Halvah . . . 186
Halvah . . . 266
Halvah, Carob . . . 266
Halvah, Marbled . . . 186
Halvah, Sesame, carob-coated . . . 69
Hazel's prune nut bread . . . 142
Health . . . 2-4, 11-15
Hearth rye bread . . . 90
Hearty whole grain black bread . . 72
Herb bread . . . 82
Herb onion bread, Vickie's . . . 216
Herb sourdough bread . . . 120
Herbs . . . 29
Hi-protein bread . . . 265
History of bread . . . 4-6
Holy granola . . . 106
Honey . . . 24
Honey cake . . . 166
Hot cross buns . . . 113
Hybrid plants . . . 6, 7
Hydrogenated, see Fats

Illness and disease . . . 3, 4, 12-13
Infant formula . . . 8
Ingredients, Substituting . . . 42-3
Irish soda bread . . . 146

Julia's favorites — raisin oatmeal cookies . . . 273
Just rye bread . . . 247

Kasha . . . 17
Kelp . . . 26, 43
Kneading . . . 33-4
Kneading surface . . . 32
Krunch bars . . . 153

Leaveners . . . 22-3, 43
Legumes . . . 27-8
Lemon coconut pie . . . 177
Lemon sesame bread . . . 231
Lemon wedding cake . . . 133
Liquids . . . 21-2

Macaroons, Coconut . . . 198
Macaroons, Golden . . . 174
Malt . . . 24
Map of bakery locations . . . 49
Maple granola . . . 105
Maple oatmeal cookies . . . 257
Maple syrup . . . 24
Marbled halvah . . . 186
Meal . . . 18
Milk . . . 21, 27, 42
Millet . . . 18
Milling flour, Methods of . . . 5, 20
Miso . . . 26, 43
Molasses . . . 24
Molasses butter cookies . . . 199
Muesli . . . 65
Muffins, How to make . . . 40, 45

Natural flavorings, colorings, and trimmings . . . 29-30
Nature . . . 4
Nine-grain bread . . . 55
Nutrition . . . 11-15
Nutritional science . . . 11-12
Nuts . . . 28
  milks and butters . . . 28, 42

Oat bread, Sweet . . . 57
Oatmeal raisin cookies . . . 129
Oatmeal sunflower cookies . . . 279
Oatmeal sunflower millet bread . 264
Oats . . . 18-19
Oils . . . 26-7
Old bread, Uses of . . . 37
Old world rye bread . . . 204
Onion crackers . . . 210
Onion rolls . . . 249
Onion rye bread . . . 268
Onion sandwich rolls . . . 270
Orange-date surprise bread . . . 189
Orange-oat cookies . . . 159
Organic farming . . . 6-7
Organic ingredients . . . 6-7
Oven . . . 31, 37
Ozark barley bread . . . 206

Pans for baking . . . 32
Papaya squares . . . 175
Patience' cracked wheat bread . . 217
Peanut butter . . . 28
Peanut butter cookies . . . 207
Peanut butter cookies with raisins or carob chips . . . 223
Peanut butter crunchies . . . 138
Peanut cashew crunch granola . . 106
Peanut granola chews . . . 100
Peanut minus cookies . . . 123
Peasant bread . . . 51
Peasant bread . . . 163
Pecan sandies . . . 259
Pecan-raisin essene rolls . . . 256
Pesticides . . . 6, 8, 19, 24, 27
Pie crusts . . . 41
Pies, How to make . . . 41
Pies, Banana cream . . . 179
  Carob cream . . . 178
  Lemon coconut . . . 177
  Pumpkin . . . 180
Pita . . . 132
Pita or pocket bread . . . 94
Pizza . . . 250
Poppy seed cookies . . . 152
Poppy seed loaf . . . 169
Poppy seed cake, Rice . . . 232
Potato buttermilk bread . . . 71
Potato dill bread . . . 53
Potato water . . . 22, 124
Preservatives, . . . 5, 13, 15, 21
  Natural . . . 21, 24, 25, 29
Processed foods . . . 6, 7, 8, 12-13
Profits . . . 6, 8, 9-10
Proofing bread . . . 36
Proofing yeast . . . 32-3
Protein, Complementary . . . 43
Prune nut bread, Hazel's . . . 142
Pudin de pan . . . 68
Pumpcorn muffins . . . 221
Pumpkin clouds . . . 219
Pumpkin cookies . . . 63
Pumpkin cupcakes and/or cake . . 61
Pumpkin pie . . . 180

Quantity, Baking in . . . 45
Quick breads, How to make . . . 40

Raisin bran bread . . . 213
Raisin bread . . . 229
Raisin date bars . . . 84
Raisin oatmeal cookies, Julia's favorites . . . 273
Raisin sunnies . . . 86
Rancidity . . . 20, 21, 26, 28
Raw fruit balls . . . 161
RDAs . . . 11-12
Recommended Daily Allowances, See RDAs
Refined Foods, See also Sugar, White flour . . . 2-3, 7, 12-13, 25
Refrigerating doughs . . . 44, 45
  loaves . . . 37, 40
Rice . . . 19
Rice bread . . . 92
Rice poppy seed cake . . . 232
Rice sourdough bread . . . 108
Rice sourdough bread . . . 120
Rice syrup . . . 25
Rich currant scone . . . 237
Rising of dough, See Dough
Roll-ups . . . 96
Rolls, How to make . . . 33, 36

Rye 19
Rye, Just 247
Rye bread 209
Rye bread, Hearth 90
Rye bread, Old world 204
Rye bread, Onion 268
Rye bread, Swedish 117
Rye crackers 211
Rye sourdough bread 120

Salt 13, 25-6, 27, 43
Sandwich rolls, Plain and onion . 270
Scented pecan balls 161
Scone, Rich currant 237
Scones, Simple 236
Scottish shortbread 150
Seed industry 6
Seeds 28, 43
milks 28, 42
Sesame chews 103
Sesame crunch bars 238
Sesame dream bars 99
Sesame garlic bagels 95
Sesame halvah, carob-coated 68
Sesame oat rolls 248
Sesame seeds 28, 42, 43, 44
Sesame soya bread 58
Seven grain bread 245
Seven grain currant muffins 136
Shaping loaves and rolls 34-6
Shortbread, Coco 195
Shortbread cookies, Walnut 176
Shortbread, Scottish 150
Shortcuts in baking 44
Simple scones 236
Sorghum 19-20
Sorghum molasses 25
Sourdough 23
Sourdough breads,
How to make 37-8
Sourdough bread 109
Sourdough, Currant-raisin 110
Rice 108
Sourdough, Basic 119
Herb 120
Rice 120
Rye 120
Sourdough Pumpernickel 224
Sourdough Whole Wheat Bread . 218

Soybeans and products 27, 42-3
Soymilk, Raw for baking 124
Spices 29
Spicy apple muffins 185
Sponge, Making the 32-3
Sprouted wheat bread 193
Sprouting 19, 39
Sprouts 28
St. John's bread 145
Starting a bakery 282
Stollen, Christmas 182
Stone-grinding 5, 20
Storing bread 37, 40
Substitutions for – dairy 42
– eggs 42
– leaveners 43
– fats 43
– sweeteners . . . 43
– wheat 43
– salt 26, 43
Sugar, refined 7, 13, 23
brown 25
confectioner's 25
raw or turbinado 25
white 25, 43
Summer wheat bread 212
Sunflower seeds 28, 42-4
Sunny date chews 64
Sunny seed cookies 137
Sunseed bread 190
Survival 4, 12
Swedish rye bread 117
Swedish tea ring 112
Sweet oat bread 57
Sweeteners 23-5, 43

Tahini 42
Tahini coffee cake 67
Tahini-raisin-oat cookies 200
Tassajara Bread Book 31, 32
Tea ring, Swedish 112
Temperature conversions 46
Third World 7-8
Three seed bread 125
Thumbprint cookies 214
Time, Ways to save 44
Toasted all grain cereal 153
Tofu 28, 43
Tofu frosting 158

Tools for baking 31-2
Trimmings for cakes 30
Triticale 20
Triticale sunflower bread 140

Ultimate oatmeal cookies 77
Unyeasted breads, How to make . 38
Upside-down cake, Fruit 167
U.S. Senate Select Committee on Nutrition and Human Needs . 3, 13
Utensils 32

Vanilla 29
Vegetables 28-9
Vegie bread 148
Vickie's herb onion bread 216
Vinegar 29

Walnut-raisin ultimate
oatmeal cookies 77
Walnut shortbread cookies 176
Warm morning cinnamon
granola bread 269
Water 21
Weights and measures 46
Wheat 8, 20-21, 43
berry 2
bran 2, 3, 21
germ 2, 3, 21
products 21
whole wheat flour 3, 20
hard whole wheat flour 20
whole wheat pastry flour 20
white flour 2, 3, 20, 21, 43
Wheat sprout crackers 121
Wheat sprouts bread 56
White flour, See Wheat
White sugar, See Sugar
Whole grains 2-8, 15, 16, 29
Whole wheat bread 116
Whole wheat-rye French bread . . 156
Whole meal flour 18

Yeast, Baking 22-3, 43
Nutritional 26, 43
Proofing the 32-3
Yeast West familia 280
Yeasted breads,
How to make 32-37, 44

Recipes by Type of Baked Good

Yeasted Breads

Anadama bread 183
Apple bread 188
Bran wheat germ bread 141
Carrot celery bread 52
Carrot herb bread 230
Challah 131
Cheddar cheese bread 149
Christmas stollen 182
Cinnamon currant bread 205
Cinnamon date bread 194
Corn rye bread 144
Daily bread 126
Date nut bread 246
Hazel's prune nut bread 142
Hearth rye bread 90
Hearty whole grain black bread . . . 72
Herb bread 82
Hi-protein bread 265
Just rye 247
Lemon sesame bread 231
Nine-grain bread 55
Oatmeal sunflower millet bread . 264
Old world rye bread 204
Onion rye bread 268
Orange-date surprise bread 189
Patience' cracked wheat bread . . 217
Peasant bread 51
Peasant bread 163
Potato buttermilk bread 71
Potato dill bread 53
Raisin bread 229

Rice bread . . . 92
Rye bread . . . 209
Sesame soya bread . . . 58
Seven grain bread . . . 245
Sourdough whole wheat bread . . 218
Summer wheat bread . . . 212
Sunseed bread . . . 190
Swedish rye bread . . . 117
Sweet oat bread . . . 57
Three seed bread . . . 125
Triticale sunflower bread . . . 140
Vegie bread . . . 148
Vickie's herb onion bread . . . 216
Warm morning cinnamon granola bread . . . 269
Wheat sprouts bread . . . 56
Whole wheat bread . . . 116
Whole wheat-rye French bread . . 156

Unyeasted and Sourdough Breads

Buckwheat bread . . . 118
Currant-raisin sourdough . . . 110
Grandpa's farm bread . . . 89
Irish soda bread . . . 146
Ozark barley bread . . . 206
Pecan-raisin essene rolls . . . 256
Sourdough bread . . . 109
Sourdough rice bread . . . 108
Sourdough, Basic . . . 119
Herb . . . 120
Rice . . . 120
Rye . . . 120
Sourdough pumpernickel . . . 224
Sprouted wheat bread . . . 193
St. John's bread . . . 145

Rolls, Crackers, Snacks

Arepas . . . 252
Bagels . . . 226
Bagels, sesame garlic or plain . . . 95
Buttermilk dinner rolls . . . 276
Cinnamon rolls . . . 74
Hot cross buns . . . 113
Onion crackers . . . 210
Onion rolls . . . 249
Pecan-raisin essene rolls . . . 256
Pita . . . 132
Pita or pocket bread . . . 94
Pizza . . . 250
Rich currant scone . . . 237
Roll-ups . . . 96
Rye crackers . . . 211
Sandwich rolls, plain and onion . 270
Sesame oat rolls . . . 248
Simple scones . . . 236
Swedish tea ring . . . 112
Wheat sprout crackers . . . 121

Quick Breads and Muffins

Applesauce cake or muffins . . . 60
Banana muffins . . . 134
Blueberry coconut muffins . . . 171
Blueberry muffins . . . 128
Bran muffins . . . 157
Breakfast bran muffins . . . 271
Carrot cake or muffins . . . 59
Corn-benne muffins . . . 157
Corn muffins . . . 127
Corn muffins . . . 135
Cranberry muffins . . . 184
Gingerbread muffins . . . 170
Pumpcorn muffins . . . 221
Pumpkin cupcakes and/or cake . . 61
Raisin bran bread . . . 213
Seven grain currant muffins . . . 136
Spicy apple muffins . . . 185

Cakes and Brownies

Apple cake . . . 277
Applesauce cake or muffins . . . 60
Banana creme cake . . . 80
Carob brownies . . . 159
Carob cake . . . 165
Carob coconut brownies . . . 62
Carob nut brownies . . . 207
Carrot cake . . . 233
Carrot cake or muffins . . . 59
Carrot cake with tofu frosting . . . 158
Cheesecake . . . 73
Coconut cake . . . 234
Devil's carob cake . . . 168
Eggless cheesecake . . . 172
Fruit upside-down cake . . . 167
Honey cake . . . 166
Lemon wedding cake . . . 133
Poppy seed loaf . . . 169
Pumpkin cupcakes or cake . . . 61
Rice poppy seed cake . . . 232
Tahini coffee cake . . . 67

Cookies, Bars, Treats

Almond crescents . . . 173
Almond rice cookies . . . 240
Apple bars . . . 258
Apple kuchen . . . 164
Apricot almond bars . . . 199
Apricot-peach bars . . . 258
Auntie Nuke's nuggets . . . 235
Best butter cookie batter . . . 199
Butter sesame cookies . . . 201
Carob chews . . . 104
Carob chip bars . . . 76
Carob chip chews . . . 87
Carob coconut clusters . . . 261
Carob halvah . . . 266
Carob mint balls . . . 241
Carob-mint cookies . . . 160
Carob nut bars . . . 122
Carob nut fudge . . . 202
Carob tofu bars . . . 85
Coco shortbread . . . 195
Coco-almond cookies . . . 160
Coconut dream bars . . . 76
Coconut macaroons . . . 198
Cream cheese carob chip cookies . . . 242
Cream cheese cookies . . . 152
Date bars . . . 196
Date bars . . . 258
Dingwall's delectable old country date bars . . . 272
Dream cookies . . . 262
Fruit bars . . . 79
Fruit and nut drops . . . 260
Ginger bears . . . 98
Ginger cookies . . . 278
Ginger snaps . . . 151
Golden macaroons . . . 174
Granola cookies . . . 151
Halvah . . . 186
Halvah . . . 266
Julia's favorites — raisin oatmeal cookies . . . 273
Krunch bars . . . 153
Maple oatmeal cookies . . . 257
Marbled halvah . . . 186
Molasses butter cookies . . . 199
Oatmeal raisin cookies . . . 129
Oatmeal sunflower cookies . . . 279
Orange-oat cookies . . . 159
Papaya squares . . . 175
Peanut butter cookies . . . 207
Peanut butter cookies with raisins or carob chips . . . 223
Peanut butter crunchies . . . 138
Peanut granola chews . . . 100
Peanut minus cookies . . . 123
Pecan-raisin essene rolls . . . 256
Pecan sandies . . . 259
Poppy seed cookies . . . 152
Pumpkin clouds . . . 219
Pumpkin cookies . . . 63
Raisin date bars . . . 84
Raisin sunnies . . . 86
Raw fruit balls . . . 161
Scented pecan balls . . . 161
Scottish shortbread . . . 150
Sesame chews . . . 103
Sesame crunch bars . . . 238
Sesame dream bars . . . 99
Sesame halvah, carob-coated . . . 68
Sunny date chews . . . 64
Sunny seed cookies . . . 137
Tahini-raisin-oat cookies . . . 200
Thumbprint cookies . . . 214
Ultimate oatmeal cookies, walnut-raisin & date-cashew . . . 77
Walnut shortbread cookies . . . 176

Granola, Cereals

Aunt Louise's coco-date granola . 106
Cashew date granola . . . 191
Coconut almond granola . . . 191
Date crunch . . . 255
Holy granola . . . 106
Maple granola . . . 105
Muesli . . . 65
Peanut cashew crunch granola . . 106
Toasted all grain cereal . . . 153
Yeast West familia . . . 280

Frostings

Carob icing 165
Coconut frosting 234
Cream cheese frosting 233
Tofu frosting..................... 158

Pies, Desserts

Apple kuchen 164
Banana cream pie.............. 179
Carob cream pie 178
Carob tofu bars 85
Cheesecake 73
Eggless cheesecake........... 172
Fruit upside-down cake........ 167
Lemon coconut pie............. 177
Papaya squares 175
Pie crusts.......................... 41
Pudin de pan 68
Pumpkin pie 180
Swedish tea ring 112
Tahini coffee cake................ 67

Miscellaneous

Baking powder, home-made...... 43
Cashew cheese 43
Date butter 43
Egg replacer 207
Flaxseed egg replacer 124
Nut milks 42
Potato water 124
Seed milks 42
Soymilk, Raw, for baking........ 124

Recipes by Special Dietary Characteristic

No Eggs or Dairy

(Since most breads, rolls, and granolas contain no eggs or dairy, they are not listed here.)

Almond crescents.............. 173
Apple/apricot-peach/date bars .. 258
Auntie Nuke's nuggets 235
Blueberry muffins 128
Bran muffins........................ 157
Carob brownies 159
Carob cake 165
Carob coconut brownies............ 62
Carob halvah 266
Carob mint balls 241
Carob-mint cookies 160
Carob nut bars 122
Carob nut brownies 207
Carob nut fudge.................. 202
Carrot cake 233
Carrot cake with tofu frosting ... 158
Coco shortbread 195
Coco-almond cookies 160
Corn-benne muffins 157
Corn muffins...................... 127
Date bars 196
Fruit bars 79
Fruit and nut drops 260
Ginger bears 98
Ginger snaps 151
Golden macaroons 174
Granola cookies 151
Halvah 266
Krunch bars 153
Lemon coconut pie.............. 177
Maple oatmeal cookies 257
Oatmeal raisin cookies 129
Oatmeal sunflower cookies 279
Orange-oat cookies 159
Peanut butter cookies 207
Peanut butter crunchies 138
Peanut granola chews 100
Peanut minus cookies 123
Pecan-raisin essene rolls 256
Pudin de pan 68
Pumpcorn muffins 221
Pumpkin pie 180
Raisin sunnies 86
Raw fruit balls 161
Scented pecan balls............ 161
Sesame crunch bars............ 238
Sesame halvah, carob-coated 68
Sunny date chews 64
Sunny seed cookies 137
Tahini coffee cake................. 67
Tahini-raisin-oat-cookies 200

No Dairy (but contains Eggs)

Applesauce cake or muffins...... 60
Bagels 226
Banana muffins 134
Blueberry coconut muffins...... 171
Challah............................. 131
Dingwall's delectable old country date bars 272
Fruit upside-down cake......... 167
Honey cake 166
Pumpkin cupcakes and/or cake .. 61
Sesame dream bars 99

No Eggs (but contains Dairy)

Apple kuchen 164
Apricot almond bars............ 199
Best butter cookie batter 199
Butter sesame cookies 201
Buttermilk dinner rolls......... 276
Carob chews....................... 104
Carob chip chews 87
Carob icing 165
Carob tofu bars 85
Cheddar cheese bread.......... 149
Coconut frosting 234
Cream cheese cookies........... 152
Dream cookies 262
Eggless cheesecake............. 172
Halvah 186
Hi-protein bread................. 265
Irish soda bread.................. 146
Marbled halvah 186
Molasses butter cookies........ 199
Patience' cracked wheat bread .. 217
Peasant bread 163
Pecan sandies 259
Pizza 250
Poppy seed cookies 152
Potato buttermilk bread 71
Pumpkin cookies 63
Raisin bran bread 213
Raisin date bars 84
Rice poppy seed cake 232
Scottish shortbread 150
Sesame chews 103
Simple scones 236
Sourdough whole wheat bread .. 218
Walnut shortbread cookies 176

No Wheat

Almond crescents............... 173
Almond rice cookies............. 240
Carob coconut clusters.......... 261
Carob mint balls................. 241
Carob-mint cookies............. 160
Carob nut fudge.................. 202
Coco-almond cookies........... 160
Date bars.......................... 196
Date crunch....................... 255
Fruit and nut drops.............. 260
Golden macaroons............... 174
Halvah 186
Just rye............................ 247
Krunch bars 153
Lemon coconut pie 177
Marbled halvah 186
Orange-oat cookies 159
Peanut granola chews 100
Peanut minus cookies 123
Pumpkin pie 180
Raw fruit balls................... 161
Rice bread........................... 92
Rice poppy seed cake 232
Scented pecan balls............ 161
Sesame halvah, carob-coated 68
Sunny date chews 64
Tahini-raisin-oat cookies 200

No Sweetener, or Fruit-sweetened

Buckwheat bread 118
Date crunch 255
Date nut bread 246
Fruit bars 79
Fruit and nut drops 260
Grandpa's farm bread 89
Hearth rye bread 90
Just rye............................. 247

Muesli ... 65
Pecan-raisin essene rolls ... 256
Pita ... 132
Potato buttermilk bread ... 71
Raw fruit balls ... 161
Rice bread ... 92
Scented pecan balls ... 161
Sourdough bread ... 109
Sourdough rice bread ... 108
Sourdough, Basic ... 119
  Variations ... 120
Sprouted wheat bread ... 193
Sunny date chews, variation ... 64
Wheat sprout crackers ... 121
Yeast West familia ... 280

No Added Oils or Fats

(may contain high-fat ingredients)

Arepas ... 252
Buckwheat bread ... 118
Carob chews ... 104
Carob halvah ... 266
Carob mint balls ... 241
Carob-mint cookies ... 160
Carob nut fudge ... 202
Cheddar cheese bread ... 149
Coco-almond cookies ... 160
Date crunch ... 255
Date nut bread ... 246
Fruit bars ... 80
Fruit and nut drops ... 260
Halvah ... 186
Halvah ... 266
Krunch bars ... 153
Marbled halvah ... 186
Onion crackers ... 210
Peanut granola chews ... 100
Peanut minus cookies ... 123
Pecan-raisin essene rolls ... 256
Potato buttermilk bread ... 71
Raisin bran bread ... 213
Rye bread ... 209
Rye crackers ... 211
Sesame chews ... 103
Sesame crunch bars ... 238
Sourdough bread ... 109
Sourdough rice bread ... 108
Sourdough, Basic ... 119
  Variations ... 120
Sprouted wheat bread ... 193
Summer wheat bread ... 212
Tahini-raisin-oat cookies ... 200
Whole wheat-rye French bread ... 156
Yeast West familia ... 280

No Baking

(may involve pre-heating or toasting)

Carob chews ... 104
Carob halvah ... 266
Carob mint balls ... 241
Carob nut fudge ... 202
Fruit and nut drops, raw ... 260
Halvah ... 186
Halvah ... 266
Marbled halvah ... 186
Muesli ... 65
Peanut granola chews ... 100
Raw fruit balls ... 161
Scented pecan balls ... 161
Sesame chews ... 103
Sesame halvah, carob-coated ... 68

No Salt, or Optional Salt

(Salt is in fact optional in all recipes; goodie recipes contain no salt, and are not listed here.)

Buckwheat bread ... 118
Cheddar cheese bread ... 149
Grandpa's farm bread ... 89
Herb bread ... 82
Onion crackers ... 210
Peasant bread ... 51
Pita ... 132
Rice bread ... 92
Rye crackers ... 211
Sourdough, Basic ... 119
  Variations ... 120
Sprouted wheat bread ... 193
St. John's bread ... 145
Vegie bread ... 148
Vickie's herb onion bread ... 216
Wheat sprout crackers ... 121

Recipes by Major Ingredients

ALMONDS
Almond crescents ... 173
Almond rice cookies ... 240
Apricot almond bars ... 199
Coco-almond cookies ... 160
Coconut almond granola ... 191
Dream cookies ... 262
Holy granola ... 106

APPLE JUICE
Apple bread ... 188
Pudin de pan ... 68
Spicy apple muffins ... 185

APPLES, APPLESAUCE
Apple bars ... 258
Apple bread ... 188
Apple cake ... 277
Apple kuchen ... 164
Applesauce cake or muffins ... 60
Fruit upside-down cake ... 167
Roll-ups ... 96
Spicy apple muffins ... 185

APRICOTS, DRIED
Apricot almond bars ... 199
Apricot-peach bars ... 258
Fruit and nut drops ... 260
Just rye ... 247

BANANAS
Banana creme cake ... 80
Banana cream pie ... 179
Banana muffins ... 134
Eggless cheesecake ... 172

BARLEY
Ozark barley bread ... 206
Seven grain bread ... 245

BLUEBERRIES
Blueberry coconut muffins ... 171
Blueberry muffins ... 128

BRAN – See Wheat Bran

BUCKWHEAT
Buckwheat bread ... 118
Nine-grain bread ... 55

BUTTER
Best butter cookie batter ... 199
Butter sesame cookies ... 201
Carob icing ... 165
Coconut cake ... 234
Cream cheese cookies ... 152
Papaya squares ... 175
Pecan sandies ... 259
Poppy seed loaf ... 169
Raisin date bars ... 84
Rice poppy seed cake ... 232
Scottish shortbread ... 150
Thumbprint cookies ... 214
Walnut shortbread cookies ... 176

BUTTERMILK
Apple cake ... 277
Buttermilk dinner rolls ... 276
Carob chews ... 104
Irish soda bread ... 146
Potato buttermilk bread ... 71
Rice poppy seed cake ... 232
Rich currant scone ... 237
Sesame chews ... 103

CARAWAY SEEDS
Cheddar cheese bread ... 149
Corn rye bread ... 144
Hearth rye bread ... 90
Irish soda bread ... 146
Old world rye bread ... 204
Rye bread ... 209
Rye crackers ... 211

CAROB CHIPS
Carob chip bars 76
Carob chip cookies 87
Cream cheese carob chip cookies 242
Dream cookies 262
Sesame halvah, carob-coated 68

CAROB POWDER
Carob brownies 159
Carob cake 165
Carob chews 104
Carob coconut brownies 62
Carob coconut clusters 261
Carob cream pie 178
Carob halvah 266
Carob icing 165
Carob mint balls 241
Carob-mint cookies 160
Carob nut bars 122
Carob nut brownies 207
Carob nut fudge 202
Carob tofu bars 85
Devil's carob cake 168
Dream cookies 262
Hearty whole grain black bread 72
Marbled halvah 186
Old world rye bread 204
St. John's bread 145

CARROTS
Carrot cake 233
Carrot cake or muffins 59
Carrot cake with tofu frosting 158
Carrot celery bread 52
Carrot herb bread 230
Golden macaroons 174
Vegie bread 148

CASHEWS
Auntie Nuke's nuggets 235
Cashew date granola 191
Date-cashew ultimate oatmeal cookies 77
Papaya squares 175
Peanut cashew crunch granola .. 106

CHEESE
Cheddar cheese bread 149
Pizza 250
Roll-ups 96

CINNAMON
Apple kuchen 164
Cinnamon currant bread 205
Cinnamon date bread 194
Cinnamon rolls 74
Raisin bread 229
Warm morning cinnamon granola bread 269

COCONUT
Aunt Louise's coco-date granola . 106
Auntie Nuke's nuggets 235
Blueberry coconut muffins 171
Carob coconut brownies 62
Carob coconut clusters 261
Coco shortbread 195
Coco-almond cookies 160
Coconut almond granola 191
Coconut cake 234
Coconut dream bars 76
Coconut frosting 234
Coconut macaroons 198
Golden macaroons 174
Lemon coconut pie 177
Raw fruit balls 161

COCONUT OIL
Almond crescents 173
Blueberry coconut muffins 171
Golden macaroons 174
Honey cake 166

CORN, DRIED
Arepas 252

CORNMEAL
Anadama bread 183
Carob-mint cookies 160
Coco-almond cookies 160
Corn-benne muffins 157
Corn muffins 127
Corn muffins 135
Corn rye bread 144
Grandpa's farm bread 89
Pumpcorn muffins 221

CRANBERRIES
Cranberry muffins 184

CREAM CHEESE
Cheesecake 73
Coconut frosting 234
Cream cheese carob chip cookies 242
Cream cheese cookies 152
Cream cheese frosting 233
Eggless cheesecake 172

CURRANTS
Breakfast bran muffins 271
Cinnamon currant bread 205
Currant-raisin sourdough 110
Irish soda bread 146
Rich currant scone 237
Seven grain currant muffins 136

DATE SUGAR
Carrot cake or muffins 59

DATES
Aunt Louise's coco-date granola . 106
Auntie Nuke's nuggets 235
Cashew date granola 191
Cinnamon date bread 194
Date bars 196
Date bars 258
Date-cashew ultimate oatmeal cookies 77
Date crunch 255
Date nut bread 246
Dingwall's delectable old country date bars 272
Fruit bars 79
Fruit and nut drops 260
Lemon sesame bread 231
Muesli 65
Orange-date surprise bread 189
Raisin date bars 84
Raw fruit balls 161
Scented pecan balls 161
St. John's bread 145
Sunny date chews 64

DILL
Potato dill bread 53

DRIED FRUITS — See also individual fruits
Fruit and nut drops 260

EGGS
Banana creme cake 80
Banana cream pie 179
Carob cream pie 178
Challah 131
Cheesecake 73
Hot cross buns 113
Papaya squares 175
Rich currant scone 237
Sesame dream bars 99

EGG WHITES
Dingwall's delectable old country date bars 272
Poppy seed loaf 169

FLAXSEED
Blueberry muffins 128
Corn muffins 127
Nine-grain bread 55
Oatmeal raisin cookies 129
Peasant bread 163

GARLIC
Cheddar cheese bread 149
Herb bread 82
Pizza 250
Sandwich rolls, onion 270
Sesame garlic bagels 95
Vegie bread 148

GINGER
Ginger bears 98
Ginger cookies 278
Ginger snaps 151
Gingerbread muffins 170
Sesame halvah, carob-coated 68

GRANOLA
Warm morning cinnamon granola bread 269

HERBS
Carrot herb bread 230
Herb bread 82
Herb sourdough 120
Pizza 250
Vegie bread 148
Vickie's herb onion bread 216

KELP
Bran muffins 157
Carob brownies 159
Carrot cake with tofu frosting 158

Coco-almond cookies 160
Old world rye bread 204
Onion crackers 210
Orange-oat cookies 159
Ozark barley bread 206
Peasant bread 51
Rye crackers 211

LEMON
Lemon coconut pie 177
Lemon sesame bread 231
Lemon wedding cake 133

MALT SYRUP
Applesauce cake or muffins 60
Bran muffins 157
Carob brownies 159
Carob coconut brownies 62
Carob-mint cookies 160
Carrot cake with tofu frosting 158
Carrot cake or muffins 59
Carrot herb bread 230
Coco-almond cookies 160
Corn-benne muffins 157
Orange-oat cookies 159
Peanut minus cookies 123
Raisin bread 229
St. John's bread 145
Sunny date chews 64
Toasted all grain cereal 153
Whole wheat bread 116

MAPLE SYRUP
Auntie Nuke's nuggets 235
Carob nut bars 122
Granola cookies 151
Maple granola 105
Maple oatmeal cookies 257
Pecan sandies 259
Simple scones 236

MILK
Banana cream pie 179
Carob cream pie 178
Coconut cake 234
Devil's carob cake 168
Hot cross buns 113
Poppy seed loaf 169

MILK POWDER
Carob icing 165
Halvah 186
Marbled halvah 186

MILLET
Bran muffins 157
Carob-mint cookies 160
Coco-almond cookies 160
Granola cookies 151
Nine-grain bread 55
Oatmeal sunflower millet bread 264
Peanut minus cookies 123
Rice bread 92
Seven grain bread 245

MOLASSES
Bran wheat germ bread 141
Corn rye bread 144
Ginger bears 98
Ginger cookies 278
Ginger snaps 151
Gingerbread muffins 170
Hearty whole grain black bread 72
Molasses butter cookies 199
Old world rye bread 204
Potato dill bread 53
Raisin bran bread 213
Summer wheat bread 212

MULTI-GRAIN BLENDS
Aunt Louise's coco-date granola 106
Holy granola 106
Maple granola 105
Muesli 65
Nine-grain bread 55
Peanut cashew crunch granola 106
Seven grain bread 245
Seven grain currant muffins 136
Simple scones 236
Toasted all grain cereal 153

NUT BUTTER, NUT MILK
Lemon coconut pie 177
Pumpkin pie 180
Sunny date chews, variation 64

NUTS – See also individual nuts
Carob nut bars 122
Carob nut brownies 207
Carob nut fudge 202
Cream cheese cookies 152
Krunch bars 153
Muesli 65

NUTRITIONAL YEAST
Patience' cracked wheat bread 217
Vickie's herb onion bread 216

OAT FLOUR
Almond crescents 173
Date bars 196

OATS
Apple/apricot-peach/date bars 258
Carob coconut clusters 261
Cashew date granola 191
Coco shortbread 195
Coconut almond granola 191
Date crunch 255
Dingwall's delectable old
country date bars 272
Fruit bars 79
Fruit and nut drops 260
Granola cookies 151
Holy granola 106
Julia's favorites –
raisin oatmeal cookies 273
Maple granola 105
Maple oatmeal cookies 257
Muesli 65
Oatmeal raisin cookies 129
Oatmeal sunflower cookies 279
Oatmeal sunflower millet bread 264
Orange-oat cookies 159
Peanut cashew crunch granola 106
Peanut granola chews 100
Sesame oat rolls 248
Sweet oat bread 57
Tahini-raisin-oat cookies 200
Toasted all grain cereal 153
Ultimate oatmeal cookies 77
Yeast West familia 280

OLD BREAD
Peasant bread 51
Pudin de pan 68

ONION
Onion crackers 210
Onion rolls 249
Onion rye bread 268
Sandwich rolls – onion 270
Vegie bread 148
Vickie's herb onion bread 216

ORANGE
Christmas stollen 182
Hot cross buns 113
Orange-date surprise bread 189
Orange-oat cookies 159
Scented pecan balls 161
Swedish rye bread 117
Swedish tea ring 112

PAPAYA, DRIED
Papaya squares 175

PEACHES, DRIED
Apricot-peach bars 258
Fruit and nut drops 260
Raw fruit balls 161

PEANUT BUTTER
Carob chews 104
Krunch bars 153
Peanut butter cookies 207
Peanut butter cookies
with raisins or carob chips 223
Peanut butter crunchies 138
Peanut granola chews 100
Peanut minus cookies 123
Sesame chews 103
Sunny date chews 64

PEANUTS
Peanut cashew crunch granola 106
Peanut minus cookies 123

PECANS, PECAN MEAL
Fruit and nut drops 260
Pecan-raisin essene rolls 256
Pecan sandies 259
Scented pecan balls 161

PEPPERMINT OIL
Carob mint balls 241
Carob-mint cookies 160

POPPY SEEDS
Orange-date surprise bread 189
Poppy seed cookies 152
Poppy seed loaf 169
Rice poppy seed cake 232
Three seed bread 125

POTATO
Just rye 247

Potato buttermilk bread 71
Potato dill bread 53

POTATO WATER
Patience' cracked wheat bread . 217
Three seed bread 125
Vickie's herb onion bread 216

PRUNES
Hazel's prune nut bread.......... 142

PUMPKIN
Pumpcorn muffins 221
Pumpkin clouds................. 219
Pumpkin cookies.................. 63
Pumpkin cupcakes and/or cake .. 61
Pumpkin pie 180

RAISINS
Breakfast bran muffins 271
Carrot cake or muffins........... 59
Christmas stollen 182
Hot cross buns.................. 113
Julia's favorites—
raisin oatmeal cookies 273
Muesli 65
Oatmeal raisin cookies 129
Peanut butter cookies
with raisins or carob chips.... 223
Pecan-raisin essene rolls 256
Pumpkin cookies 63
Pumpkin cupcakes and/or cake .. 61
Raisin bran bread 213
Raisin bread 229
Raisin date bars.................. 84
Raisin sunnies 86
Raw fruit balls 161
Swedish tea ring 112
Tahini-raisin-oat cookies 200
Ultimate oatmeal cookies 77

RICE
Grandpa's farm bread 89
Rice sourdough 108
Rice sourdough bread 120
Seven grain bread 245

RICE FLOUR, FLAKES
Almond rice cookies............. 240
Hi-protein bread................ 265
Poppy seed cookies 152
Rice bread 92
Rice poppy seed cake 232
Scottish shortbread 150

RYE FLAKES
Aunt Louise's coco-date granola . 106
Holy granola 106
Maple granola 105
Muesli 65
Peanut cashew crunch granola.. 106
Toasted all grain cereal........ 153
Yeast West familia 280

RYE FLOUR
Coco-almond cookies 160
Corn rye bread 144
Grandpa's farm bread 89
Hearth rye bread 90
Just rye......................... 247
Old world rye bread............. 204
Onion rolls...................... 249
Onion rye bread 268
Rye bread....................... 209
Rye crackers.................... 211
Rye sourdough................... 120
Seven grain bread 245
Swedish rye bread............... 117
Whole wheat-rye French bread .. 156

SESAME SEEDS
Butter sesame cookies 201
Corn-benne muffins 157
Date crunch 255
Krunch bars 153
Lemon sesame bread............. 231
Peasant bread 163
Sesame chews 103
Sesame crunch bars.............. 238
Sesame dream bars 99
Sesame garlic bagels............. 95
Sesame halvah, carob-coated 68
Sesame oat rolls 248
Sesame soya bread................ 58
St. John's bread 145
Three seed bread 125

SOY FLOUR
Apple/apricot-peach/date bars .. 258
Golden macaroons 174
Hi-protein bread................ 265
Nine-grain bread 55
Patience' cracked wheat bread .. 217
Rice bread 92
Sesame soya bread................ 58
Sweet oat bread.................. 57
Vickie's herb onion bread 216

SOYMILK
Blueberry muffins 128
Corn-benne muffins 157
Corn muffins.................... 127
Daily bread 126
Pumpkin pie 180

SOY POWDER
Carob halvah 266
Halvah 266

SPICES
Apple cake...................... 277
Applesauce cake or muffins...... 60
Carrot cake 233
Carrot cake with tofu frosting . 158
Gingerbread muffins 170
Pumpkin cookies.................. 63
Pumpkin cupcakes and/or cake .. 61
Raisin bread 229
Rice poppy seed cake 232

SOUR CREAM
Dream cookies................... 262

SUNFLOWER SEEDS
Carob chip bars.................. 76
Date crunch 255
Fruit and nut drops............. 260
Oatmeal raisin cookies 129
Oatmeal sunflower cookies 279
Oatmeal sunflower millet bread . 264
Peasant bread 163
Raisin sunnies 86
Sunny date chews 64
Sunny seed cookies 137
Sunseed bread 190
Three seed bread................ 125
Triticale sunflower bread 140
Yeast West familia 280

TAHINI
Carob halvah 266
Halvah 186
Halvah 266
Marbled halvah 186
Poppy seed cookies 152
Tahini coffee cake............... 67
Tahini-raisin-oat cookies 200

TOFU
Carob tofu bars 85
Pizza 250
Tofu frosting................... 158

TOMATO
Pizza 250
Roll-ups 96
Vegie bread 148

TRITICALE
Nine-grain bread 55
Triticale sunflower bread 140

VEGETABLES
Pizza 250
Roll-ups 96
Vegie bread..................... 148

WALNUTS
Carob brownies 159
Carob-mint cookies 160
Carob nut bars 122
Carrot cake 233
Carrot cake with tofu frosting . 158
Christmas stollen 182
Date nut bread 246
Fruit bars 79
Raw fruit balls 161
Walnut-raisin ultimate
oatmeal cookies 77
Walnut shortbread cookies 176

WHEAT, CRACKED
Patience' cracked wheat bread .. 217
Summer wheat bread............. 212

WHEAT BRAN
Bran muffins.................... 157
Bran wheat germ bread 141
Breakfast bran muffins 271
Carob halvah 266
Granola cookies 151
Halvah 266
Hi-protein bread................ 265
Peanut granola chews 100
Raisin bran bread 213

WHEAT FLAKES
Granola cookies 151
Granolas. 105-6
Muesli 65
Toasted all grain cereal. 153

WHEAT GERM
Bran wheat germ bread 141
Coconut dream bars. 76
Hi-protein bread. 265
Julia's favorites –
raisin oatmeal cookies 273
Pumpkin cookies. 63
Toasted all grain cereal. 153

WHEAT SPROUTS
Essene bread 38
Pecan-raisin essene rolls 256
Sprouted wheat bread 193
Wheat sprout crackers 121
Wheat sprouts bread 56

YOGURT
Apple cake. 277
Eggless cheesecake. 172

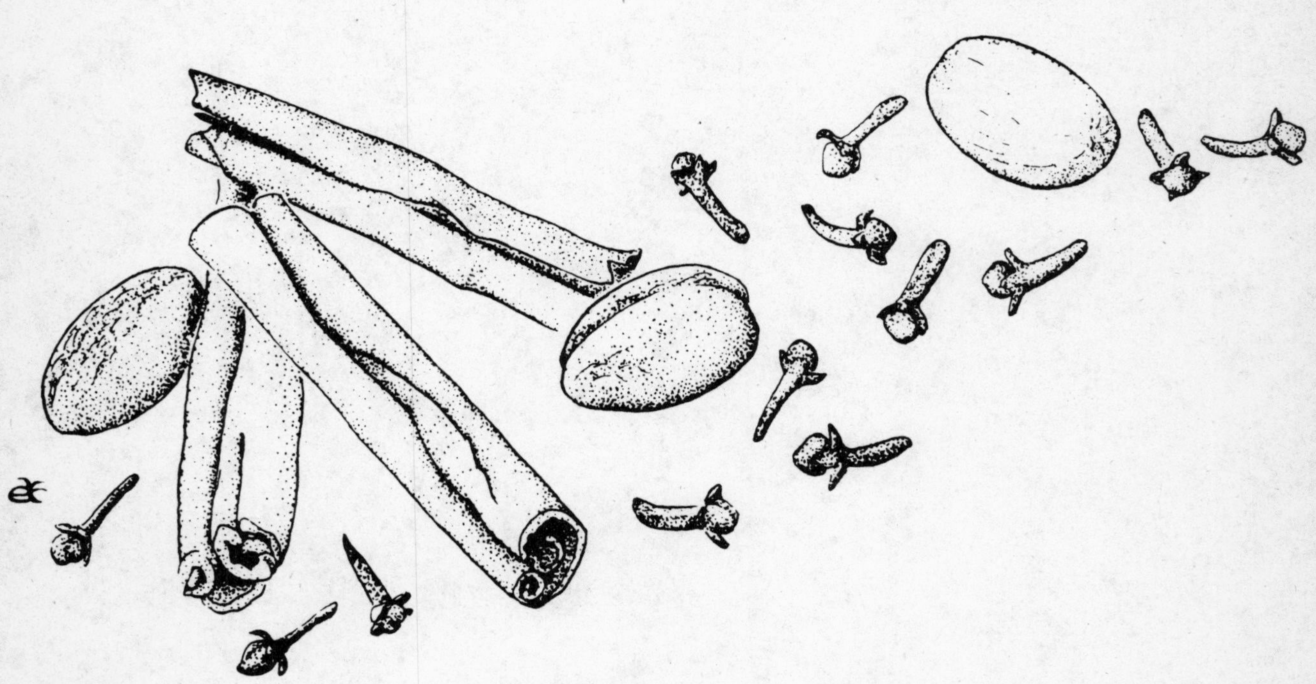